Who Put The Bots In The Tort$?

—A Legal Farce

iBooks
Habent Sua Fata Libelli

iBooks
Manhanset House
Shelter Island Hts., New York 11965-0342

bricktower@aol.com • www.ibooksinc.com
All rights reserved under the International and Pan-American Copyright
Conventions. Printed in the United States by J. Boylston & Company, Publishers,
New York. No part of this publication may be reproduced, stored in a retrieval system,
or transmitted in any form or by any means, electronic, or otherwise, without the prior
written permission of the copyright holder.
The iBooks colophon is a registered trademark of
J. Boylston & Company, Publishers.

Library of Congress Cataloging-in-Publication Data
Morrison, T. C.
Who Put The Bots in the Tort$?—A Legal Farce
p. cm.

1. Humor—Topic—Business and Professional. 2. Fiction—Legal.
3. Fiction—Humorous—Black Humor. 4. United States—Fiction
Fiction, I. Title.
ISBN: 978-1-59687-929-4, Hardcover

October 2024

Who Put The Bots In The Tort$?

—A Legal Farce

T. C. Morrison

Acknowledgments

I wish to thank my good friend Paul Depaolo for his help on all things computer-related and for suggesting I delve into the fascinating world of AI for this book. I also wish to thank my friend Peter Becket for his strong proofreading skills; any errors in proper punctuation are mine, not his (like my protagonists, I don't believe in rules).

Thanks also to Jennifer Vance and her colleagues at Books Forward for their strong promotional efforts on *Send In The Tort Lawyer$*. And finally, thanks to my publisher John Colby for his continued belief in this series and his suggestion that my heroic lawyers take on some of the nonsense that occurs in municipal politics.

Dedication

To the many friends and colleagues who have read the earlier books in this series and encouraged me to continue writing. And to the officers and staff of the Americn Museum of Tort Law in Winstead, Connecticut, the museum founded by Ralph Nader, the most famous tort lawyer in America. Their hospitality and sale of my books proves that even tort lawyers have a sense of humor.

Other books by T. C. Morrison

Tort$ "R" Us

Please Pass the Tort$

Send in the Tort Lawyer$

(Semi-Finalist for the Mark Twain Humor
and Satire Book Award)

"I've never met a lawyer I didn't like."
—Will Rogers

"One enchanted evening, you will see a lawyer across a crowded room."
—Oscar Hammerstein

"One nation, under God, with attorneys and lawyers for all."
—Pledge recited in all US schools

"It was impossible to get a conversation going, everyone was talking too much."
—Yogi Berra

Critical Praise for SEND IN THE TORT LAWYER$

"The laughs keep coming as fast as the torts and the wild settlements. No one with the slightest interest in law, life, or shenanigans should miss this third volume of the Pap and Pup series."
—Mike Abram, Retired Labor Lawyer

"The laughs never stop, as T.C. Morrison has once more struck comedy gold."
— Jack Isler, Retired Physician

"WARNING TO READERS: This book is not intended to be consumed in a public space! Readers should find a quiet corner where others will not be disturbed by unexpected outbursts of loud laughter."
—Richard Gilbert, College Professor

"I wonder if the legal profession can ever be this much fun? I'm delighted that T.C. Morrison has given his readers a third book about the Peters Brothers and their small class action firm in New York."
—Janet Graaff, Retired College Professor

"The dynamic legal team of Pap and Pup and the escapades of Chip and Lydia continue at a fast pace. The wit and word play keep you laughing. The legal cases are a hilarious reflection on current events and culture."
—Chris Kaiser, Retired Medical Executive

"T. C. Morrison gives his readers a master class in legal lunacy. No one captures the absurd side of legal practice better than Mr. Morrison."
—Andrew Schau, Retired Litigator and NY City Law Firm Partner

Table of Contents

1	Rough Landing	1
2	Arrested	7
3	Next Up	14
4	The Congressman	23
5	Super Pacs	30
6	Holly	37
7	Orville and Virgil	44
8	Belle and Mona	55
9	The Professor	56
10	The Heiress	72
11	AI Galore	79
12	Hon. Samuel Spade, III	89
13	Bridget	101
14	The Bathhouse	109
15	Sue the Bots	116
16	Martha and Moe	125
17	The Ledger	139
18	Holly Nails It	145
19	Mow On	160
20	Pac Men	167
21	*Ex Parte*	184
22	Bad Luck	189
23	Badd Boogle	200
24	Pigcasso	212
25	Prey Tells	220
26	Fifty/Fifty	236
27	Press Conference	250
28	Happy Thanksgiving	258
29	Autumn	271
30	Paige	288
31	Lydia	304
32	Orinthology	322
	About The Author	333

Chapter 1

ROUGH LANDING

"Why are we landing here?" Pap shouted to the pilot of the balloon that was now descending over the football field of Staples High School in Westport, Connecticut. "We're supposed to land back at the park at Compo Beach, where we took off from."

It was the second Saturday in May. Patrick A. Peters, III, known to one and all as "Pap," and his wife Piper had decided to do something different for their annual "Spring Fling" party. Instead of dinner on their patio in the Green Farms section of Westport, they would hire some hot air balloons and treat everyone to a leisurely flight along the coast of Long Island Sound.

The plan was to take off from the park area at Westport's Compo Beach at 11:00, fly south along the coast down to Greenwich, and then come back to Compo by about 1:00, where they would have a lavish picnic lunch that Piper had ordered from Balducci's.

The guests included eight of their oldest friends. There were Stacey and Daisy Spacey, Ray and Bunny Rabbitz, Mona and Hamilton Lott and Laurel Ann Hardy and her boyfriend, Milo Nulow. Laurel's husband Harry had died tragically five years ago when he fell off the big white horse he was riding on the merry-go-round at Oak Bluffs on Martha's Vineyard. Laurel had been dating Milo for a couple of years. Although she thought he was a bit of a wuss, he was knowledgeable about cultural things and, at least for the time being, that was good enough for Laurel.

The other two couples were newer friends. William and Hilary Fund were neighbors who lived nearby in a mansion overlooking Long Island Sound. After they bought the mansion, they bought the large house next to it and proceeded to tear it down, thereby giving them two large tracts of land overlooking the water. Fund ran a large hedge fund, the Fund Fund, and Pap had long hoped to convince him to finance one or more of his law firm's cases.

Because the firm's cases were mainly class action lawsuits which it handled on a contingency basis, the firm only received a fee once the case was successfully resolved. As a result, the firm always had to bear the enormous cost of prosecuting a class action case against a well-heeled corporate defendant. As it was generally pursuing several cases at a time, Pap was always looking for ways to raise money to finance them. Hence his friendship with William Fund.

The other new couple was Peachy and Harley Keane. The Keanes, who lived in next-door Southport, had shown up unexpectedly at last year's Spring Fling, having been invited by Mona Lott, who neglected to tell Piper that she had invited them.

But everyone liked the lively and still lovely Peachy, and so she and Harley became a permanent part of the group. In fact, as the result of a chance conversation at that party, Peachy became the plaintiff in a class action lawsuit the firm filed against Godiva for falsely labeling its chocolates as "Belgian Chocolates" when they were actually made in Reading, Pennsylvania.

The group also included Pap's twin brother Prescott Underwood Peters, known since childhood as "Pup," and his wife Priscilla. They lived down in Greenwich, where Pap and Pup had grown up, but they frequently spent much of the weekend with Pap and Piper.

Like Pap, Pup was a lawyer. In fact, he had been a very well-paid partner at Oliver and Cromwell, the bluest of New York City's blue chip law firms. But Pap, who was then a partner at the litigation firm Rogers and Autry, had convinced Pup that the two of them should start their own firm; it would be a small firm devoted to plaintiff's class action cases. He promised Pup that they would have more fun, and make more money, than they would if they stayed forever at their respective firms.

Both families had brought along their respective twins. Pap and Piper had twin boys, Patrick A. Peters, IV (known as "Little Pap") and Henry Alden Peters ("Hap"). The boys, now ten, were excited about the balloon ride, they'd been talking about it for weeks.

Pup and Priscilla had twin girls, Tiffany Ann Peters ("Tap") and Bethany Ann Peters ("Bap"). The girls, a half-year older than their cousins, hated their childhood names. Now that they were grown up, they insisted that everyone call them by their proper names, Tiffany and Bethany. Those were beautiful names, befitting their status as proper young ladies.

After considerable investigation, Piper had decided to hire balloons operated by Brothers Brothers Balloons, LLC, a relatively new company that promoted its balloon rides up and down the coastline of Long Island Sound.

The company was operated by three brothers, Fred, Ted and Ned Brothers. Each of them piloted a balloon named after his wife. Fred's balloon, bright red and white, was named "Jennifer." Ted's, a brilliant blue and white, was named "Gwyneth." And Ned's, green and white, was named "Danielc."

Pap and his boys were riding in Jennifer, which was being piloted by Fred Brothers. Pap called again to Fred, who seemed not to have heard his earlier question.

"Why are we landing here? We're supposed to land back at Compo where we started. That's where we all left our cars – and all the food for our picnic lunch."

Fred shouted back to Pap, who was at the back of the balloon. "The lady in the blue and white balloon – Gwyneth – asked us to land here."

Pap knew immediately that the lady Fred was referring to was Mona. None of the ladies in Gwyneth – or any of the balloons for that matter – would have dared to change the flight plan.

Mona Lott was a tedious but amusing neighbor who always managed to get herself embroiled in one controversy or another. She had once telephoned Pap on a Saturday morning, while he and Piper were having breakfast, to insist that he come get her out - she was in jail in Bridgeport where she had been taken for allegedly shooting at a pair of geese, and also at her neighbor, Nina Nosenyorbus, with an assault rifle.

The "assault rifle" turned out to be a BB gun belonging to one of her now grown kids. She had been using it to try to get the geese off her pond where they had just landed with considerable fanfare. Mona's mugshot, taken as part of her arrest, had, thanks to Nina, been posted all over the town of Westport. That led to one of the firm's first big cases, an invasion of privacy lawsuit against the company that had posted Mona's mugshot on a website filled with mugshots of criminals arrested around the country.

"That's Mona Lott you're referring to" Pap shouted to Fred. "But why did she want you to land here?"

"You'll have to ask her. All I know is she promised each of us two hundred dollars cash if we landed here."

"But couldn't you get fined for landing here? Don't you have to have some sort of approval to use the places where you take off and land? I know my wife made sure the town was okay with using the park at Compo for the takeoff and landing."

"The lady said she'd cover any fines we got. Also, she said the press would be waiting here at the football field, they would likely mention us in any story they ran. We need all the publicity we can get, we're just getting our business off the ground."

At that point Fred shouted out instructions to the riders. "We're about to land. Everyone bend you knees, then crouch down. And turn your back toward the direction we're heading. There'll be a little bump when we land, then maybe a short skid. The basket may tip slightly to one side. But don't worry, it seldom tips over."

Jennifer, Fred's balloon, was the first to touch down. It did so smoothly, with scarcely a bump or skid. Gwyneth, Ted's balloon, landed next, with a slight bump and a skid of ten or twelve feet. Both balloons had landed near midfield.

But Daniele, Ned's balloon, had a much rougher landing. It bumped up and down three times, then skidded twenty or thirty yards downfield before almost tipping over.

"We're going to crash!" shouted Milo, who was frantically holding onto the top of Daniele's basket. "We're all gonna fall on top of each other when the basket tips over."

Pup and his daughters were also in Daniele. "Wow, this is exciting!" yelled Bethany as the basket skidded downfield toward the end zone.

"We're gonna score a touchdown!" shouted Stacey Spacey. "Another ten yards and we're in!"

But Daniele did not tip over. Everyone, except Milo, calmly stepped out of the basket and looked for the other two balloons. Milo staggered out of the basket and dropped to his knees. "Thank God we made it down" he said repeatedly. "Thank God we made it down."

Milo had not only panicked when they began to land, he had been visibly nervous during the entire flight. Claiming he suffered from extreme vertigo, he had wormed his way to the innermost section of the basket, so that he was enveloped on all sides by his fellow passengers. Standing anywhere close to the edge of the basket made him ill.

The Daniele passengers began making their way toward midfield, where the passengers from the other two balloons were congregating. But they were now attracting attention from others who were not in their party. Several people who had been walking or jogging around the track began walking toward the two balloons that had landed at midfield.

"Why are you landing here?" one of them shouted.

"Where did you come from?" shouted another.

"Are you Chinese spies?" shouted a third.

Hap and Little Pap were full of excitement, running back and forth from one yard-line marker to another. Tiffany and Bethany were more composed, walking calmly from where the Daniele had landed up toward midfield.

It was Tiffany who first spotted the men and women holding notepads and smartphones; one pair was holding a camera and mic.

"Uncle Pap" she shouted, "I think the press is here. Did you and Daddy arrange that?"

"No, Tiffany, we didn't. I think someone else in our group did."

Pap quickly located Mona. "Mona, what on earth is going on? Why did you tell the pilots to land here? They could be subject to fines for landing without permission. You can't just land a group of balloons in the middle of a high school football field."

"Why not?" she responded. "What could be safer for a landing? There's over a hundred yards of nice soft grass here."

Piper was angry. "We were supposed to land back at Compo. You knew that. That's where we're supposed to have lunch. All the food and wine is sitting in the cars, it could spoil by the time we get back there."

"I can explain everything" said Mona breathlessly. "But first I need to speak with all those lovely people from the Westport media. It was so nice of them to show up and watch our landing."

Chapter 2

ARRESTED

Mona immediately took charge. Standing at the fifty yard line, midway between the Jennifer and Gwyneth balloons, she motioned for the media folks to approach.

She recognized Ali Starr, the smart, impeccably groomed reporter for News 12 Connecticut, the region's cable news channel. She also recognized Barney Burner, the loud and excitable announcer for WWPT, the local radio station.

Three other reporters were also there, although Mona didn't know them. There was a reporter from *Westport Journal*, an online newspaper. And one from the *Westport Daily Voice*, a daily online paper covering Westport and its inland neighbor Weston. And finally there was a reporter from *Westport Magazine*, a monthly that covered Westport, Weston and other nearby towns.

"Where's the demonstration?" shouted Barney Burner. "You said there would be a demonstration here after the balloons landed."

"The demonstration's right here" answered Mona. "And it starts right now." With that, she proceeded to unfurl a long red and white banner. With her friend Peachy Keane holding up the other end, the banner displayed the following message:

7

MAKE OUR LAWNS GREAT AGAIN!

"I don't get it" said Ali Starr. "You dragged all of us here on a Saturday afternoon for a demonstration about lawns?"

"Is there something wrong with the lawns in Westport?" asked Barney Burner.

Mona grabbed the mic that Ali was carrying and began to explain.

"There certainly is something wrong with our lawns. It all started last year when the town's Planning and Zoning Commission passed an ordinance prohibiting lawn mowing on weekends. That regulation's ridiculous! When do they expect us to mow our lawns?

"Everybody mows their lawn on the weekend. Except those wealthy elites who've been buying weekend homes in Westport. Those people have so much money they can afford to hire a lawn service company to mow their lawn during the week. But regular people like me and my husband can't afford to do that."

"But that ordinance only prohibits mowing on Sundays and Saturday afternoon after two o'clock" said Ali Starr.

"That's not true" said Mona.

"But it is true. You can mow your lawn on Saturday up until two o'clock. I know because News Twelve covered the story last year."

"It's not true that I can mow my lawn then" said Mona. "Ham and I play golf every Saturday morning. We play with Peachy and her husband Harley. This is Peachy here holding up the banner and that's Harley over there next to the blue and white balloon.

"They live in Southport and we have a standing ten o'clock tee time every Saturday at the Southport Golf Club. So it's mid-afternoon before I can get out my John Deere X57 Select – that's one of those nice riding mowers - and begin mowing. The P and Z should have taken that into account before they adopted that regulation."

Ali Starr was incredulous. "You're having a demonstration because the town won't let you mow your lawn on Saturday afternoon? On your fancy John Deere X57 Select riding mower?"

"But that's not all" said Mona. "This year they adopted yet another stupid regulation. This one prohibits all mowing during the month of May."

"That's right" said Barney excitedly. "And Westport is now at the forefront of this movement, it's called 'No Mow May.' It's an environmentally-friendly idea that's being pushed nationally. Most people I've interviewed are proud that Westport's in the vanguard of this movement."

"Talk about the environment" said Mona with a snort. "Go around town and see what everyone's lawn looks like right now. It's only the second week of May and the lawns are already looking like the dickens.

"And just wait until the end of the month. All the lawns will be totally overgrown, they'll look like wild prairies in the middle of Kansas. This isn't the way we want Westport . . . ."

Just then, two police cars with their sirens blazing drove onto the track surrounding the field. They raced to the bend at the west end of the field and paused. Seeing that they were at the wrong end of the field, they restarted their cars and raced around to the east end of the field.

After they came to a stop, they realized they were no closer to the people congregated in the middle of the field than they had been when they were at the other end of the field. So they restarted their engines and continued around the bend onto the straightaway until they came to the fifty yard line, where they stopped.

Turning off their engines and sirens, they alighted from their vehicles and walked to the middle of the field where everyone was congregated.

"What are you doing here?" demanded Mona as she approached the first policeman.

"I'm Patrolman Wood" said the policeman. "Chuck Wood. And this here" he said as he pointed to the policeman behind him, "is Patrolman Moss. Pete Moss.

"We got a call from a lady saying that some hot air balloons were landing here and she thought it was probably illegal, this being the town's High School."

"Who's the lady that called?" demanded Mona.

"We didn't speak with her" said Patrolman Wood. "But I think the dispatcher said her name was Nina. Nina something or other."

"It's that bitch Nina Nosenyorbus" said Mona irritably. "She's always trying to get me and my husband in trouble. That's my husband there, Ham, taking pictures of everything. He can tell you a thing or two about that troublemaker.

"But tell me, how would that slut know our balloons were landing here?" she said as she looked at Patrolman Wood.

"She probably saw them coming in to land" he responded. "It's not everyday that balloons fly over Westport and then land on the football field.

"Now" he continued patiently, "if someone phones in a complaint – doesn't matter if she's a nice lady or, as you say, a slut – it's our job to find out what's going on. See whether any laws are being broken. So, we've got to ask you folks, what . . . . " He was quickly interrupted as everyone started talking at once.

"That Nina's nothing but a trouble-making slut" shouted Mona.

"We were just out for a nice quiet balloon ride" said Ray Rabbitz. "What's the harm in that."

"Would you like to ride back to Compo in the balloon with us?" asked Ray's wife Bunny.

"We were having a political demonstration" said Stacey Spacey indignantly. "We have a constitutional right to demonstrate."

"It's in the First Amendment" added his wife Daisy. "The one they're always talking about on the radio."

"Are you going to arrest us?" asked Peachy. "I've never been arrested before. I'm not sure about my husband, you'll have to ask him."

Milo Nulo walked up to the patrolmen and gravely announced: "We were nearly killed when that balloon back there landed" he said as he pointed to Daniele, which was sitting by itself back at the twenty yard line. "It didn't just land. It crashed."

"Is that a real gun?" asked Little Pap, pointing to the gun on Wood's waist.

Patrolman Wood had had enough. He raised his arm and shouted "Will everyone stop talking at once! I only wanna hear from one of you. Now, who's in charge here?"

Seeing Mona starting to raise her hand and step forward, Pap quickly spoke up. "I'm Patrick Peters. I'm a lawyer. My wife and I organized this event for our friends. We were scheduled to land back at the park at Compo Beach, where we took off from, but circumstances forced us to land here."

"What circumstances would those be?" asked Patrolman Wood skeptically.

"I think the wind changed direction. This was the nearest open space."

"I see that there are members of the press here" Wood responded. "I doubt they knew that the wind was suddenly going to change direction and force you to land here. Looks to me like this was all planned. Where are the pilots? I need to hear from them."

Fred, Ted and Ned Brothers stepped forward. They all began talking and gesticulating at the same time.

"I can't hear you when you're all talking at the same time" said Patrolman Wood. "Let me hear from you" he said as he pointed to Fred. "What's your name?"

"Fred Brothers" said Fred Brothers. And these are my brothers, Ted and Ned. Their last names are also Brothers. We're the owners of this business. Brothers Brothers Balloons." He then turned and nodded to Barney Burner: "Your listeners will want to know who we are. Well, we just started up this business and . . . ."

"Never mind that" said Patrolman Wood. "Just tell us how you happened to land here. In the middle of Staples High School football field. Without advance clearance."

"Well . . . ."

"Was it really a change in wind direction that forced you to land here?"

"Well, yes and no."

"Whad'ya mean, yes and no. It's gotta be one or the other."

"Chuck" interrupted Patrolman Moss, "What about this here demonstration? They're clearly holding some sort of demonstration." Looking at Mona, he added "Lady, can you put down that banner, it's distracting everyone."

"Pete" said Wood, "that's a good point. About this bein' a demonstration." Turning back to Pap he asked: "You folks have a permit to hold a demonstration here? With that there banner and the press bein' here and all, it sure looks to me like you're havin' some sort of demonstration."

"I don't think we need a permit to hold a demonstration" said Pap. "Not that we were actually having a demonstration. We were just milling about after the balloons were forced to land here because of the change in wind."

"Look" said Patrolman Wood, "five reporters don't just show up to watch a bunch of people milling about on a football field. This was plainly a planned demonstration. And in Westport you can't have a demonstration on public property without a permit."

Wood paused, then looked at Patrolman Moss and said, "Pete, I think we've got to arrest them all. Maybe you should start getting everyone's name and address."

Turning to address the entire group, Patrolman Wood pulled himself up straight and dramatically announced: "I'm arresting the lot of you for holding an unlawful demonstration and for trespassing on public property.

"And as for you Brothers guys, I'm arresting you for landing your balloons on public property without advance permission. Now, we can't do anything here, we'll have to take you all downtown to police headquarters and book you there."

"You can't arrest us here" said Pap. "We need to get back to Compo, where all of our cars are parked. Besides, there's twenty-three of us, you can't get all of us in your two police cars."

"So maybe we'll have to make a couple of trips" said Patrolman Wood.

"Look" said Pap. "We've got three hot air balloons sitting here. You can't ask the pilots to just leave them. You want to be responsible for damage to – or maybe even the theft of - three expensive hot air balloons?"

"Well . . . ."

"And besides, we've all got to get back to Compo at some point. The simplest thing would be for all of us to get back in the balloons and fly back to Compo. You can meet us there and take our names and addresses and give us summonses for whatever we're being charged with."

"I'm not going back up in that balloon" said Milo as he approached Pap and Patrolman Wood. Holding out his wrists to the patrolman, he said "Here, you can cuff me now. Take me wherever you want in your squad car. But I'm not getting back up in that balloon."

"This is perfect" said Pap to Wood and Moss. "You guys take Milo with you. He can be a sort of hostage to guarantee our cooperation. You won't have to release him until you finish with us at Compo."

"Chuck" said Pete Moss to Chuck Wood, "that sounds like a pretty good solution to me. And this guy's right" he added as he pointed to Pap. "We can't have these balloons left here unattended. The town would be on the hook for any damage to them."

"So it's a deal" said Pap as he shook hands with the two patrolmen. "You can take Milo with you as a hostage. The rest of us will take the balloons back to Compo and you can meet us there.

"And I'll tell you what. When you get to Compo, you can join us for lunch. We have a very nice picnic lunch waiting for us there. Piper, what is it we're having for lunch?"

"Roast chicken, potato salad, French bread and pasta salad. All from Balducci's. And tiramisu and cookies for dessert."

"Terry what?" asked patrolman Moss.

"Tiramisu" said Piper. "It's a rich Italian dessert, sort of like a pudding. I'm sure you'll like it."

"Sounds good. But what's to drink?"

"I'm glad you asked" said Piper. "We've got several bottles of a great Rose. It's from California."

"We can't drink" said Patrolman Wood. "We're on duty."

"We brought along some lemonade for the kids. You can have some of that."

"What do you say, Pete?", said Wood, "should we join 'em?"

"Sure. Wait 'til I tell my wife. She always says the food at Balducci's is the best in town. But we can't afford it."

"Okay" announced Patrolman Wood. "Everyone back in the balloons. Except you" he said as he pulled Milo aside. "You can ride with us."

Chapter 3

NEXT UP

On the Monday morning following the ill-fated balloon party, all the lawyers assembled in Pap's office for their weekly meeting. Pap and Pup, the firm's partners, were joined by their four associates.

Melissa Muffett, known behind her back as Little Miss Muffett, was their smartest associate. She had worked with Pup at Oliver and Cromwell when Pup had been a partner there.

Then there was Brandon Muffinsky and Charles Powell Pierpont, III, both of whom had worked at Rogers and Autry with Pap. Brandon was a straight-laced hardworking associate who could be counted on to do any of the boring work the others didn't want to do.

Charles Pierpont, known to everyone as "Chip," had been a star quarterback at Dartmouth. Tall, dark and ruggedly handsome, he had a string of success with beautiful women that had not been seen since JFK's days at Choate and Harvard. Pap had brought Chip with him from Rogers and Autry, primarily because of his connections in the New York financial and media world.

The firm's newest associate was Helen Healer. Helen was married to Keith Keeler, an investment banker at Moreland Shanley. Helen and Chip had dated when Helen was at Wesleyan. Chip would drive down from Dartmouth to Wesleyan where he would spend Friday night and all day Saturday with her. On Sunday, he would head down to Vassar where he would spend the day in bed with Christine Keeler, Keith Keeler's sister.

Helen's mother, Faith Healer, had been one of the three mothers – the other two being Kiki Keeler, Christine's mom, and Fanny Pak, the mother of Penelope Pak, Chip's Dartmouth girlfriend – who, as a result of their daughters' relationships with Chip, knew of his legal career. Years later, the three of them had suggested Chip's law firm, Peters and Peters, to Dr. Hazel Nutt, the plaintiff and class representative in the firm's highly successful Corny Flakes case.

When all the lawyers were seated, Pap began by saying "I was in the Worry Room last Friday and I . . . . "

"What were you doing in the Worry Room?" asked Melissa. "I thought you never worried about our cases."

"I don't. I was taking a nap. That's one of the authorized uses of the Worry Room. It's a place where you guys can go to worry about our cases. And where I can go to take an afternoon nap. But that's it. That room's not to be used for anything else, especially not for sexual liaisons."

"Except in emergencies" said Chip. "You said it could be used for sexual liaisons in an emergency."

"Look, Chip, prearranged sexual encounters are not emergencies. I've told you that a hundred times."

"Let's hear what Pap was going to say about the Worry Room" said Melissa.

"Well, I noticed that there are two new photos on the Wall of Fame. That brings the number up to ten. Some of you may not have been in the Worry Room lately, I thought you'd all want to know about the additions."

"Are you kidding?" said Melissa. "We all go there every day to see if anyone new has been added."

Three years ago, Pap and Pup had begun posting in the Worry Room framed, autographed photos of women that Chip had bedded. But only if the women had some connection with the firm or one of its cases. The first to be posted was Candy, the firm's voluptuous paralegal

Chip had bedded in the Worry Room during the firm's first month in business.

Her photo was quickly followed by Lydia Lowlace, the former lap dancer Chip had met at a strip club. Lydia had gone on to be a Playboy Centerfold and was now the firm's most famous client, having been the plaintiff in no less than four of the firm's cases.

Then there were signed photos of Chip's three college girlfriends – Helen, Christine and Penelope – all of whom, unbeknownst to them at the time, played a role in the firm's representation of Hazel Nutt in the Corny Flakes case.

Then there were the Tuney twins - Melony Harmony Tuney and Harmony Melony Tuney. They were members of the class in the Bunny Hop electronic video game case. The game's producer, Erotic Arts, had used the Playboy spreads of Lydia, the Tuney twins and several other Centerfolds without their permission.

The last photo was Francoise Fournier, Chip's live-in girlfriend who worked at the UN as a translator. Francoise had played a key role in enlisting the hapless Pierre Dupre, a member of France's UN delegation, to serve as the class representative in the firm's case against the Russian government and its intelligence services. The Russians had succeeded in ensnaring Dupre, as well as a US Congressman and several other prominent figures, in a classic Honey Trap.

Melissa continued: "I think we all know that one of the new additions is Candy Lande." Candy was a reporter for Tech Tok, an online news service that covered the tech industry. Chip had recruited her as a last-minute back-up plaintiff in the Belgian Chocolates case; they had been worried the court would not allow Peachy Keane to serve as the class representative.

"Didn't Chip ah, know her, so to speak, when she was at Bennington?" asked Brandon.

"That wouldn't count" said Melissa. "Chip knowing her – as you so delicately put it – when she was at Bennington has nothing to do with our cases. There has to be a connection between the lady and the firm."

"Actually there is a connection" said Chip. "It was because I knew her from college, and knew that she liked chocolates, that I thought of her for the Belgian Chocolates case."

"Anyway" Melissa resumed, "after he recruited her he worked closely with her, supposedly to prepare her for the hearing. They worked several late nights together."

"As long as they weren't working in the Worry Room, I'm okay with that" said Pap.

"So who's the other new dame on the wall?" asked Brandon.

"Dee Jon" said Pap. "She was a lawyer at Knotts and Boltz, the firm that got us involved in the Madison Square Circle case."

"Chip" Melissa said, "didn't you tell us she offered you a picture of her and her daughter in their Brownie uniforms, but you didn't think that was appropriate for the Wall of Fame?"

"That's true" said Chip. "But then Dee called me last month and invited me to join her and her daughter for the Easter pageant at Radio City. I told her the Easter pageant wasn't really my cup of tea. But she said her daughter wanted to meet the lawyer who made it possible for her mother to attend Radio City. And then Dee added that she would make it worth my while. How could I say no to that?"

"And did she make it worth your while?" asked Melissa.

"She did."

"And she gave you a photo of herself, without her daughter or the Brownie uniform?"

"Exactly."

* * * *

Pup spoke up for the first time. "All right, now that we've got all that straightened out, can we get down to business?" Pup hated these long jocular exchanges that consumed part of every meeting. They never had them at Oliver and Cromwell. In fact, he couldn't recall anyone ever having laughed at Oliver and Cromwell.

"Okay" said Pap. "I should first update everyone on Mona's lawn mowing case." And he proceeded to explain that, last October, he had given the proposed complaint, that Helen had prepared, to the town's First Selectman and urged her to use it as leverage to convince the Planning and Zoning Commission to rescind the weekend mowing regulation.

But that hadn't worked. Not only did the Commission refuse to rescind the regulation, it adopted a new one prohibiting all mowing in May. Mona, of course, ignored both regulations and had resumed mowing on Saturday afternoons as she always had. She mowed it twice in May, meaning that she now had four citations: two for mowing on Saturday after 2:00 and two for mowing at all in May.

That's when Mona had come up with the idea of having the balloons – which Pap and Piper had arranged for their annual Spring Fling – land at the Westport High School football field where she would hold a press conference to denounce the regulations. Which had led to all of them being arrested and given citations for demonstrating without a permit and trespassing on public property.

"You and Pup got arrested?" said Melissa. "That won't look good for the firm."

"We can beat this" said Pap. "And when we do, we'll look good for protecting our client's right of free speech. As you all know, we don't just care about lucrative class action cases. We also care about everyone's civil rights."

"Including apes" said Chip, referring to the firm's unsuccessful attempt to free the chimpanzees in the Bronx Zoo.

"Chip, those weren't apes. They were chimpanzees. And Peters and Peters proudly stepped up to protect their civil rights."

"And we failed. Twice" said Pup, who had always been against representing apes.

"Well, we're not gonna fail on this case. Helen, you need to take the complaint you prepared last Fall and add a new section covering the 'No Mow May' regulation. Then prepare a motion for a preliminary injunction enjoining both ordinances pending a final ruling in the case.

"And by the way, add a new claim: the May ordinance violates Mona's right to freedom of expression under the First and Fourteenth Amendments to the Constitution."

"Right of expression?" asked an incredulous Helen.

"Sure. Mona wants to keep her lawn nice and neat. That's her form of expression. Expression's protected under the First Amendment. You can look it up."

Melissa spoke up. "That's only gonna help Mona's case against the town. I don't see how it will help you and Pup avoid the consequences of your arrest."

"Look. The mass arrests were a violation of everyone's First Amendment rights. We were punished for joining in the demonstration, which we had a First Amendment right to do."

"Well" said Pup, "we didn't exactly participate in the demonstration. Its just that, after the balloons landed, we got out and found ourselves listening to Mona's speech to the press."

"We were assembling" said Pap. "We were assembling for the demonstration, which never happened because the police came and broke everything up. The right to assemble is in the First Amendment. You can look that up too."

"What about the unlawful landing charge?" said Melissa.

"I think that charge is only against the three pilots. But we'll claim Act of God on their behalf."

"What's God got to do with it?" asked Helen.

"He caused the winds to change. So the pilots had no alternative but to make an emergency landing at the first open space they could find. Wind, tornadoes, hurricanes – those are all Acts of God and can justify what would otherwise be a breach of contract or other unlawful act. You guys should know that."

* * * *

Just then Pap's secretary, Vera Pesky, opened the door and waved to Pap.

"You've got a . . . ."

"I'll call them back. Miss Pesky, I've told you a hundred times not to interrupt me when we're in a meeting."

"But . . . ."

"No buts. I'm not taking the call now.

"Okay, now where were we? Oh yes, as I said last week, we need to talk about finding some new cases. I hope one of you has an idea."

"I do" said Brandon. "Monkey dog racing."

"What's that?" asked Melissa.

"It's a type of racing that's really popular at state fairs. Dogs race with monkeys on their back acting as jockeys. The monkeys are even dressed in silks, like real jockeys."

"So what's the issue?" asked Melissa.

"New York just passed a law banning it. The legislature . . . . "

"Not another animal rights case" said Pup. "Look at all the money we lost on the chimpanzee case. Besides, there's no claim here. The state has the authority to regulate horse racing. Surely it can regulate dog racing as well – especially if the dogs have monkeys on their back."

"Pup's right" said Pap. "We've done our bit for animal rights. Besides, there's no money here. We would only be suing to enjoin the new law."

"I thought we cared about animal rights" said Brandon. "Isn't that what you said at your press conference in the chimpanzee case?"

"Brandon, we care about animal rights if there's money to be had by caring about them. Otherwise, who cares? Besides, we need something new. No more food or animal rights cases. We need something new and exciting. Peters and Peters should always be known for breaking new legal ground."

"What about that Congressman from Long Island?" said Helen. "Sandoza. Gregory Sandoza. I just read a story suggesting that he may have fabricated his entire background. From his family to his education to his professional career before he ran for Congress."

"Yeah, I've been reading about that" said Pap. "It's really interesting. But isn't it a matter for Congress? A question of whether he should be expelled? Besides, who would we sue and for what?"

"We could sue on behalf of all the people who gave him campaign money" said Helen. "If what they are saying is true, he would have gotten that money under false pretenses."

"But suing Sandoza to get the donors' money back wouldn't amount to much. He probably only raised a few hundred thousand and, from the looks of it, he's not gonna have much of that money left."

Helen persisted. "What if he had a PAC – a Political Action Committee – behind him? They could have collected a million or more. And even if they spent most if it, they're probably in the process of collecting money for his next campaign."

"Okay" said Pap. "Melissa, Helen's going to be busy with all the papers in Mona's case. Can you look into this? See if Sandoza has a PAC and, if so, whether it has any money?"

Pup spoke up. "I understand we need some new cases. That's obvious. But we need to look for something that's really cutting edge. Maybe something involving AI."

"What's AI?" asked Brandon.

"Artificial Intelligence. Jeepers, Brandon, have you been living under a rock? AI is everywhere these days.

"Students use it to write papers that they turn in as their own work. Hollywood uses it in numerous ways, sometimes even to help with screenplays. In fact, screenwriters are worried AI will eventually be used to write entire scripts, putting them out of work."

"All the Internet search programs use it" said Melissa. "They accumulate huge amounts of information from traditional sources and then regurgitate it in response to a search. Publishers are up in arms about it, they say their stories are being used without their being compensated."

"Right" said Pup. "That's why we need to get into this area; there's going to be hundreds of cases involving AI in the next year or two."

"Does AI include robots?" asked Brandon.

"Absolutely. There are all kinds of robots, like that one named Optimis created by Tesla, that perform tasks in factories that used to be performed by humans."

"I think they had AI Santas last Christmas" said Chip.

"And AI lawyers" said Helen. "I just read about a start-up company that developed an AI lawyer program for people going to traffic court. At first it just gave out advice – such as the typical fine for the infraction in question. But now they offer an AI lawyer who can actually speak up and represent people in traffic court."

"If the robot goes to court, does it have to wear a suit" asked Chip.

"I'm not sure you have to wear a suit in Traffic Court" said Helen.

"Listen to this" said Melissa. "An AI lawyer just made the list of the top one hundred lawyers in Florida. Someone invented a name for the lawyer – Oliver Homes they called him – and then used AI to generate a resume for him. They submitted his name and CV to the company that publishes the top one hundred list. Oliver made the list."

"This doesn't sound good" said Pap. "We can't have robots taking away factory jobs from human workers. Or AI Santas taking work away from real Santas. And we certainly can't have AI lawyers taking work away from real lawyers. Where will this all end?"

"Well" said Melissa, "according to an article I saw last week, there was a survey of several hundred researchers working in the AI field. Five per cent of them said there was a chance that AI will eventually cause the extinction of the human race."

"Maybe that's why all those rich tech guys are building doomsday structures" said Helen. "They build them in remote places they can use in the event there's an AI apocalypse. The bunkers are stocked with food, gold bars and guns."

"Gold bars and guns?" said Brandon. "You've got to be kidding."

"Look" said Pup. "We're lawyers. What do we care if those tech guys want to build doomsday structures and stock them with food and guns. Probably pornographic movies too. But we can't worry about where AI is going. We're only concerned with where it's at right now. And right now it's the hot new thing and its loaded with scores of legal issues. We need to get involved in it. We need to be at the forefront of AI litigation."

"Okay" said Pap, "let's look into it. Brandon, Chip, why don't you two start poking around in the AI field and see what you can come up with. Pup's right, it would be good for the firm to start making a name for itself in the AI field.

"In the meantime, Melissa you need to follow up on Sandoza, see if there's a big PAC supporting him. And Helen, you focus on the complaint and motion papers in Mona's case. You gotta keep Pup and me out of jail.

"Okay, I think we're done for now. Let's all get to work. And don't forget to stop by the Worry Room and see the two new photos. We don't want Chip to think his efforts aren't appreciated."

Chapter 4

THE CONGRESSMAN

The following Monday, they assembled once again in Pap's office for their weekly meeting.

"I hope one of you has some good news" Pap began. "Pup and I, as well as our wives and kids and twelve of our friends, are going to have to appear in Connecticut Superior Court in Bridgeport in a few weeks. We're all gonna be charged because of that balloon business. Helen, how are you coming on the papers?"

"Not to worry" said Helen. "We've got some arguments you can make with a straight face, although I can't guarantee they will prevail."

"Great, Helen. I knew we could count on you to come up with arguments I can make with a straight face. Even if they aren't good enough to keep me and Pup and our wives and children out of jail. Now, anyone else have some good news?"

"I do" said Melissa. "Its about Congressman Sandoza. What I found will blow your mind. Pup, you said the firm needed a case in the AI realm. Well, this is it."

"What's Sandoza's phony background got to do with AI?" asked Pup.

"Everything. Gregory Sandoza is literally the Congressman from AI. His entire education and background, his every speech and constituent communication, were all fabricated by AI."

"How can that be?" asked Pap.

"Well, it's not known how it started or whose idea it was. But it was recently discovered that Sandoza and his campaign team used an AI program called BotsUp? That's B-O-T-S-capital U-P followed by a question mark. It's an AI platform put out by Boogle, the tech giant in Silicon Valley.

"Now, BotsUp? can be used for all kinds of things, from background research to any kind of writing: school papers, letters to the editor, speeches, short stories, you name it. Its marketing slogan is: 'When the chips are down, our Bots are up to it.'

"So, when he decided to run for Congress, Sandoza used the program to concoct an entire persona for himself. And then he used it to generate everything: campaign announcement, speeches, letters and emails to constituents, even his speeches in Congress. Anything he ever said was actually prepared by BotsUp?"

"How was this discovered?" asked Pup.

"Someone at Boogle, probably a disgruntled employee, made an anonymous call to *Newsday*, the newspaper that covers Long Island. *Newsday* ran the story and neither Sandoza nor his campaign denied it.

"Now, getting back to the story. Sandoza wanted a persona that would be popular in the Third District, where he was living at the time. The district has over eight hundred thousand residents. Sixty percent are white but eighteen percent are Hispanic. The district includes tony towns like Glen Cove, Roslyn and Oyster Bay. But it also has some blue collar towns, such as Levittown, Hicksville and Port Washington.

"So the first thing he needed to do was create a family background that would appeal to voters in that district. BotsUp? decided that he should be a first generation Hispanic American with a wife and two kids. Now, it appears that he's actually gay, he's said to have participated in several cross-dressing drag shows in Brazil a few years ago. He only got married a year or so before he ran and doesn't yet have any children. Nobody seems to have ever seen his wife.

"As for his parents, here's where it really gets wild. His campaign biography says that his parents were from Brazil, where they settled after his grandparents died in the Holocaust. He even gave a speech on the Senate floor on Holocaust Remembrance Day; he said his grandparents were Ukrainian Jews who died in one of the camps.

"When someone looked into his genealogy, they found that he had no Ukrainian heritage and that Sandoza was a common name for Hispanics in Brazil.

"The other interesting family fabrication involves his mother. A year ago, on the fifth anniversary of her death, he put out a press release and a Twitter feed saying that she died from the effects of nine-eleven; he claimed she had been working in the North Tower that day and suffered various ailments from the attack. But it turns out his mother was in Brazil on nine-eleven and there is no record of her ever working at the World Trade Center.

"As for his education, his bio claims that he graduated from Horace Mann School. And that he received an undergraduate degree from Baruch College, where he was in the top five percent of his class and a shortstop on the baseball team. He also claimed to have an MBA from the NYU Stern School of Business."

"Is any of that true?" asked Helen.

"None of it. All he has is a high school equivalence diploma.

"And then we have his alleged career before he decided to run for Congress. He claims that he started out at Citibank and then moved on to Golden Slacks where he became quote 'a seasoned Wall Street financier and investor.' Needless to say, neither Citibank nor Golden Slacks has any record of Sandoza having worked for them.

"He then moved to Florida. That part was true, he did live in Florida for a few years. And he did work, as his bio claimed, for an investment firm there called Harbor Capital.

"He worked briefly for that firm but there's no evidence that, as he claimed, he managed a one-point-five-billion-dollar investment fund that realized annual returns of twelve to twenty-six percent. In point of fact, the SEC sued Harbor Capital, claiming it was nothing more than a Ponzi scheme and had stolen over fifteen million dollars from its investors."

Everyone in the room was speechless. For the first time in the history of Peters and Peters, no one had anything to say.

So Melissa continued. "There's a third and final leg to his pre-political career. A few years ago he moved back to Long Island from Florida and bought a small house in Hicksville.

"His bio claims that, after moving back, he joined a business development company called Landbridge Investments. He claims he was a vice-president and brought in over a million dollars in revenue during his first six months at the firm. But Landbridge's founder told *Newsday* that Sandoza was merely a freelancer who sold event sponsorships. And he did so solely on commission.

"Finally, to create an image that he was a warm and caring person, Sandoza claimed that he helped fund a not-for-profit animal rescue service called 'Pet Friends.' He claims the organization helped rescue over two thousand dogs and cats. But nobody can find any registration for such an organization in either New York or New Jersey and there's no record of any IRS filing by the group and no mention of it on any social media site.

"Once he was elected, Sandoza used BotsUp? to generate all his public statements as well as all communications with his constituents. One of the most notorious examples was a speech he gave in Congress regarding the danger posed by Communist China. Sometime after that speech, he took to social media to claim that China had threatened him with assassination.

"Moreover, he claimed that his five-year-old niece had disappeared from a Queens playground and was subsequently discovered on a surveillance camera in the presence of two Chinese men. He then issued a press release saying that, while he didn't generally like to engage in conspiracy theories, he believed that the Chinese government was targeting him and his family as a result of his China speech.

"Did the police look into it?" asked Brandon.

"According to *Newsday*, there is no police record of any threat made to him or the disappearance of his alleged niece."

"When I first read about him" said Helen, "it was in connection with his lavish lifestyle, which his critics believed had been funded by campaign money."

"Yes, that's another of his many vices" said Melissa. "He was always taking lavish vacations to Atlantic City, Las Vegas and the Caribbean. And he made constant purchases at high-end retail stores: Tiffany, Hermes, Burberry and Ralph Lauren. He also spent thousands of dollars on Botox treatments."

"I thought only women get Botox treatments" said Brandon.

"Brandon, you're stereotyping again" said Melissa. "Why should women be the only ones to get Botox treatments?"

"Just sayin'" said Brandon.

"Wait a minute" said Chip, "this is the first time I've heard of a guy getting Botox treatments. I don't think Brandon meant to be sexist."

"I agree" said Pap. "Besides, stereotyping isn't sexist."

"You guys are hopeless" said Melissa. "But let's get back to Sandoza. His bank account never seemed to have more than a few hundred dollars in it and his credit cards were always maxed out. That's why they suspect he must have been using campaign funds to support his lifestyle.

"So what we have" said Melissa as she wrapped up, "is the first US Congressman created entirely by AI. Sandoza used AI to create his background and credentials and to generate every speech and constituent communication he ever made. And besides being a phony, he was a crook, stealing money from campaign funds to finance a lavish lifestyle."

"Wow" said Pap. "This is incredible. It's tailor-made for Peters and Peters. A lawsuit based on this will be front-page news. And it will put us at the forefront of the whole AI discussion."

"But who would we sue?" asked Brandon. "It's no use suing Sandoza, he's not going to have any money."

"We certainly would sue him" said Pap. "But not to get money. We need to take his deposition to find out whose idea this was, who all knew about the scheme, and whether Boogle knew he was using BotsUp? to get himself elected."

"Okay" Brandon replied, "but who do we sue that might be able to pay a judgment?"

"Everyone we can find" said Pap. "Sandoza must have had a PAC raising money for him. Melissa, see what you can find out about that. And we'll sue Boogle, we can't have tech companies creating

Congressmen out of AI. And besides, Boogle's one of the wealthiest companies in the world, they'll be our deep-pocket defendant."

"We should also see if Sandoza got money from a Super PAC" said Pup. "That's where the big money in politics comes from these days. Super PACs can't give money directly to a candidate, so they use their money to generate ads for candidates they prefer."

"Great idea" said Pap. "It would be great fun to sue one of those Super PACs, they're parasites. Worse than class action lawyers."

* * * *

As Chip got up to leave, Pap said "Now, we haven't heard from Brandon or Chip. You two were supposed to look for other AI issues. Chip, what did you come up with?"

Chip reluctantly sat back down. "Frankly, not too much. I've been pretty busy."

"Doing what? I'm not aware that we have any big cases that are active right now."

"Well, I spent last week helping Helen with the papers in Mona's case. You said you wanted to get a restraining order . . . . "

"I didn't know you were working on Mona's case" interrupted Melissa. "I haven't seen the two of you working together, or even talking, in the office."

"That's because we're working at Helen's apartment, mostly in the evening. It's quieter there. No phones, no email."

"Helen, what about your husband, Keith I believe is his name? He'd hardly want you and Chip working together in your apartment. Especially at night."

"He's in Tokyo right now. He's head of Moreland Shanley's Japanese operation and spends lots of time in Tokyo."

"So" said Pap, "you and Helen worked on Mona's case every night last week?"

"No" said Chip. "Keith only left on Tuesday. We worked on the case Tuesday and Wednesday night."

"What about Thursday?"

"Thursday night I took Candy to the Knicks game. I had promised to take her to a game if the Knicks made the playoffs. I always try to keep my promises."

"You were away overnight three nights last week?" said Brandon. How did you explain that to Francoise?"

"She was in Paris all week. The UN was in recess, so she took the opportunity to visit her family in France."

"Chip" said Pap, "I don't care how you spend your evenings. But what you've told us doesn't account for the workday. You're supposed to be working for the firm during the day."

"Well, Monday was pretty much taken up with our morning meeting. On Tuesday I started looking into this AI stuff. But then Helen asked if I could help her with the papers in Mona's case. That pretty much took up the next few days. I was doing research during the day so I could help Helen with the papers at night."

"What about Friday? That's still a working day around here. I don't recall saying we were going to a four-day workweek."

"I had to be in Shelter Island on Friday. I was meeting with a broker helping me find a rental for August."

"Okay, but you could have made up your lost Friday time on Saturday. Lots of lawyers work on Saturday. Especially if they didn't work on Friday."

"I had to pick up Francoise at JFK. As you know, with all the traffic it takes the better part of a day to go out there and back."

"And you spent Sunday with Francoise because you hadn't seen her for a week."

"Exactly. I'm glad you understand."

Pap decided to wrap up the meeting. They weren't getting anywhere beyond the Sandoza matter.

"Okay. Melissa, you need to keep focusing on Sandoza. See if you can turn up any Super PACs we can sue. Brandon and Chip, keep looking into AI, see if there's anything else out there for us. Let's reconvene Wednesday morning."

Everyone got up and headed for the door. They were heading for the Starbucks across the street to bring back their morning expresso drinks. The ones from the firm's coffee maker were terrible. No associate at Peters and Peters would be caught dead drinking the firm's coffee, even if it was free.

Chapter 5

SUPER PACS

On Wednesday morning, everyone convened in Pap's office. Pap and Pup took their usual seats behind Pap's desk while Melissa, Brandon, Chip and Helen sat on chairs placed in a semicircle in front of the desk.

Without allowing time for anyone to start up the usual banter and jokes, Pap launched right into business. "Okay, Melissa, what did you turn up in terms of PACs that supported Sandoza?"

"First of all" she began, "Sandoza had a small PAC that supported his campaign. It's called Goldstone Strategies. I suspect it was BotsUp? that came up with that name, it sounds solid and impressive. It raised about one-and-a-half million for his campaign, and spent all but about a couple hundred thousand. So, there's not much there to go after.

"But Pup was right, it's the Super PACs we want to focus on. And there are two big ones here. Between them they put about five million into Sandoza's campaign. I know that seems hard to believe, a first-time candidate getting that kind of money. But we're going to be playing in the big league of Super PACs.

"The first one is the conservative Super PAC, Take America Back. It's one of the largest Super PACs supporting Republican candidates. It was started by a guy named Dusty Rhodes; he made a fortune in road building in the Northeast.

"And this is what's ironic. He made most of his money from road-building contracts with public authorities – states and cities, even the federal government – but he's an arch-conservative. In the last election, Take America Back took in eighty-two million and disbursed about seventy-nine million. It gave an average of two million to forty different Congressional candidates. It looks like Sandoza's campaign got a little over two million."

Brandon interrupted: "If they took in eighty-two million and disbursed seventy-nine million, there won't be anything left."

"Brandon" said Melissa, "they have an ongoing operation. They'll be raising another eighty million for the next election cycle. It's a continuous inflow and outflow of money."

"Sounds like they should have at least three million left after the last election" said Pup. "We could ask the court to freeze that amount pending the outcome of the litigation."

"What did Take America Back see in Sandoza?" asked Helen. "It seems like he was always a shady character, and a complete novice at politics."

"He was a conservative Latino" said Melissa. "It doesn't get much better than that for Republicans."

Just then the door to Pap's office opened and his secretary, Vera Pesky, walked in and motioned to Pap.

"Sorry to interrupt" she said, sounding not the least bit sorry. "But you've got a phone call you have to take."

"Miss Pesky, how many times have I told you, I don't take calls during our meetings. Just tell whoever it is that I'm in a meeting and I'll call them back."

"But it's Mona. I told her you were in a meeting but she insisted it was urgent."

"Miss Pesky, I'm not interrupting a meeting to take a call from Mona Lott."

"But she's a client. You owe it to your clients to take their calls when they need to speak with you. Especially if they say it's urgent."

Pap hated these exchanges with Miss Pesky. In fact he hated Miss Pesky. She was always insisting he drop everything and speak with whoever was calling him. Why on earth had he brought her with him from Rogers and Autry? It was the dumbest thing he had ever done.

"Look. Tell Mrs. Lott this is a meeting I dare not interrupt. Tell her I'm meeting with three attorneys from the Justice Department's Civil Rights Division. They're threatening to sue the firm unless we hire some attorneys from Somalia and Bangladesh. This could threaten the firm's future."

"Right" Chip piped in. "If the DOJ sues us, the firm could go out of business. Then we couldn't represent her any more. She'd have to find new lawyers."

"That she'd have to pay" added Pap. "Now please leave us, we have important matters to discuss."

"No need to get snippy" huffed Pesky as she walked out and slammed the door.

"Now, where were we?" asked an exasperated Pap.

"We were identifying the Super PACs that supported Sandoza" said Melissa. "I just finished telling you about the Republican one, Take America Back."

"Right. And I believe you said there was a second large one involved?"

"Yes, and that's the really interesting part of the story. The other one is Democracy Now, the huge liberal Super PAC."

"Isn't that the one founded by that Hungarian guy, George Taurus?" asked Helen. "The financial guru who made a fortune in currency trading and now gives away billions of dollars a year to ultra-liberal causes?"

"Yes" said Melissa. "He's one of the richest people in the world. Forbes puts his net worth at over eight billion. So he can afford to lavishly fund Democracy Now. Last year, it gave over one-hundred-twenty-five million to various progressive candidates. About three million of that went to the Sandoza campaign."

"But why would George Taurus donate three million dollars to the campaign of a conservative Republican?" asked Helen.

"I'm not sure" said Melissa. "It's possible they liked the fact that he was a Latino. But I can't find a record of Democracy Now ever supporting a Republican candidate."

"Maybe they knew he was a phony" said Pap. "And knew that, after he got elected, this whole story would come out. It would be a huge black eye for Republicans. And it could even result in Sandoza being forced to resign and a Democrat taking his seat in a special election. That seat would stay Democratic for years."

"You know" said Pup, "if we could show through discovery that this is in fact what happened, we could sue them for more than the three million they poured into the Sandoza campaign. We could go for damages, arguing that they're guilty of election fraud. I'm not sure what the exact claim would be, I know some states have specific laws regarding election fraud."

"That would be rich" said Pap. "Democracy Now guilty of election fraud."

"But what if that wasn't the case?" said Brandon. "What if they simply wanted to see a Latino win. Would we have a claim?"

"Sure" said Pup. "The same claim we have against Take America Back. They were negligent in not investigating this guy before they supported his campaign with all that money."

"And we'll be on the side of the angels here" added Pap. "People hate these Super PACs, they think they're putting way too much money into elections.

"But look, before we get too far ahead of ourselves, we need to think about how we're going to find someone to bring this case."

Pap paused, then corrected himself. "I mean, how will someone who wants to bring a case against Sandoza and the Super PACs find us? As you know, we never find people to bring a case. We represent people who find us to bring a case for them."

"Absolutely" said Melissa, "that's how we do it. But look, I know from my research that Sandoza had a handful of major donors who gave to his PAC. One of them was a husband and wife team, Ray and Faye Wray. They each gave Goldstone Strategies fifteen thousand – although the money probably all came from Ray, not Faye."

"Isn't Faye Wray a famous actress?" asked Brandon.

"Yes" said Melissa. "She was a famous actress a hundred years ago. I don't think that Faye Wray is the one who's married to Ray Wray."

"Besides" said Helen, "she couldn't be married to Ray, she's already engaged to King Kong."

Ignoring Helen's bad joke, Melissa continued. "Ray and Faye Wray live in Roslyn, that's a tony village on the North Shore. If they live in Roslyn and can give thirty thousand to Sandoza's campaign, they're probably fairly wealthy. They're the ones we should start with."

"I know them" said Chip.

"You know them?" said an incredulous Pap.

"Sure. I met them last summer at a cocktail party on Shelter Island. Francoise and I spent a week there last August. That's why the day I took off last Friday, to look for a Shelter Island rental for August, could actually be seen as being in furtherance of firm business."

"He's probably going to put in for reimbursement of his rental from last summer" said Melissa.

"That would only be fair" Chip responded. "After all, that rental allowed me to meet the Wrays. And if I'm not mistaken, Pap is about to ask me to introduce him and Pup to them."

"Chip" said Pap, "have I ever told you how much you mean to the firm?"

"Actually you haven't. But you could show me how much I mean to the firm by reimbursing me for this summer's rental."

"Not only that" said Melissa, "but if Faye turns out to be good looking, we could add her photo to the Wall of Fame."

"Don't even think about that" said Pap. "We'll need Faye and Ray to be totally focused on the case. No monkey business with Faye Wray, okay?"

Pap paused and then said: "Look, if we can pull this off, it could be our most famous case yet."

"I thought all our cases were famous" said Melissa.

"They are, but this one could be even more famous. Everybody loves a political scandal. And this scandal has AI at its center."

"We'll be known as the firm that specializes in apes and bots" said Brandon.

Pup broke in. "I think we're missing something here. The Wrays and any other donors we locate would only be suing to get their money back. That's going to be a finite amount. Maybe a million or two at most.

"What we need to focus on are all the voters who voted for Sandoza in the belief that he was who he said he was. Melissa, as I recall you said there are about eight hundred thousand voters in that District?"

"Right. But they won't all have voted, and certainly they all won't have voted for Sandoza."

"That's okay" said Pup. "Maybe only two or three hundred thousand voted for him. That's an awful lot of voters who were defrauded. And also disenfranchised, if Sandoza is eventually thrown out of Congress."

"Pup, that's a great idea" said Pap. "All we need to do is find one person who voted for Sandoza and persuade him or her to sign on as our plaintiff."

"You mean" corrected Melissa, "all we need to do is to have one person who voted for Sandoza find us and persuade us to represent them in a class action."

"That's exactly what I said" said Pap. "And once we have a class certified, thousands of Third District voters will undoubtedly sign on to be in the class."

"I think I can help" said Chip.

"I'm sure you can" said Melissa as she looked at Chip. "You've probably bedded a score of women in Sandoza's district. But you probably didn't bother to ask them if they were Democrats or Republicans."

"No, I'm bipartisan" said Chip.

"So how can you help?" asked Pup.

"Look, I don't know anyone in that district but I think Candy probably does."

"Candy lives in Manhattan" said Melissa. "And she grew up in Staten Island. She can't possibly . . . ."

"Not our Candy, the other Candy. Candy Lande. The one from the Belgian Chocolates case – someone just put her photo up on the Wall of Fame. She's from somewhere in Nassau County, Oyster Bay I think. I'm sure she would know lots of people who live in that district."

"He'll probably take Candy to lunch at Le Bernardin and then, if she comes up with a candidate, charge it to the firm" said Melissa.

"And then he'll have to take the other Candy, our Candy, to Le Bernardin to even things up" said Brandon.

"Look" said Pap, "if Chip can get a resident of the Third District to be our plaintiff, he can charge the firm for fifteen lunches at Le Bernardin."

"It's a deal" said Chip.

"He can take me next" said Helen. "I haven't been there since you and Pup took me there when you were recruiting me."

"Okay" said Pap. "Chip's going to introduce Pup and me to the Wrays. And then he's going to take Candy, Candy Lande, to lunch at Le Bernardin. And then he'll take our Candy and God knows who else to lunch there as well.

"Well, I think we're done for now. On your way out, would one of you tell Pesky to get Mona on the phone."

Chapter 6

HOLLY

One week later, Chip stood at the entrance to the Red Salt Room, the dining room at the Garden City Hotel. The hotel was a lavish five-star resort in the heart of Garden City, which was on the western edge of Nassau County.

Chip broke into a broad grin as a gorgeous blonde in a light blue sleeveless summer dress approached.

"You must be Mister Pierpont" she said. "I'm Holly Gonightly, Candy's friend. We grew up together in Oyster Bay."

"You can call me Chip. That Mister Pierpont stuff makes me feel old."

After they were seated at a quiet table in the corner, Chip said: "Candy told me you were childhood friends. And that you were probably a Republican and may have voted for this Sandoza guy. But she didn't tell me you were gorgeous."

"Well, my mother Molly was quite beautiful. She did a handful of shows on Broadway, then spent several years doing TV commercials. Whenever they had a commercial where they needed a classy lady, they called her."

"What happened to her career?"

"She married my father Walter. Walter Clark. He's a fairly well-known ad executive. She had shot a commercial for one of his clients, Teflon, the big cosmetics company. They fell in love and she married him and they settled down in Oyster Bay to raise a family."

"If your father's last name is Clark, how come your name is Gonightly?"

"I changed it when I decided I wanted to follow in my mother's footsteps as an actress. I have a degree in theater performance from NYU. And I know I'll have to do some modeling until my career takes off, so I've recently signed on with a modeling agency. It's called the Big Top Modeling Agency.

"Anyway, I didn't think the name Holly Clark would get me very far, it certainly wouldn't turn any heads. So I had the lawyer for my father's ad agency help me legally change my name."

"But how did you come up with Gonightly?"

"It's in honor of my great uncle, Truman Coyote, the famous writer. Holly Gonightly was the heroine of his most famous story, Breakfast at Tierney's."

"Wasn't that Breakfast at Tiff...."

"No, Breakfast at Tierney's. It's a Jewish deli on the Upper West Side. Everybody used to go there in the morning for their bagels. Tierney's was famous for its bagels. Anyway, after I got out of school, I had my name changed to Gonightly."

After they had ordered, Chip launched into the history of Peters and Peters, how it was started up by the Peters brothers, Pap and Pup. He explained that the brothers had left lucrative law firm practices in order to start up a small firm specializing in plaintiffs' class action cases. All but one of the four associates had been with Pap or Pup at their prior firms.

He told Holly about some of the successful cases the firm had brought, including the Corny Flakes case three years ago and the cryptocurrency and Belgian Chocolates cases just last year. And of course the numerous successful cases the firm had brought on behalf of its most famous client, Lydia Lowlace.

Over dessert of blueberry tarts and cappuccino, Chip explained the firm's discovery that Congressman Sandoza's political career had been invented by the use of an AI program put out by Boogle, the tech giant. He explained that this was a fraud on both Sandoza's donors and his constituents.

"We think his donors and constituents have been cheated and are likely outraged. We think they'd like to see Boogle, Sandoza and his financial backers punished. The partners are meeting with a couple who gave lots of money to Sandoza's campaign, we think they'll want us to help them get their money back."

"I'd sure like to help" said Holly. "But I couldn't afford to give Sandoza any money, my modeling career hasn't yet taken off. So I don't know that I can help you."

"That's where you're wrong" said Chip as he nudged his knee against Holly's under the table. "We want to bring a class action on behalf of all the people who voted for Sandoza, whether or not they gave him any money. You'd be one of hundreds, probably thousands, of voters suing Boogle, Sandoza and the political action committees that supported him."

"What would I have to do?"

"Just allow us to make you the lead plaintiff. As the lead plaintiff, you'd be the representative of all the hundreds of constituents who were fooled by Sandoza. Your name would be the first name in the complaint: Holly Gonightly et al. versus Gregory Sandoza et al.

"We might even decide to list Boogle as the first defendant, so then the case would be known as Holly Gonightly versus Boogle. The case will undoubtedly be covered in all the newspapers and by local radio and cable media.

"And we always have a press conference where we announce our new cases, we'd probably want you to participate, say a few words to the press."

"Well, that would probably be good for my career. The trick is always to get noticed."

"Right. The lady I mentioned earlier, Lydia, spoke at the firm's press conference announcing the first case we brought on her behalf. She went on to become a Playboy Centerfold and now she's quite a celebrity."

"Didn't you say she started out as a stripper? I don't want to be known as a stripper."

"Not a stripper. She was a lap dancer when I discovered her at a club. And now she's famous. Just think about this as opening a career path for you."

"What were you doing in a strip club?"

"Holly, I assure you they weren't strippers. Just lap dancers. It was a club where some of my banker friends – they work at Golden Slacks, one of the top investment banks in New York - like to hang out. They insisted I join them that night.

"Anyway, that's not important. What's important is that Lydia was totally unknown when I first met her and our firm proceeded to make her famous. We could do the same for you. Especially when the media realizes you're related to Truman Coyote."

"What would happen besides the press conference?"

"Well, eventually the defendants' attorneys would take your deposition. We'd be in a conference room and they'd ask you a bunch of questions. What do you know about Sandoza? Did you give any money to his campaign? Why did you vote for him? Why are you suing? That kind of thing."

"That sounds kind of tricky. How would I know how to answer the questions?"

"I'll be there beside you all the way. Pup and I will prepare you long before the deposition takes place. We'll tell you .... "

"What about the other guy, Pap? Will he be there too?"

"No, Pap never does depositions. Says they're boring, he always falls asleep. But he's great in court. Wait until you see him in action.

"But getting back to your preparation. We'll tell you what questions they're going to ask and we'll tell you what answers you should give. Nothing will be left to chance. And we certainly won't let anyone bully you. You can trust me on that."

"You think we'd win the case?"

"We always win the cases we bring. Except when we sue to advance animal rights. We didn't do so well when we tried to get some chimpanzees in the Bronx Zoo released so they could be sent to a nature preserve in Florida."

"You guys represented a bunch of chimpanzees?"

"Yeah. Pap – he's sort of the head partner – thought it would be good publicity for the firm, even if we lost. Which, of course, we did. Actually, we won the case – twice – in the trial court. The judge really liked our case and ruled for us twice. But both times she got reversed by the appellate court."

"So you actually lost that case twice?"

"Right. But we've won all of our other cases and we've always gotten tons of money for the members of the class. And the class representative – which you would be – always gets a whole lot more than the other members of the class."

"I don't care all that much about the money. Daddy pays my rent, which is my biggest expense. But if my role in the case generates publicity and helps spark interest in my career, I'm all in."

"I'm sure it will. If we can make a stripper from McKeesport, Pennsylvania famous, we can certainly make you famous."

"I thought you said she wasn't a stripper."

"Right. As I said, she was a lap dancer. And a very good one, by the way."

"Did she do a dance in your lap?"

"Yes, that's how she came to my attention."

"Did she do anything else for you?"

"Look, I can't answer that. She's a client. And everything that transpires between a client and her lawyer is privileged."

Holly smiled. "Still" she said, "I'm worried about saying the wrong thing in that deposition. Or in court. Would I have to testify in court?"

"Yes, if the case isn't settled before then. But I told you not to worry. I'll be right there with you all the time. I'll make sure you know what to say."

Holly nudged her knee against Chip's and said "Maybe we should get a head start."

"What do you mean?"

"Well, maybe we should start my preparation this afternoon."

"Where? We can't sit here in the restaurant all afternoon. The maitre'd is already giving us looks like he wants us to leave."

"This is a hotel, isn't it?"

"Right. What a great idea, Holly. I'll check with the front desk and see what's available."

* * * *

The following Monday, the associates assembled in Pap's office for their weekly meeting.

Pap began by announcing that, thanks to Chip's introduction, he and Pup had met with the Wrays at their home in Roslyn. The Wrays were really steamed about the whole Sandoza thing. They had given thirty thousand to a candidate who was an absolute phony and who was likely to be kicked out of Congress, thereby endangering the Republicans' already thin majority in the House.

In fact, they were so steamed about the matter that they had invited their best friends, Adam and Eve, to the meeting.

"Adam and Eve?" said Helen. "You've got to be kidding."

"It's no joke" said Pap. "The husband's name is Adam. Adam Eaves. He's a stockbroker in the City. His wife's name is Eve. Her maiden name is Eve Adams."

"So now she's Eve Eaves?" asked Brandon.

"No, she's a writer, and wanted to keep the name she was known by – Eve Adams – before she married Adam. So she did. According to the Wrays, everyone just calls them Adam and Eve."

"The point is" said Pup, "Adam and Eve gave a total of twenty thousand to Sandoza's PAC and they're furious. So we now have two sets of plaintiffs: Ray and Faye Wray and Adam Eaves and Eve Adams."

"Right" said Pap. "We're all set on plaintiffs for the donor class. So Chip, did you have any luck coming up with a plaintiff for the voter class?"

"Yes, you might say I had some luck."

"You want to tell us about it?"

"I first had lunch with Candy – Candy Lande that is – and she told me about her childhood friend Holly. Holly Gonightly. She and Candy grew up together in Oyster Bay and she's a Republican who voted for Sandoza. She's our plaintiff."

"Holly Gonightly?" said Helen. "What kind of a name is that?"

"Well, it's a long story. She explained it all to me over lunch at the Red Salt Room in the Garden City Hotel."

"Is that the day you left the office at eleven and never came back?" asked Melissa.

"Yes. We had a lot to talk about."

"You talked all afternoon in the Garden City Red Salt Room?"

"Well, she was nervous about having to answer questions at a deposition, and then in court. I needed to help her get over her fears."

"How did you do that?" asked Brandon. "We need to learn how to deal with a witness who's reluctant to get involved in a case."

"For heaven's sake, Brandon, how do you think he dealt with her?" said Melissa. "He did his usual thing and it obviously worked."

"You mean . . . ."

"I don't care how he did it" said Pap. So long as he recruited her to be our plaintiff. That was his mission."

"I always try to carry out my mission" said Chip.

"You'd better get an autographed photo of her" said Melissa. "We need to add it to the Wall of Fame."

"What about the lunch?" asked Chip. "The Red Salt Room is pretty expensive. The firm will reimburse me for it, won't you? That would only be fair."

Chapter 7

ORVILLE AND VIRGIL

On the third Thursday in June, Pap, Pup and all the participants in the ill-fated balloon party trudged up the steps of the Connecticut Superior Court in Bridgeport. They headed for the courtroom of Judge Orville Rite. The courtroom was quite small and so their entourage quickly filled the entire spectator section.

Judge Rite's bailiff, Virgil Trucks, seemed to be running the proceedings. At the counsel table nearest the jury box was Belle Towles, the local prosecutor. Dressed in a gray skirt and black jacket, and with a look of utter seriousness on her face, she did her best to convey the image of a seasoned prosecutor.

Judge Rite quickly disposed of three routine matters, two misdemeanor charges and a continuance in a sentencing proceeding. At that point bailiff Trucks called the case of State versus Mona Lott, et al.

Led by Pap, the entire spectator section rose and advanced to the front of the courtroom where they crowded around the table opposite prosecutor Towles's table.

Who Put the Bots in the Tort\$?

Transcript of Proceedings:

The Court: Virgil, who are all these people? And why are they all standing around the defense table?

Mr. Trucks: I think they're all defendants.

Ms. Towles: That's correct, Your Honor. They all received citations for trespassing and holding a demonstration without a permit. Down in Westport at the local high school.

The Court: How many are there?

Ms. Towles: Twenty of them received citations for trespassing and holding a demonstration without a permit.

The Court: Is that right, Virgil? We got twenty defendants in this case?

Mr. Trucks: Well, let's see. According to this charge sheet, we got Mona and Hamilton Lott; Patrick and Piper Peters; Prescott and Priscilla Peters; William and Hillary Fund; Stacey and Daisy Spacey; Ray and Bunny Rabbitz....

The Court: Bunny Rabbits?

Mr. Trucks: That's what the charge sheet says, Bunny Rabbitz. That's R-A-B-B-I-T-Z. I think she's Ray Rabbitz's wife.

(Long Pause)

The Court: Okay, Virgil, please continue.

Mr. Trucks: Then we've got Laurel Ann Hardy and Milo Nulow, I can't tell if they're married.

Voice from Crowd: Certainly not.

Mr. Trucks: Okay, I guess you must be Ms. Hardy and Mr. Nulow, next to you, is not your husband. Now, Judge, we've also got Peachy and Harley Keane.

The Court: Peachy?

Voice from Crowd: It's actually Peggy Myhart Keane but everyone calls me Peachy. You see, it's because when . . . .

The Court: Yes, I can see why they call you Peachy. No need to elaborate. Now, how many is that Virgil?

Mr. Trucks: That's sixteen. But we've got four more. We've got Tiffany and Bethany Peters and then Patrick Peters the Fourth and Henry Alden Peters. They must be related to one of the two Mr. and Mrs. Peters, I'm not sure which ones go with which, they all look alike.

So that brings the number up to twenty. But there are still three more.

The Court: Now you're telling me there are more than twenty defendants in this case?

Mr. Trucks: Yes, there's the three balloon pilots. Fred Brothers, Ted Brothers and Ned Brothers.

The Court: They're charged with trespassing too?

Mr. Trucks: No, I think they're charged with unlawfully landing their hot air balloons.

The Court: What do you mean unlawfully landing their balloons?

Ms. Towles: They were piloting the three hot air balloons in which the other twenty defendants were riding. They didn't have a permit or advance permission to land where they did.

The Court: Where did they land?

Ms. Towles: On the football field at Staples High School in Westport.

The Court: What's wrong with that? It's summer, there couldn't have been any football games going on at the time. Hot air balloons need to land somewhere in the open, a high school football field seems like a good place for them to have landed.

Ms. Towles: But you need a permit from the town to land a hot air balloon on pubic property.

The Court: Ms. Towles, I fly an airplane on weekends. I always have in mind one or two open spaces where I can land in an emergency.

Ms. Towles: You have an airplane?

The Court: Yes, a Baby Ace. My brother and I assembled it from a kit put out by Ace Aircraft.

Ms. Towles: You and your bother assembled an airplane?

The Court: Certainly. My brother Wilbur and I assembled a Baby Ace airplane. We call it "The Kittyhawk." It only seats one, so we have to take turns flying it.

Ms. Towles: You and Wilbur made a real airplane from a kit? And it flies?

The Court: Yes. Of course we had to supplement what was in the kit with some additional parts, such as an engine. But yes, it certainly flies.

I'll admit it took several tries getting it off the ground. The first few times it only flew fifty feet or so. But we kept working on it and now it flies just fine. We keep it in a private hanger over at Sikorsky Airfield in Stratford. We generally fly along the coast of Long Island Sound, beautiful views. I'd offer to take you up for a ride but, as I said, it only seats one person.

Ms. Towles: Thank goodness for that. But we need to get back to the charges. These three pilots didn't have clearance to land their balloons at Staples High School. They did have a permit to take off from and then land back at Compo Beach. But they had no permit to land on the Staples High School football field.

The Court: Well, as I said before, good pilots – whether flying an airplane or a hot air balloon – always have in mind one or two places where they can land in an emergency.

Maybe that's what happened here. Maybe the balloons had some sort of emergency and needed somewhere safe, like a football field, to land. Is that what happened?

(Several defendants begin speaking and gesticulating all at once. Mass confusion.)

(The Court bangs its gavel several times.)

The Court: For heaven's sake, you can't all speak at once. Which one of you is the lawyer here?

Unidentified Voice: I am.

The Court: Who are you?

Same Voice: I'm Patrick Peters, one of the defendants. My brother and I practice law in New York City. I wish I could say we also fly airplanes, but I'm afraid we only play golf on weekends.

Ms. Towles: Your Honor, he's only admitted in New York, he's not admitted in Connecticut. So he can't appear as an attorney in this case.

Mr. Peters: I'm pro se.

Ms. Towles: What's pro se?

The Court: Pro se means "for himself" or "on his own behalf." Parties can always represent themselves in a lawsuit, even if they're not attorneys. You should know that, it happens a lot here.

Ms. Towles: Well, maybe he can represent himself but he can't represent all the others.

Mr. Peters: Then the others can all represent themselves pro se.

The Court: Virgil, aside from Mr. Peters, how many defendants are there?

Mr. Trucks: Let's see, we had twenty-three but take away Mr. Peters and we got twenty-two.

The Court: Mr. Peters and twenty-two other defendants, each acting as their own attorney. Ms. Towles, do you really want to prosecute a case with twenty-three pro se attorneys on the other side?

Ms. Towles: Well, I don't see any alternative. But that shouldn't be a problem, they'll probably all say the same thing.

The Court: You think twenty-three people acting as their own attorney are all going to say the same thing?

Ms. Towles: Why don't we ask them.

The Court: Are you crazy? You want me to ask twenty-three defendants what their defense is going to be? We'd be here all week.

Mr. Peters: Your Honor, I have a suggestion. Just for today, why don't you let me speak for the others. That will help move things along.

The Court: Good idea. I'm appointing Mr. Peters – for purposes of today's hearing only – as the representative for all the defendants.

Ms. Towles: Does that include the four kids?

The Court: You're prosecuting four kids?

Ms. Towles: Yes. They were part of the unlawful demonstration. And they were also trespassing on the football field.

The Court: I seriously doubt that four children were part of a demonstration. Or that they knowingly recognized that they were trespassing. But before we go any further, would the four children please step forward.

(Two boys and two girls step to the front of the table.)

The Court: Virgil, how old are they? And why do they all seem to look alike?

Mr. Trucks: You'll have to ask them. But I believe they are nine or ten. And I'd say the boys are twins. Same with the girls. You can tell by looking at them.

The Court: Okay (Court smiles at the children). Now there's no need to be frightened. Could you please tell me your names and ages.

(All four children answer at once)

The Court: No, no, one at a time. You (pointing at boy on the far left): What's your name?

Boy on Left: I'm Patrick Aldrich Peters the Fourth. And I'm ten.

The Court: Do your friends call you something other than Patrick Aldrich Peters the Fourth?

First Peters Boy: Well, Sir, everyone calls me "Little Pap." You see, my initials are P-A-P, the same as my father's. He's Patrick Aldrich Peters the Third, but everyone just calls him Pap. So, to avoid confusion, they call me Little Pap.

The Court: And the one next to you, he must be your twin brother?

First Peters Boy: Yes (pointing), this is my brother Henry Alden Peters. His initials are H-A-P so everyone calls him Hap. He's also ten.

The Court: Yes, I figured that. Twins are usually the same age. Now, let's move on to the girls. What are your names?

(Both answer at once.)

The Court: No, haven't you been listening? You can't both talk at the same time. Lets start with you (pointing).

Peters Girl: I'm Tiffany Ann Peters and I'm ten-and-a-half. When I was little everyone called me by my initials, Tap. But I'm grown up now and I prefer my real name, Tiffany. Don't you think that's a pretty name?

The Court: It certainly is, Tiffany. Now, that must be your sister next to you, what's her name?

Peters Girl: Her name's Bethany Ann Peters. We used to call her Bap but now we call her by her real name. Bethany is a very pretty name, just like Tiffany. And she's ten-and-a-half also.

The Court: The boys said they were ten. How could your mother have two sets of twins six months apart?

Peters Girl: Oh, Aunt Piper isn't our mother. Our mother is Priscilla, that's her there (pointing).

The Court: So who's Aunt Piper?

Peters Girl: She's married to Uncle Pap. The one you said could be everyone's lawyer.

The Court: I see. So who's your father?

Peters Girl: Pup. That's him next to my mother. He's Uncle Pap's brother. He's a lawyer too.

The Court: So your father and your uncle are both lawyers?

Peters Girl: Yes. They have a firm in New York City. They sue companies for lots of money. Mother says they're famous.

The Court: Ms. Towles, look at what you've gotten us into. Twenty-three defendants, two of them New York City lawyers who go around suing people. And who are apparently famous.

Ms. Towles: Well, this is a serious case and . . . .

The Court: I'm not so sure it's a serious case. At the moment it's more like a circus.

Ms. Towles: Well, if we could just . . . .

The Court: No, here's what we're going to do. First of all, I'm dismissing the case against the three pilots. Virgil, what are their names again?

Mr. Trucks: Fred Brothers, Ted Brothers and Ned Brothers.

The Court: Are they brothers?

Mr. Trucks: Yes. They're the Brothers brothers. In fact, I believe that's the name of their balloon business: Brothers Brothers Balloons.

The Court: Gentlemen – by that I mean the three Brothers brothers – I'm dismissing the charges against you. Your first duty as balloon pilots is safeguarding the lives of your passengers. You seem to have done that well.

The Brothers (In unison): Thank you, Your Honor.

A Brother: And on behalf of the three of us, Your Honor, we admire your skill in building your own airplane.

The Court: It wasn't just my skill. My brother Wilbur and I built it together, I really needed his help. That's why I have to let him fly it every other weekend.

Another Brother: You could come and fly with us on the weekends you can't take up the plane. We could really use a fourth pilot.

The Court: I'll give that some thought.

Now, getting back to the other defendants, I'm also dismissing all charges against the four children. The Connecticut Superior Court is not in business to prosecute ten-year-old kids for riding in a hot air balloon. It's not their fault the balloons landed on a high school football field. So now, Virgil, that leaves us with sixteen defendants, is that correct?

Mr. Trucks: That's correct. Sixteen adults. No kids, no pilots. They're all charged with trespassing and demonstrating without a permit.

The Court: Look, Ms. Towles, we're not gonna prosecute sixteen adults in this court for such petty offenses. But I'll let you select one of them to prosecute, sort of a representative defendant. We'll take a short break. When we resume, you tell me which one of them you want to pursue the charges against.

Ms. Towles: You're letting the other fifteen off the hook?

The Court: Not exactly. I'll dismiss the charges against them without prejudice.

Ms. Towles: What do you mean, "without prejudice"?

The Court: My God, where did you go to law school?

Ms. Towles: I went to the . . . .

The Court: That wasn't a question. It was a rhetorical question. Maybe Virgil can explain to you what a rhetorical question is, you can talk with him during the break. But "without prejudice" means that if I find the representative defendant guilty of one or both of the charges, you're free to reinstate charges against some or all of the other fifteen.

Now, we'll take a ten-minute recess. Ms. Towles, please be prepared to let us know who the representative defendant will be. And as for all of you (pointing at the people around counsel table), you can resume your seats in the spectator section. Okay, we're in recess until eleven thirty.

Chapter 8

BELLE AND MONA

(Hearing resumes at 11:35 am)

The Court: Okay, we're back on the record. Ms. Towles, have you selected the defendant against whom you wish to proceed?

Ms. Towles: Yes. Mrs. Lott. Mona Lott. She was clearly the ringleader behind the balloons landing at the high school and also the ensuing demonstration.

The Court: What did she have to do with the balloons landing at the high school?

Ms. Towles: The Westport police don't believe it was an emergency landing. They think she planned it so they could have the demonstration there. That's why several members of the Westport press were there when the balloons landed.

The Court: And the demonstration, what was it all about?

Ms. Towles: It was about lawn mowing in Westport. And it wasn't really a big demonstration, it was mostly Mrs. Lott. The other people were just standing around and listening.

The Court: What did Mrs. Lott do?

Ms. Towles: Well, after everyone climbed out of the balloons, she unfurled a large banner saying "Make Our Lawns Great Again." And then she began addressing the members of the press - she had apparently arranged to have them there when the balloons landed. She launched into a speech about why she needed to mow her lawn on Saturday afternoons.

The Court: She was arrested because she made a speech about mowing her lawn on Saturday afternoons?

Ms. Towles: Well, it was really a speech complaining about a couple of Westport zoning ordinances that regulate lawn mowing.

The Court: We're having a criminal proceeding with sixteen defendants because Mrs. Lott made a speech about Westport's lawn mowing regulations?

Ms. Towles: Well, it's more than that. You see, she's repeatedly been given citations for mowing her lawn on Saturday afternoon but she just keeps on doing it.

The Court: What's wrong with that? That's when I mow my lawn. That way, I can take The Kittyhawk up all day Sunday. Well, every other Sunday. Wilbur gets to fly it on half the Sundays.

Ms. Towles: Well, there's probably no law in Bridgeport against your mowing your lawn on Saturday afternoon. But there is in Westport. They have a zoning regulation that prohibits lawn mowing on Saturday afternoon and all day Sunday.

The Court: That sounds like something a bunch of rich folks with second homes in Westport cooked up.

Ms. Towles: I don't make the laws. I'm only here to enforce the laws made by other people.

The Court: Those other people are the ones who ought to be defendants here. Don't you think so, Virgil?

Mr. Trucks: Absolutely.

Ms. Towles: That's not all, Your Honor. So far this year Mrs. Lott has been seen mowing her lawn every other weekend in May.

The Court: Yes, you just said she mows it on Saturday afternoons and that's against some crazy ordinance.

Ms. Towles: It's more than that. Westport also has a zoning ordinance that prohibits all lawn mowing in May. It's called the "No Mow May" ordinance.

The Court: That's ridiculous. Why can't people in Westport mow their lawns in May?

Ms. Towles: Your Honor, it's been discovered that mowing your lawn in May is harmful to the bio-environment. It inhibits the growth of weeds and flowering plants, plants that provide nectars and pollens that nourish bees and other pollinators.

They even say that No Mow May has, in some communities, led to a resurgence of wildlife. People have spotted woodchucks, racoons and snakes in the tall grass. One plant expert in Delaware reported finding almost twelve hundred species of moths on his property when he stopped mowing. I think he had ten acres.

The Court: This is nuts. This is America. People have a right to mow their lawns in May – that's when your grass is growing the fastest. It'll get out of hand if you don't mow it then. Besides, why do we need racoons and snakes in everyone's front yard?

Ms. Towles: Well, that's the law in Westport and Mrs. Lott can't just ignore it.

The Court: This is a waste of everyone's time. We've got real criminal issues to deal with in Bridgeport: burglaries, robberies, carjackings, rapes, sex trafficking, crack cocaine. We don't have time to deal with issues involving lawn mowing.

Ms. Towles: I'm sorry, Your Honor, but . . . .

The Court: Why don't you just withdraw the charges against Mrs. Lott? I'm sure she'll agree to behave (nodding at Mrs. Lott, now standing with Mr. Peters at the counsel table).

Mrs. Lott: Yes, Your Honor. I promise I won't cause any more balloons to land at the high school. And I'll agree not to mow any more in May – at least not until next year.

Ms. Towles: So you admit that you're the one who caused the balloons to land on the high school football field? I remind you, you're under oath.

The Court: Ms. Towles, she's not under oath. She's not even on the witness stand.

Ms. Towles: Oh, I see. But she still should tell the truth. So, is it true, Mrs. Lott, that you're the one who caused the balloons to land on the football field?

Mrs. Lott: Yes, of course. That's where the reporters were waiting. I couldn't very well ask the reporters to come to the football field if we were going to land back at Compo. And besides, I've just agreed with this nice judge that I won't make any more balloons land at the football field.

Ms. Towles: Right. But as for mowing in May, you're only promising not to more any more in May this year?

Mrs. Lott: That's correct. I agree not to mow this weekend, I'll wait until June. One week without mowing won't hurt.

Ms. Towles: But no promises about next year?

Mrs. Lott: That's right. My grass will grow five feet tall if I don't mow it at all in May. And like you said, it will attract woodchucks, racoons and snakes. Who wants to send their kids out to play in a yard filled with snakes?

Ms. Towles: You have young kids?

Mrs. Lott: No, they're all grown by now. Most people think I look too young to have grown kids, that's probably what you thought.

Ms. Towles: That's not what I thought. What I thought was that there wouldn't be any young kids for the snakes to bother.

The Court: Ms. Towles, Mrs. Lott may not have any young kids but I'm pretty sure there are some young couples with kids somewhere in Westport. Now can we . . . .

Ms. Towles: There's still the Saturday afternoon mowing. She's received numerous citations for mowing her lawn on Saturday afternoons. So I need to ask her about that. Now, Mrs. Lott, in order to resolve this case, are you willing to stop mowing your lawn on Saturday afternoons, as required by your town's zoning ordinance?

Mrs. Lott: Of course not. That's the only time I can mow it.

Ms. Towles: You could mow it on Saturday morning. Any tine up to two o'clock.

Mrs. Lott: But I've already explained this to the town and they wouldn't listen. Ham and I play golf every Saturday morning. We have a standing game with Peachy and Harley.

Ms. Towles: Who's Peachy?

Mrs. Lott: Peachy Keane. She's married to Harley Keane. They're two of the nice people you're trying to put in jail. That's them back there (witness points). Next to the four children that you also tried to prosecute. You should be ashamed of yourself.

Ms. Towles: The law's the law. If the law says you can't mow your lawn on Saturday afternoon, you'll just have to mow it on Saturday morning.

Mrs. Lott: Do you mow your lawn on Saturday mornings?

Ms. Towles: That's irrelevant and immaterial. I'm not the one on trial here.

The Court: That's true. But I'd like to hear your answer to Mrs. Lott's question.

Ms. Towles: No, I don't.

Mrs. Lott: Why not?

Ms. Towles: That's when I have my mindfulness sessions.

Mrs. Lott: Mindfulness sessions?

Ms. Towles: Certainly. Every Saturday, except in the winter, Gladys, Iris and I go down to the beach and practice mindfulness. It's a zen-like thing. Helps put you in touch with your innermost self. And with the environment.

Ms. Lott: It takes you all Saturday morning to get in touch with your inner self?

Ms. Towles: We also mix in some yoga. Yoga goes well with mindfulness.

Mrs. Lott: So then you must mow your lawn on Saturday afternoon?

Ms. Towles: No, but my husband does.

Mrs. Lott: Why doesn't he mow it on Saturday morning?

Ms. Towles: He can't. That's when he plays tennis. He's part of a foursome, they have a standing doubles game every Saturday morning.

Mrs. Lott: If you and your friends can practice mindfulness every Saturday morning, and your husband can play tennis every Saturday morning, why can't I play golf on Saturday morning?

Ms. Towles: Nobody says you can't. They just say if you want to cut your grass on Saturday, you need to do it before two o'clock.

The Court: I don't see why she shouldn't be able to mow her lawn on Saturday afternoon if that's when she wants to do it.

Ms. Towles: Your Honor, the laws's the law. We can't have rich people in Westport deciding which laws they will obey and which ones they won't.

Mrs. Lott: I'm not rich. I make documentaries. Everyone knows that no one except Ken Burns has ever made any money from making documentaries.

Ms. Towles: Your Honor, her husband Hamilton Lott is a big shot banker. He's with Smith Blarney in New York. They have a large house, its probably an estate, in a tony section of Westport. They even have a name for it, they call it "Hamalot."

The Court: So you want to prosecute this lady because her husband's a banker and they have an estate in Westport that they call Hamalot? When this is over she'll probably make a documentary about the whole thing. We'll all look ridiculous.

Mrs. Lott: That's a great idea, Your Honor. I've been looking for a subject for a new documentary. But I promise I won't make you look ridiculous. No promises about her (witness points to Ms. Towles).

Ms. Towles: Your Honor, the law's the law. And . . . .

The Court: You keep saying that. But I'll bet Mr. Peters here will have eighteen reasons why those lawn mowing ordinances are invalid.

Mr. Peters: That's correct, Your Honor. In fact, we plan to file a motion next week for a restraining order suspending enforcement of the ordinances until the Court can make a final ruling on the merits.

Ms. Towles: He can't file such a motion. He may be able to represent himself – per se or whatever it's called – but he can't represent Mrs. Lott.

Mr. Peters: My good friend Sam Snake, of Snake and Rolle – their office is right here in Bridgeport – will appear as attorney of record for Mrs. Lott.

The Court: Mr. Snake's a friend of yours? His firm has a fine reputation in this court.

Mr. Peters: Sam and I both got our start in the New York DA's office. I stayed in New York but Sam came up here. We've worked together several times, we'll do the case together.

Ms. Towles: But Mr. Peters isn't admitted in Connecticut. He can't participate in the case on behalf of Mrs. Lott.

Mr. Peters: I'll be filing a motion for admission Pro Haec Vice. That would allow me to fully participate in the case.

Ms. Towles: What's pro haec vice?

The Court: It means "for this turn, for this one case." Out-of-state attorneys appear on that basis all the time. You really should learn these Latin terms, they're used all the time.

In any event, if Mr. Peters files for admission pro haec vice, I'll grant it. And if he and Mr. Snake file a motion for a restraining order, I'll likely grant that as well.

So, Ms. Towles, I strongly suggest you sit down with Mr. Peters, or with Mr. Snake if you prefer, and try to resolve this matter. Virgil, put this matter over for three weeks, that should give them plenty of time to talk. If the case hasn't been resolved by then, we'll reconvene and I'll hear the motion for a restraining order.

* * * *

As everyone spilled out of the courthouse, Pap spotted Sheriff Horace Ryder crossing the street and heading in their direction. Ryder was the Bridgeport sheriff who had been involved in Mona's arrest five years ago for her alleged use of an assault rifle to shoot at some Canadian geese that had landed on her pond.

"Mr. Peters" said Ryder, "what brings you to Westport? I hope it's not another case involving that eccentric lady, Mona . . . I forget her last name."

"Lott. Mona Lott" said Pap. "Nice to see you again sheriff. Unfortunately, it does involve Mrs. Lott – along with twenty-two other defendants, myself included."

Pap, proceeded to explain how a dispute over two lawn mowing ordinances in Westport had led to three hot air balloons landing on the high school football field in Westport. Which then led to charges against twenty defendants for demonstrating without a permit and three balloon pilots for alleged unlawful landings.

"Who's the judge?" asked Ryder.

"Orville Rite. Turns out he has a brother named Wilbur and they built a small airplane from a kit. Rite's interest in aviation worked to the advantage of the three guys who were piloting the balloons. Rite let them off."

"Who's the prosecutor?"

"Belle Towles. She seemed to be unnecessarily strident; and she kept irritating Judge Rite."

"She's incompetent. She never wins the really important cases she brings. Why, just a few months ago, she lost an airtight case against Slick Wick, the leading drug pusher in Bridgeport. He was arrested for trying to sell thirty ounces of crack cocaine to an undercover officer. The entire encounter was recorded on the officer's body cam."

"How could she lose a case like that?"

"Wick belatedly claimed alibi. Said that was not him on the video. Claimed he had been in Buffalo at the time."

"He claimed alibi in a drug transaction that was filmed on a body cam?"

"Yeah. He testified that he had been in Buffalo to watch his nephew's participation in a Christmas pageant. Said his nephew was playing the part of the camel."

"I think there's usually a donkey, not a camel, in those pageants. And anyway, couldn't she have had someone check out the alibi?"

"She didn't have much to go on. Wick claimed he couldn't remember the name of the church, just knew it was somewhere in

Buffalo. Towles never bothered to ask for an adjournment to check the story out, she just barged ahead. The jury acquitted him. He's back on the street pushing cocaine and meth."

"Well, I think our case will have a happier ending. Rite's dismissed the charges against the three pilots and against Pup and my kids. And he dismissed charges, without prejudice, against everyone except Mona. If Towles won't drop the charges, I'll have to file a motion for a restraining order against the lawn mowing ordinances."

"I'm on good terms with Judge Rite. In fact, I'll be seeing him next week, I've got a case in front of him. I'll put in a good word for you. Mona too, she didn't deserve to get arrested for that BB gun thing. I'm sure Towles will try to bring that up."

"What's your case about?"

"It's a car-jacking case. Actually a double car-jacking case. A couple of dopey kids tried to hijack a Mercedes SUV. Turned out the Mercedes had just been hijacked by three gang-bangers at a nearby shopping center. The guys in the Mercedes opened fire on the kids, they never knew what hit 'em."

"Well, it sounds like Judge Rite has more serious stuff to deal with than a fight over lawn mowing in Westport. He probably doesn't need a nudge from you, but I'd appreciate any word you could put in if you find an appropriate opening."

"Happy to help. You take care now."

"Thanks, Sheriff. If there's ever anything I can do for you, just let me know."

Chapter 9

THE PROFESSOR

On the first Wednesday in July, the lawyers assembled in Pap's office for their weekly meeting. The firm had been closed on Monday and Tuesday as Tuesday was the Fourth of July.

"I hope everyone enjoyed the long weekend" Pap began. "Pup and I got in lots of golf."

"I hope the two of you didn't play against your wives" said Chip. "You told us they beat you the last time you played against them."

"They cheated" said Pup petulantly. "I explained that to you guys last year."

"That's why we never play against them anymore" said Pap. "Pup lets their antics get under his skin. Throws him off his game."

"Speaking of being off your game" said Melissa. "Chip, what on earth's up with your new desk calendar? Each month has a picture of fans. Small fans, large fans, floor fans. Every kind of fan under the sun. I thought you always used a Sports Illustrated Swimsuit calendar."

"Candy gave it to me for April Fool's Day" said Chip. "It's called the 'Only Fans' calendar. The cover has a photo of a sultry brunette in a low-cut top with a 'come hither' look. But it turns out the cover's just a come-on. The interior pages don't have any pictures of sultry women in low-cut tops with a 'come hither' look. They only have pictures of fans. That's what the company makes. Fans."

"Could be a case of false advertising" said Brandon.

"Not if the name on the cover says 'Only Fans'" said Melissa. "Fans are what's inside. In fact, I looked through it the other day and there are only pictures of fans. So the name of the calendar, 'Only Fans,' is absolutely truthful."

"Why were you looking through my calendar?" Chip asked.

"Candy wanted me to find out how many lunches you had scheduled with our new plaintiff, Holly Gonightly."

"But why'd Candy give you the calendar in the first place?" asked Brandon.

"As I said, it was an April Fool's Day joke. And the joke was on me. I think Candy's still sore at me for standing her up at last year's Christmas party."

"I thought the two of you had made up" said Brandon. "Didn't you tell us you took Candy to a Knicks game that week when you spent two nights with Helen working on Mona's case?"

"Yeah, I took her to the game. But she wouldn't let me stay with her afterward, so I just went home. Wasted the cost of dinner and tickets. Those playoff tickets are really expensive."

* * * *

"Okay" said Pap. "Now that we know Candy's still sore at Chip, we need to get down to business."

"I think you should tell everyone about our meeting with Nick Urbacher" said Pup.

"Right. Nick Urbacher is the embodiment of New York City's upper class. He's the managing director of Lazard and he's quite rich. He's also a friend of Bill Fund.

"You remember Fund, he's my neighbor in Westport, runs the Fund Fund. He's the one that put us onto the cryptocurrency case. Well, Urbacher's a close friend of his. Apparently he helped Fund recruit investors when Bill was starting up the Fund Fund.

"Urbacher's a really wealthy guy. He has a luxury condo on the Upper East Side and a summer place in East Hampton. Last September, his daughter Olivia got married at their East Hampton place. Urbacher and his wife Penelope threw a lavish two-day party. They invited dozens of friends and colleagues. A few of them even stayed overnight.

"The day after the wedding, his wife discovered that fifty thousand dollars worth of heirloom jewelry, which she kept in a drawer in her bedroom, was missing.

"When Urbacher spoke with the various overnight guests, one of them said he had seen a nice-looking older man, probably in his seventies, walking around on the second floor near Penelope's bedroom. When he confronted the guy, the guy said he was interested in interior design and was admiring the molding and wainscoting in the upstairs hallway.

"Urbacher and his wife went over the guest list one by one. They determined that only one guest met that description: Barkley Prey, a retired Georgetown political science professor. Prey was at the wedding with his socialite girl friend – Urbacher's not sure if they're married. The socialite's name is Ava Borokin, a Swiss heiress with a multi-million-dollar trust fund.

"Urbacher's wife had met Borokin at a gallery opening in New York and they became friends.

"All that Urbacher knows about Borokin is what Penelope told him. She divides her time between Manhattan, DC and East Hampton. In DC she lives in the most expensive hotel in the city, the Waldorf-Astoria; it's the building that used to be the post office. LeRumpe bought it before he became president and converted it into a luxury hotel.

"Prey, on the other hand, is just a regular guy. He's apparently a real gentleman. He always dresses like a professor at a nineteen fifties Ivy League school. He showed up at a reception held the day before the wedding wearing a navy blazer, gray slacks, a bow tie and tassel loafers.

"Urbacher says his wife told him that Borokin had met Prey in Georgetown; he had been a long-time professor at Georgetown University. At first they lived at the Hay-Adams, a ritzy hotel on Lafayette Park, just across from the White House. When the Waldorf took over the LeRumpe Hotel, Borokin and Prey moved in there.

"Urbacher says Prey has impeccable manners and is extremely polite. He even signed their East Hampton guest book with a warm thank you message on behalf of himself and Borokin."

"Did Urbacher report the theft to the police?" asked Helen.

"No. He wasn't sure what to do. He only had a suspicion that Prey was the culprit, and that was based solely on the guest's second floor encounter with the person thought to be Prey. Urbacher knew it would be embarrassing if his suspicion proved not to be true.

"Besides, his wife had a close friendship with Borokin. She was always inviting Penelope to important art and film events in New York. Urbacher didn't want to burn Penelope's bridges with Borokin based only on a suspicion.

"But Urbacher did continue looking into it. He talked with several of his friends – all of them are quite wealthy – and asked if anyone else had experienced a jewelry theft. Turns out one of them had.

"Urbacher's a close friend of Averell Harrington, the wealthy banker and former diplomat, you've probably heard of him. Harrington and his wife have a summer place in Newport. Last July, following a cocktail party, his wife discovered that her favorite brooch – I think it was a platinum, diamond and sapphire brooch - was missing. It's apparently worth close to ten thousand dollars. Harrington told Urbacher that Prey had been at the cocktail party, although he had no basis to believe that Prey was the thief.

"What was Prey doing in Newport?" asked Helen. "Didn't you say this Borokin lady has a summer place in East Hampton?"

"She apparently rented a place in Newport for the summer. Harrington told Urbacher that she and Prey were there for three months – June, July and August. By September they were back at Borokin's place in East Hampton; that's when they attended Urbacher's daughter's wedding."

"This is a fascinating story" said Melissa, "but I don't see why we'd want to get involved." Melissa was not only the firm's smartest associate, she was also the most practical. And she never shied away from challenging Pap when she thought his ideas were cockeyed.

"Urbacher doesn't want to turn this into a criminal matter" said Pap. "But he wants to know if there's enough here for him to sue to get the jewelry back. He knows we only do class actions, but he thinks he could get Harrington to join the suit, so there'd be at least two plaintiffs."

"I still don't see why we would get involved" said Melissa. "Two plaintiffs doesn't make a class action. And a couple of pieces of jewelry, even expensive jewelry, doesn't make for much of a recovery."

"Well, I told Urbacher we'd have our private investigator look into it."

"We have a private investigator?" said an astonished Helen.

"Yes. Rollie Fingers. I got him sent up for wiretapping years ago when I was in the DA's office. After he got out I helped him get a job with a private security firm. Now he has his own firm, Fingers Security it's called. We use him from time to time when we need information we can't get by conventional methods."

"So we have an ex-con working for us?" said Brandon.

"He's actually a good guy" said Pap. "He got mixed up with a corrupt union boss who was extorting money from companies his union was bargaining with. Rollie had no idea about the extortion."

"So what's he going to be looking for in this investigation?" asked Melissa.

"Pup and I want him to take a close look at Prey and Borokin. But more importantly, we want him to look at police reports in Manhattan, Georgetown and Newport over the past year or so. See if he can find any further thefts from wealthy society people."

"But still" insisted Melissa, "we'd only be talking about four or five victims. That's not enough to justify a class action."

"Melissa" said Pap, "these are important people. The managing director of Lazard. A wealthy banker and diplomat. They're both well-connected. Clients like this don't turn up around here every day. We can't spend all our time representing apes and strippers. We need to up the quality of our client base."

"They weren't strippers" insisted Chip. "Lydia was a lap dancer. She was never a stripper. You think I'd date a stripper?"

"Right" said Pap. "We represent apes and lap dancers but not strippers."

"That's right" said Melissa. "We have our standards."

Pap resumed his explanation. "Look, Bill Fund really wants us to take on the case. Fund said he would pay our retainer and cover our out-of-pocket expenses. He feels a deep sense of gratitude to Urbacher for helping him start up his fund.

"Besides, we need to have a good relationship with Fund. I've been trying for some time to get him to finance one of our cases. This is a good way to start."

When there were no further comments or questions, Pap said "Okay, we need to get to work. We've got to start preparing the Sandoza case. We'll be having our initial conference with the judge later this month.

"And we need to get our motion papers filed in the Bridgeport case. We've gotta get that case dismissed. You don't want Pup and I going to jail over that stupid balloon incident."

"We'd come visit you" said Chip. "Every day if you like."

"Would they let us have our Monday morning meetings in your cell?" asked Melissa. "You think it would be big enough?"

"How many months do you think you'd spend in jail?" Brandon asked.

Pap stood and said "What I think is that all of you should get to work."

Chapter 10

THE HEIRESS

Their next meeting wasn't until the third Monday in July. Pap immediately got down to business.

"We've got lots of news on the Prey and Borokin matter. We received Rollie's report on Friday, and it's a real doozy."

"How could he issue his report so quickly?" asked Melissa. "You just told us about this matter when we met the day after the fourth."

"Rollie had already started by then. Urbacher first came to meet with Pup and me in June, right before the hearing in Bridgeport. So, he's been on the job a full month.

"Now, the first thing Rollie turned up was a large number of other jewelry thefts. All the victims were wealthy people and all of them appear to have a connection with Prey."

Pap opened the report and began going down the list.

"There were numerous thefts in New York City. A seventy-five hundred dollar Buccellati brooch and a pair of Buccellati earrings worth thirteen thousand. A Verdura brooch worth over twenty-two thousand. A thirty-five-hundred dollar ring from Van Cleef and Arpels. An eighteen thousand dollar platinum sapphire ring. And twelve pieces of jewelry with a combined value of more than seventy thousand dollars.

"Then there were several thefts in Georgetown. A seventeen-thousand dollar diamond ring. A ten thousand dollar Patek Phillipe watch. A pair of diamond earrings worth forty-seven-hundred dollars and three sets of earrings with a combined value of fifty-seven-hundred dollars.

"But listen to this. There were two thefts of extraordinarily expensive stuff in Newport. Both occurred during the three months Prey and Borokin spent there last summer. One was a Himalaya Birkin handbag from Hermes. Those bags are made from crocodile hide and cost anywhere from fifty thousand to eighty thousand bucks. They're considered the Holy Grail for handbag collectors.

"The other big ticket item was a Richard Mille watch. They cost a million dollars and up. They're the 'go to' watch for celebrities. The actress Michelle Yeoh wore one at the Oscars ceremony. And the Formula One race car driver Carlos Sainz frequently wears one under his racing uniform."

"How do we know that Prey was the culprit in all of those thefts?" asked Melissa.

"Rollie doesn't yet have proof that all of them can be traced to Prey. But he's gone through the police reports for each of the thefts. Each of them occurred at the home of a wealthy couple. And in each case, the theft occurred when the victims were hosting some sort of society event.

"Rollie hasn't yet spoken to all the people who were victimized. But once he does, I suspect we'll be able to place Prey at most of the events in question."

"What would he do with all that stuff?" asked Chip. "He might give one or two of the items to his heiress friend, and maybe he'd risk wearing the Richard Mille watch. But otherwise, what's he gonna do with everything else?"

"The police reports on two of the stolen items show that they wound up at an auction house, Boyle Auctioneers and Appraisers. They have an auction house here in New York on the upper east side. So he's obviously selling the stuff to dealers and auction houses.

"If he was clever, he would have spread the goods around among several different places. It would look awfully suspicious if he took everything to a single buyer. We need Rollie to find out where all these items wound up.

"Rollie thinks that a couple of the less expensive items may have been sold to a dealer in the Diamond District here in New York. There's a store that buys diamonds, Diamond's Best Friend it's called. Rollie thinks they wouldn't be overly concerned about the provenance of the items they buy.

"A lot of this stuff may have been resold by now, but Rollie thinks some of it could still be in the hands of the dealers and auction houses that bought it."

"What about that Borokin lady, the heiress you told us about?" asked Melissa. "Was she involved? Wouldn't she have been the one to have connections with all those wealthy people?"

"Well, this is where the story gets really interesting. Rollie tracked down a former friend of Borokin, a lady named Rachel LeRoche Billings. She's a former photo editor at *Vanity Fair*.

"Billings had met Borokin at a cocktail party in New York and they became friends. Borokin took Billings along to art openings, fashion shows and cocktail parties in Manhattan. She even took her on a vacation to Morocco.

"But Billings started to get suspicious. Borokin was always claiming that she forgot her credit cards and would ask Billings if she would mind picking up the tab, saying she would reimburse her later. But of course Borokin never reimbursed her.

"And on their Morocco trip, where they stayed at the Four Seasons in Casablanca, Borokin insisted they depart the hotel on short notice without bothering to check out. On top of that, Borokin never paid back the twenty thousand dollars Billings had loaned her for the trip.

"Billings also noticed that Borokin was always changing the hotel she lived in. When they first met, Borokin told her she lived in The Jefferson Hotel; that's an upscale hotel on Sixteenth Street near Logan Circle. Several months later Borokin told her she had moved to a suite at the Fairmont Hotel, a swanky hotel on Embassy Row in northwest DC.

"By the time of the Morocco trip, Borokin was living at the Hay-Adams near Lafayette Park. It's one of DC's top luxury hotels.

"So, after Morocco, Billings broke off the relationship. And she asked Borokin to pay her back the twenty thousand she had loaned her to pay for the trip. When Borokin refused, Billings threatened to sue.

"At that point, some high-priced DC law firm sent Billings a letter threatening to sue her for defamation. Billings had apparently told some of her friends she was suspicious of Borokin, and that she didn't seem to be what she claimed. When that got back to Borokin, she called in the lawyers.

"Billings wanted no part of a lawsuit filed against her by some high-powered Washington firm. So she decided to drop the entire matter and forget about the money she had lost during her time with Borokin. She told herself it was her own fault for being so trusting.

"Well, as you can imagine, after meeting with Billings, Rollie was really curious. So he started digging into Borokin's background. And what he turned up is simply amazing.

"First of all, Ava Borokin is not Ava Borokin. Her real name is Gladys Delray. And she's not from Switzerland, she's from Fort Lee, New Jersey. And her father was not, as she told everyone, a wealthy Swiss banker who had funded the scientific research that led to development of the radar used by the Allies in World War Two. Her father was just a truck driver. And of course there was no trust fund.

"Rollie also discovered that Borokin had made up most of her claimed professional background. For example, she had not started up the wine department at Krispies in London. Nor was she ever an editor at *Purple*, the French fashion magazine. She had merely worked in the magazine's New York office for a few weeks."

Everyone in the room was now thinking the same thing. But Melissa was the first to verbalize it. "If Borokin wasn't an heiress and had no trust fund, how was she able to maintain such a lavish lifestyle?"

"According to Rollie" Pap began, "she used some software program to create fake bank statements and other financial documents; those documents showed that she had over sixty million in Euros in various Swiss bank accounts.

"She then used the fake documents to secure bank loans and lines of credit. As you know, the Swiss jealously guard the secrecy of their bank records, so none of the lending banks were able to verify that she really had sixty million Euros in Swiss bank accounts.

"So what we have here" Pap concluded, "is a series of thefts from numerous wealthy people in New York, Georgetown and Newport. And the thefts were committed by two very clever people, one of whom is not who she purports to be. If ever there was a juicy, high-profile lawsuit, this is it."

"Yes, but I thought we were a class action firm" said Brandon. "I don't see how we can make a class action out of this."

"By the time Rollie finishes" said Pap, "we could have fifteen or twenty plaintiffs. He hasn't yet talked to any of the other victims. He's going to start that this week; he'll go to each city and try to speak with the victims in person. He might even be able to get them to join the lawsuit, once he explains that Nick Urbacher and Averell Harrington were also victims. Then we . . . . "

"Are we allowed to do that?" Brandon interrupted. "Solicit plaintiffs to join a lawsuit?"

"Brandon, we do it all the time. How do you think we get all our cases? You think people just walk in off the street and ask us to file a class action on their behalf?"

"Okay" said Helen "we all understand that. But it looks to me like we've got an even bigger problem. It doesn't seem like Prey and Borokin are going to have money to pay a large judgment. In fact, they'll probably be in jail."

Pup spoke up for the first time. "You're right, Helen. And that's why we need a deep-pocket defendant. And we've got one, Boyle Auctioneers and Appraisers. They're one of the biggest and most prestigious auction houses in the country."

"And I think we'll find that many of the items found their way into the hands of other major auction houses as well" Pap added.

"But are they liable?" asked Helen. "Why would they be liable for a series of thefts carried out by two grifters, even if some of the stolen goods wound up in their hands?"

"That's what you're going to pin down, Helen. You need to do some creative legal research and come up with a way to hold the auction houses liable. For taking possession of stolen property and reselling it. Auction houses must be under some obligation to conduct due diligence before they take possession of expensive jewelry and artwork."

"What if the law is unclear?" asked Brandon. "I've read about this issue in connection with art thefts. As I recall, the law in this area is very murky."

"Murky's good enough. So long as there's no clear bar against suing the auction houses, we'll sue them. And once we sue them, they'll settle. Trust me.

"Helen" Pap continued, "you've got a couple of weeks to work out the legal basis for the lawsuit. Rollie needs time to talk with all the victims and make sure we can link the thefts to Prey or Borokin."

"But won't the two of them face criminal charges for the thefts?" asked Melissa. "And once charges are filed against them, they'll take the Fifth Amendment at their depositions. We'll never be able to find out how they disposed of all the jewelry."

"Pup and I have thought about that and we've come up with a plan. I still have contacts in the Manhattan DA's office; remember, I worked there for several years after law school. I think I can get one of them to get us a meeting with Braggert. He's...."

"Alvin Braggert?" said Melissa. "The DA that George Taurus helped get elected? He doesn't believe in prosecuting anyone. Certainly not someone who steals jewelry and watches from rich people."

"Melissa, that's why Braggert will be perfect for us. He'd never spend time investigating a case like this. And he certainly won't have any interest in putting Prey or Borokin behind bars.

"So, we'll let Rollie complete his investigation. Then we'll offer it to Braggert on a silver platter. He won't have to do any work, just file an indictment based on the thefts Rollie can document. And we'll let him take all the credit for the investigation. It'll be a big story, he'll love all the publicity.

"And then, once he agrees to file charges, we'll have him offer Prey and Borokin a sweetheart deal: minimal jail time, maybe even just a fine and some community service. A light sentence like that will appeal to Braggert.

"But that deal would be conditioned on the two of them cooperating with us in our lawsuit. They'll have to agree to disclose everything about the thefts and the disposition of the goods. What auction houses they sold or consigned them to. What was said when they offered the goods to them. Whether the houses did any sort of investigation as to how they, Prey and Borokin, came into possession of the goods.

"Once all that information is laid out in their depositions, we'll have the auction houses dead to rights. They'll have no option but to settle. Otherwise, we file the lawsuit naming them as defendants and detailing their gross negligence. They'll do anything to keep that from happening."

"Pap" said Melissa, "this is brilliant. It may be your best idea ever."

"Pup and I worked it out over the weekend while we were playing golf. I do some of my best thinking on the golf course. That's why I always write off my country club dues as a business expense."

"They didn't teach us this kind of stuff in law school" said Helen.

"Just stick around for a while" replied Melissa. "You'll learn lots of stuff they didn't teach you in law school."

Chapter 11

AI GALORE

"Keith and I just had the most amazing experience" said Helen as soon as everyone had sat down the following Monday for their weekly meeting.

"For almost a year, we've been on a two-thousand-person wait list for a table at that hot new steakhouse – Mehren's Steakhouse – on the lower east side. It's received hundreds of glowing reviews which it displays on its website. Most of the reviews were originally posted on various social media platforms.

"All of Keith's banking colleagues had their names on the wait list. Last week, we finally got a phone call saying we made it off the wait list and they had booked us a table for seven-thirty Friday evening."

"Was it worth the year-long wait?" asked Brandon.

"Well, yes" said Helen. "But not for the reasons we expected. You see, there is no Mehren's Steakhouse on the lower east side. Or anywhere else for that matter. It turns out that a bunch of twenty-year-old guys created the restaurant as a prank."

"A prank?"

"Yes. They started by creating an elaborate website for the restaurant. Then they solicited all their friends to post favorable reviews on all the major social media platforms, and those reviews were then added to the website. This generated a terrific buzz among upscale diners looking for the next great restaurant. They even managed to get the restaurant's location posted on Google Maps."

"So you went to the location and nothing was there?" asked Brandon.

"That's the really odd part. There was an actual restaurant there. And there were well over a hundred diners. The restaurant had white tablecloths and dozens of waiters dressed in tuxedos.

"We entered and walked down a long hallway between the front door and the dining room. It was hung with framed photos of the chef – Chef Mehren – posing with numerous famous guests over the years: JFK, Marilyn Monroe, Albert Einstein, Barack Obama. I can't remember all the others except I know one showed him with a bunch of gangsters."

"Probably from New Jersey" said Chip. "That's where all the gangsters are from these days."

"The photos should have been a tip-off" Helen admitted. "The restaurant was only a year old but the people in the photos were either ancient or dead."

"Did this place serve food?" asked Brandon. "Was it a restaurant or not?"

"Oh yes, they served food. It was a prix fixe five-course steak dinner. I think Keith said it cost one hundred sixty dollars per person. There were five courses and each of them was tied to something they called The Bovine Circle of Life.

"As part of the bovine concept, several of the waiters walked around carrying pitchers of milk as though they were fine bottles of wine. Our waiter told us the milk came from a cow in Uganda named Phillip."

"A milk-producing cow named Phillip?" asked Melissa.

"Yes, the cow's name was definitely Phillip. Mehren himself paraded around the room all evening with his hands clasped behind his back. He explained to anyone who asked that Phillip was a common name for a female cow in Uganda."

"So did you actually have dinner?" asked Brandon.

"Yes. Other than the bovine theme, it was just like dinner at any high-end restaurant in Manhattan. Everyone was either chatting or looking at their neighbors to see if their neighbors were looking at them. And of course everyone was constantly checking their cell phone. Keith was working his most of the time, he always does that. I don't know why he even bothers to take me out."

"I never work my cell phone when I take Francoise out to dinner" said Chip.

"What about when you take Candy out?" asked Melissa.

"Same thing there. But we haven't gone out for quite a while, except for that night I took her to dinner and the Knicks game. And came away with nothing to show for it."

"What about Holly?" asked Melissa. "Didn't you have lunch with her at that fancy hotel in Garden City?"

"Melissa, I had just met her. I wasn't about to work my cell phone during our first meeting. That could have spoiled everything."

"He never works his cell phone when he's with me" said Helen. "He has much better manners than my husband."

"Lots of women have remarked on my good manners" said Chip.

"So, Helen" said Brandon, "was this Mehren's place a real restaurant or not?"

"It was. But only for one night. Mehren's Steakhouse was a one-night pop-up restaurant. The guys behind the hoax had rented the space for a single day and night. They got a one-day liquor license and food handling permit. According to the story in the *New York Post*, all the waiters and staff were friends who agreed to participate in the hoax. It was really quite an experience."

"Well" said Pap, "it sounds like you and Keith got to participate in a really clever joke. Now, if the *Post* is covering the story, they could run it for another few days, they like to keep a good story going. You might want to let them know you were there, you could get your name in the paper. Just be sure you mention the firm's name, tell them we do class action litigation."

* * * *

"All right, we need to get down to business" said Pap. "I know we're starting to get busy again. But it's going to be a few weeks before either the Gray or the Sandoza case are really active. So let's take a little time to see if anyone has an idea for a new case."

"I've got the perfect case for us" said Brandon. "Oreos. Everyone's up in arms about them."

"Up in arms about what?" asked Pap. "The boys are perfectly happy with them, they eat 'em every day for lunch. A half dozen at a time."

"Priscilla and I don't allow the girls to eat them" said Pup. "Too much sugar. They have apples for lunch instead of cookies. Maybe a peach when they're in season."

"That's what they get for having a father who went to Harvard and Yale" said Pap. "Those girls will never know the joy of eating Oreos for lunch. You probably don't let them eat donuts either."

"Of course not, why . . . ."

"So what's the big issue with Oreos?" asked Helen.

"It's the creme filling" said Brandon. "They've apparently cut back on the amount of creme. People say the current version has far less creme than traditional Oreos. They say you have to buy the more expensive Double Stuf Oreos to get ones with the same amount of creme as the original version."

"I don't think . . ." said Pup before Brandon interrupted.

"You have any idea how many people eat Oreos? They're the best selling cookie in America. There could be tens of millions of people in the class."

Pup was not swayed. "Who cares whether or not Oreos have less creme in their filling than they used to. And even if they do, what's the legal claim? There's no law saying that Oreos must have the same amount of creme filling as they did fifty years ago."

"There's not?" said Chip.

"Pup's right" said Pap. "And besides, as I've said before, we've had our run of food cases. Peters and Peters is not going to be known as food ingredient lawyers."

"Even if millions of Americans want something to be done about their Oreos?" said Brandon.

"Yes. No more food cases. We need to focus on new areas of the law where we can set new precedents and be on the cutting edge. That's what will get us the publicity we deserve."

"And also the money we deserve" said Melissa. "We can't forget about the money."

"Right" Pap agreed. "The money's also important. After all, we have to pay your outrageous salaries. Have I ever told you what Pup and I made when we were first out of law school?"

"Only about a hundred times" said Melissa.

"We're getting a bit off track here" said Pup. "We need to talk about the kinds of cases the firm needs. Like I've said before, we need to find some AI cases.

"Now, in that connection, you wouldn't believe the number of calls we've received since we held that press conference announcing the Sandoza case. Everyone seems to have a gripe about AI. Pap doesn't like to take calls from people he doesn't know, so Miss Pesky has been directing them to me."

"Are any of them worth pursuing?" asked Melissa.

"One of them definitely is and a second one might be. But let me run through them and see what you guys think.

"The first call was from a guy in Texas who called to complain about something called Ambien Games. A company in California has started sponsoring online skill-based games. Traditional card games like Poker, various forms of Bingo, and so forth. People place bets on themselves and then test their skill against other players.

"But it turns out they aren't playing against other players, they're playing against bots. So they lose much more frequently than they do on other online game platforms. They thought they were playing against real people but instead they're playing against bots. And of course the bots are far more skillful than real players"

"What did you tell him?" asked Brandon.

"I told him if he's losing money playing Poker, he should take up Canasta. I don't think anyone's ever lost money playing Canasta. By the way, I ran this one by Pap and he agreed: we don't want to represent online gamblers."

"Right" said Chip. "Our chimpanzee clients would never stand for it."

Pup continued. "Now, the next guy had a more interesting case. He's a computer scientist who generated a large artwork solely by use of his computer. 'Entrance to the Underworld' I think he called it. It depicted a couple of beat-up trucks going down into a hellhole."

"That's Pup's kind of art" said Pap. "He loves that avant garde stuff."

"Very funny" said Pup. "But here's the issue. This guy tried to get it copyrighted but the Copyright Office twice rejected his application. They said that artwork had to have human authorship in order to be copyrightable. He wanted us to appeal that ruling to the federal courts."

"So what did you tell him?"

"I told him we were a class action law firm and that, unless he could come up with lots of other artists in the same boat, we wouldn't be able to take his case."

"It's a fascinating legal issue" said Pap. "But even with multiple artists in the case, we'd just be suing to get the artworks copyrighted. The Copyright Office wouldn't be liable for damages. We can't get involved in that."

Pup resumed his narration. "Another call was worthless but nevertheless amusing. It was from a guy in Brooklyn. He was complaining about a virtual dating coach he found on an App called Gidget. Gidget was supposed to mentor him on what to say when he tried to pick up girls. But he said the lines Gidget fed him never worked. All the women he used them on said they'd heard that line a hundred times."

"Maybe you should have referred him to Chip" said Melissa. "I'm sure he would have had some good suggestions."

"I never pick up women" said Chip. "They just seem to fall into my lap."

"That's how he met Lydia" said Melissa. "She was doing something or other on his lap at a strip club. I don't think she fell."

* * * *

Pup was anxious to move on. They would talk about Chip and Lydia for hours if someone didn't keep things on track.

"Listen" he said, "the next call hit the jackpot. "It was from a guy named Arnold Benedict. He's the Boogle employee who tipped off *Newsday* about the Sandoza scam. He was fired by Boogle, they must have identified him as the anonymous tipster. He's now living somewhere in Napa Valley. He suggested he could help us with the case."

"I'll bet he wants to be paid" said Melissa. "If he's out of a job he probably needs the money."

"Yes, he did want to be paid for helping us."

"We can't pay fact witnesses. Fact witnesses have an obligation to come forward and tell whatever they know. But they can't be paid. Only expert witnesses can be paid."

"That's why we made him an expert witness" said Pap. "I had Pesky send him a letter making him an expert witness for us."

"But all he can talk about are the facts" insisted Melissa. "Such as how Boogle generated and disseminated the BotsUp? program to Sandoza. That's fact testimony."

"Melissa, you've got to look at this creatively. We don't know anything about AI, except what we've read in the papers or online. We've no idea how a company like Boogle creates AI or how it matches that AI to the needs of its customers. Benedict was an AI creator. He can help us understand the technical side. So he's an expert."

"I hope the firm doesn't get in trouble over this. Your argument sounds pretty lame to me."

"I wouldn't worry about it if I were you" Pap replied. "But if you do want to worry about it, do it in the Worry Room. That's what it's there for.

"Now, Helen, I'll have Pesky give you Benedict's contact information. I want you to set up a meeting with him and see what you can find out."

"Sure, I'll be happy to go out to Napa Valley and meet with him."

"Maybe I should go along" suggested Chip. "He'll be more forthcoming if there's two of us."

"I don't think that's a good idea" said Pup. "I don't think much work would get done if the two of you go together."

"Nobody's making any trip anywhere" said Pap. "We'll have Benedict come to New York. Put him up in one of those inexpensive tourist hotels on Seventh or Eighth Avenue.

"And we'll give him fifty dollars a day for food. If we sent one of you to Napa Valley you'd insist on staying in some luxurious five-star hotel. And you'd spend fifty dollars a day just on breakfast."

"None of this gets us a new case" pointed out Melissa. "I thought that's what we're trying to do."

"Right. Pup, why don't you tell them about that author who called. I was at lunch when she called so Pesky directed the call to Pup."

"You weren't out to lunch" said Pup. "It was four in the afternoon. You were out playing golf."

"I was playing with a client."

"You were playing with Mona, one of our nonpaying clients."

"One of?" said Brandon. "I wasn't aware we had any other nonpaying clients besides Mona."

"The chimps" said Pup. "They never paid us a dime for all our work."

"Look" said Pap. "Mona and Ham had been scheduled to play with Peachy and Harley at the Keanes' club in Southport. Harley suddenly had to go out of town and so they asked me to be the fourth. I felt I needed to stay on good terms with them so I accepted. It was clearly a legitimate business outing."

"Right" said Pup. "You spent four hours of non-billable time playing golf with a client who has never paid us a dime for our work."

"Pup, you're forgetting that when we settled Mona's case regarding the publication of her mugshot, we got a really nice fee out of the settlement."

"That's right" said Melissa. "And the members of the class got some great benefits too. Laminated cards with Miranda warnings printed on them. And some 'Get Out of Jail Free' Monopoly cards as I recall."

"Melissa, all the class members except Mona were hardened criminals" said Chip. "That's why their mugshots had been taken. Those settlement benefits were really useful to them."

"Okay" said Pup, "now let me tell you about the call.

"It was from a lady named Paige Turner. She's written several books in the self-help category. She wanted to sue one of the big AI companies, OpenApp, for what she called 'cyberburgling.' She claimed that OpenApp was using material from her books without permission in order to regurgitate material from them in response to search inquiries."

"Sounds like it could be a great case" said Melissa. "If OpenApp is using material from her books for their AI service, they must be doing the same to other authors."

"They are. And that's why they're already being sued by some famous authors, including John Grimshaw, the guy who writes those legal thrillers, and others. So we're too late. However, if Grimshaw's case doesn't turn into a class action, we might have an opening there. Someone should follow that case and see what happens.

"Now the final call worth mentioning involved some dubious, maybe even porn-like, AI program. It was from an aspiring actress, she said her name was Autumn. Autumn Sleaves. She said she's been in some off-Broadway plays, maybe a commercial or two.

"She complained that her voice was being used by some AI App that provides virtual girl friends to lonely guys. She said some of the dialogue that used her voice was extremely racy; she said she never talks that way in real life."

"How could her voice be used to create a virtual girl friend?" asked Brandon.

"All they need are a few snippets of your voice" said Pup. "One TV commercial would probably be enough. They feed that voice into a computer program, and then use some sort of algorithm to spit out conversations, speeches, and all kinds of verbal communications using that voice. It's really amazing."

"If this sort of thing is happening" said Melissa, "there could be lots of other actresses and celebrities whose voices are being used without their permission."

"Yes, I thought of that" said Pup. "But I don't know if this is the kind of thing we want to get involved in. The conversations are probably loaded with sexual innuendo, if not downright vulgarity. I don't know that we want to become known as a firm that works in the porn arena, even if it is just audio porn."

"But look" said Chip, "if there are lots of women actresses and celebrities who've been victimized by this, we would be doing a good deed by getting involved. Maybe we should think of it as our feminist protection initiative."

"Pup" said Pap, "Chip's right. I don't think we should dismiss this thing out of hand. Let's poke around and see what we can find. Melissa's really good at Internet research, let's have her spend a couple of days looking at this App and see what she comes up with."

"I could do that" Melissa said. "But it's going to look awfully funny if a woman tries to access an AI App that offers female companionship to lonely guys. Perhaps one of the guys should do it."

Brandon immediately protested. "I can't have Brenda discover that I'm using some AI App to find a virtual girl friend. This is more up Chip's alley."

"What do you say, Chip?" asked Pap. "I realize you have no need for a virtual girl friend. And you certainly don't want Francoise, or any of your live girl friends, to know about it. But someone here's got to do it. Look at it as taking one for the team."

"Sure" said Chip. "You know I'll always do anything for the team."

Chapter 12

HON. SAMUEL SPADE, III

Three days later, Pap, Pup and Melissa were riding out to Long Island in an Executive Limousine Town Car. While the associates all used Uber when they needed a car for their personal use – which was pretty much every time they had to go more than six blocks – Pap insisted that everyone in the firm use Executive Limo when on firm business.

The associates were allowed to take an Executive Limo home when they worked past eight o'clock. So they generally worked until 8:05, called for a car and left for home. If they ordered dinner in, or ate out after leaving work past eight, they were permitted to charge it to the firm. The firm's outlay for dinners would have fed Patton's Third Army for months.

The three of them were on their way to the sleek and relatively new federal courthouse in Central Islip. Located in Suffolk County, the easternmost county on Long Island, it was part of the Eastern District of New York. It heard all cases originating in Nassau and Suffolk Counties. Today would be the initial hearing in the Sandoza case.

"So Melissa" said Pap, "tell us about Judge Spade."

"He should be a good judge for us. His grandfather was Sam Spade, the famous private detective in Los Angeles. He was legendary, they even made movies about him. The judge's father, Sam Spade, Jr., followed in the grandfather's footsteps. He spent his entire career as a detective with the Los Angeles Police Department.

"The father wasn't as famous as the grandfather, but he did work on several major cases over the course of his career. For example, he was one of the detectives on the OJ Simpson case."

"That case didn't turn out so well for the LAPD" said Pup.

"Right" said Pap. "If it doesn't fit, you must acquit. That's what Simpson's lawyer kept telling the jury."

"If what doesn't fit?" asked Melissa.

"The glove. The glove the killer was said to have worn when he committed the murders. The prosecutors had Simpson put it on in front of the jury and it didn't seem to fit, Simpson couldn't get his hand in it. Jesus, those prosecutors really botched it. They should have had him try it on before the trial. You can't do a stunt like that for the first time in front of the jury. How stupid . . . . "

"I think we should get back to Judge Spade" said Pup.

"Okay" Melissa resumed. "Judge Spade is Samuel Spade the Third. He grew up in LA and graduated from USC."

"That's where Simpson played. He was an All-American running . . . . "

"I think Melissa knows that" said Pup. "We need to get back to . . . . "

"Judge Spade" said Melissa quickly. "He put himself through college by working summers and holidays as a detective intern in the LAPD. I'm sure he got the job through his father's influence. After USC, he came East and went to law school at Fordham."

"Then he's like me" said Pap. "Bright enough to get into Fordham Law but not bright enough to get into Columbia, Harvard or Yale. You gotta be as smart as Pup to get into one of those schools."

"What's interesting" Melissa continued, "is that Spade spent his summers working as an investigator in Morgenthau's office." Robert Morgenthau was the legendary Manhattan DA who seemingly held that office forever; Pap had started his career as a prosecutor in Morgenthau's office.

"After law school, Spade joined Morgenthau's office as a prosecutor. He was there three or four years, then left to go into private practice in Garden City. He became active in the Nassau County Republican party and was eventually appointed to the bench by former President LeRumpe."

"What's his reputation as a judge?" asked Pap.

"He's said to be a 'no nonsense' judge. Moves cases along, doesn't like to get bogged down in peripheral issues. Lawyers say he always tries to get to the bottom of things. He should be good for us."

* * * *

Fifteen minutes later, the three of them were sitting in Judge Spade's fourth floor courtroom. Although their case was the only one on the calendar, the courtroom was jam-packed.

Judge Spade and his Courtroom Deputy, Beau Garte, emerged from the robing room. As the judge took the bench, Garte announced that the United States District Court for the Eastern District of New York, Central Islip Division, Honorable Samuel Spade Junior presiding, was now in session.

Transcript of Proceedings:

The Court: The case of Wray et al. versus Boogle et al. is the only case on this morning's calendar. I see we have multiple parties and multiple counsel. So counsel, please take your seats. I'm afraid some of the lawyers for defendants may have to find seats behind the counsel table.

Okay, first, let's get everyone's appearances. We'll start with counsel for plaintiffs.

Mr. Peters: Good morning, Your Honor. I'm Patrick Peters and this is my partner Prescott Peters and this is our associate Melissa Muffett. We represent the five named plaintiffs: Ray and Faye Wray, Adam Eaves and Eve Adams, and Ms. Holly Gonightly. The Wrays and the Eaves were donors to Congressman Sandoza's campaign and seek to represent a class of campaign donors. Ms. Gonightly is a Nassau County voter and seeks to represent a class of fellow citizens who voted for Sandoza.

The Court: Mr. Peters, I see you held a press conference the day you filed your complaint. I hope you don't plan to try this case in the press. That's not the way we do things out here.

Mr. Peters: Your Honor, I assure you we won't be trying this case in the press. However, it's undeniable that there is an enormous public interest in Congressman Sandoza's situation. And there's a real public interest in the way he used artificial intelligence to get himself elected. I don't think we've ever seen anything like it before. So I'm afraid we're in for major press coverage of the case.

The Court: Yes, I can see that. In fact, I think we have numerous members of the press in the courtroom right now, so you seem to have accomplished your purpose.

Now, let's get the appearances for the defendants. Perhaps we should start with Congressman Sandoza.

Mr. Sadly: I'm Omar Sadly. I'm a solo practitioner in Garden City. I'll be representing Mr. Sandoza as well as his Political Action Committee, Goldstone Strategies. Just so the record is clear, I'm being paid by Goldstone; sad to say, Mr. Sandoza is virtually bankrupt now.

The Court: Mr. Sadly, I'm happy to say that solo practitioners are always welcome in this courtroom. Okay, now who's next?

Mr. Thyme: I'm Mark Thyme, from the Palo Alto firm Sage, Rosemary and Thyme. With me is my partner Rosemary. We'll be representing Boogle.

The Court: Is Rosemary your partner's first or last name?

Mr. Thyme: Legally, it's her first name. Her maiden name is Rosemary Baybe – that's spelled B-A-Y-B-E. But she's been married several times and so, instead of changing her professional name – not to mention our firm's name – every time she remarries, she simply goes by the name Rosemary.

It would be confusing to our clients if one week the firm is known as Sage, Baybe and Thyme, the next as Sage, Rudd and Thyme and then a month later as Sage, Roper and Thyme.

The Court: Yes, I can see that. But do I address her as Miss Rosemary or Mrs. Rosemary? Or maybe Ms. Rosemary?

Rosemary: You can just call me Rosemary.

The Court: Right. Now, who's next?

Mr. Waters: I'm Walt Waters of Underbridge and Waters. As you know Judge Spade, we're located in Garden City. We'll be representing Take America Back, a Super PAC, which unfortunately spent lots of money on Mr. Sandoza's campaign without knowing that everything about him had been fabricated.

The Court: I suspect that what your client knew and when it knew it will be one of the main issues in the case. I'm sure we'll get to the bottom of it.

Mr. Goode: Your Honor I'm Gordon Goode of Goode and Badd in New York City. Sitting back there (pointing) is my partner Barry Badd. We'll be representing Democracy Now. Like Mr. Waters' client Take America Back, Democracy Now had no idea Mr. Sandoza's entire persona had been fabricated by artificial intelligence.

The Court: Is your client the Super PAC that's funded by George Taurus? The guy who goes around the country pouring money into the campaigns of progressive DA candidates who promise that if they're elected they won't prosecute anyone?

Mr. Goode: Yes, Mr. Taurus is the founder of Democracy Now. But your characterization of what the PAC does is unfair. Democracy Now is dedicated to seeing that truth and justice prevail in both our political system and our criminal justice system. So it supports candidates for public office who stand for truth and justice.

The Court: Seems odd that your client supported Congressman Sandoza's campaign. It looks like there wasn't much truth or justice there.

Mr. Goode: Your Honor, as I said a moment ago . . . .

The Court: We're not going to discuss the merits of the case now. This is a Rule 16 hearing and I just want to sort out the parties and see where the case is going. So, let me start with counsel for plaintiffs. Mr. Peters, is there something you would like the Court to focus on at this initial stage?

Mr. Peters: Your Honor, we have three priorities. First, we're anxious to have the class certified so that other Third District voters and donors can join in the case. We expect there will be scores, maybe even hundreds, in the donor class. And we believe there will be thousands in the voter class.

Now, we realize that defendants will want to take the deposition of the proposed class representatives before the class is certified. So we're willing to produce them for deposition at a mutually convenient time in the next thirty days.

The Court: Mr. Peters, the Court appreciates your forthrightness in offering your clients up for prompt depositions. Most attorneys try to delay their client's deposition, which then leads to endless motions and arguments having nothing to do with the underlying merits of the case.

Now, did you say there are two other items you wish to pursue at this stage?

Mr. Peters: Yes. After defendants have taken our clients' deposition, we want to take the deposition of the two Super PACs. They poured millions of dollars into Mr. Sandoza's campaign and we need to find out what they knew about him and why they spent all that money on his campaign.

The Court: The Court is certainly anxious to hear what they have to say. It will be interesting to see if they had any inkling that things weren't quite right about Mr. Sandoza.

Mr. Peters: Exactly. Now the final item we want to pursue right away is an order freezing the assets of the three political action committees. This is necessary to ensure they will have funds available to pay any judgment issued in this case. We see no need for such an order against Boogle, they're one of the wealthiest companies in the world.

Mr. Sadly: Your Honor, I strenuously oppose any motion to freeze the assets of Goldstone Strategies. They're the only source for payment of my fee.

Mr. Waters: Your Honor, Take America Back can't have its assets frozen. Its entire reason for being is to make contributions to the campaigns of political candidates, particularly conservative ones.

Mr. Goode: That's also true of Democracy Now. An order freezing its assets would prohibit it from making campaign contributions and that would clearly be unconstitutional.

The Court: Mr. Peters, you seem to have stirred up a hornet's nest here. I don't want to see this case get sidetracked over motions relating to the freezing of assets.

Mr. Peters: Your Honor, the order wouldn't have to be as draconian as my colleagues fear. For example, we've no desire to keep Mr. Sadly from being paid. But I don't think Goldstone Strategies should be spending any more money on Mr. Sandoza's behalf. So we could easily have an order freezing its assets subject to quarterly, or even monthly, payments to Mr. Sadly.

As for Take America Back and Democracy Now, we've no desire to cut off their regular funding of candidates. But we don't want them disbursing all their money and suddenly going out of business. So, we need to find a way that allows them to continue their funding activities but still preserves a significant amount of assets to pay a final judgment.

Mr. Waters: He's assuming there's going to be a final judgment against my client. There's no reason to make that assumption.

The Court: There's also no reason to assume there won't be a final judgment against your client. There might be, there might not be. But if there is, Mr. Peters is entitled to make sure there's money available to pay the judgment.

I'll tell you what. Why don't you, Mr. Peters, sit down with these gentlemen, one at a time or all together, whichever you prefer. See if you can come up with an agreed upon order that satisfies the needs of both sides.

But I'll say now that the Court is inclined to impose some sort of asset freeze. If the plaintiffs prevail in this matter, the damages could be quite extensive and plaintiffs are entitled to assurance that there's money available to pay the judgment. Now, lets move on. Mr. Sadly, do you have any immediate issue you wish to pursue?

Mr. Sadly: We think the case should be dismissed against both Mr. Sandoza and Goldstone Strategies. This entire matter belongs in Congress. Congress should decide whether Mr. Sandoza should stay or be expelled from office.

The Court: Mr. Sadly, I don't think the Complaint is about whether Mr. Sandoza should be expelled from Congress. That's up to

Congress. What we're concerned with here is the fraud – I'm sorry, the alleged fraud, I don't want to prejudge the case – that got him elected. And which appears to have enticed lots of people to contribute to his campaign.

Mr. Sadly: But we don't believe Mr. Sandoza broke any laws. There's no law saying a politician can't use artificial intelligence to help with his campaign.

The Court: Did you say he used AI to "help" with his campaign? According to the complaint, he used artificial intelligence for more than helping his campaign. He seems to have used it to invent his entire persona. But look, if you want to make a motion to dismiss the complaint, go right ahead. But I don't think that would be a good use of your clients' remaining funds.

Okay, Mr. Thyme. Is there anything Boogle wishes to pursue at this time?

Mr. Thyme: We think the case against Boogle should be dismissed. Boogle's AI program, BotsUp?, merely provides information and data in response to a customer's request. Boogle can't be responsible for how the customer uses that information and data.

The Court: But Mr. Thyme, in this case Boogle didn't simply provide information and data to Mr. Sandoza. It created his entire public persona, which he then used to solicit campaign contributions and get himself elected to Congress. What's next, an AI-generated presidential candidate?

Mr. Thyme: Boogle is working on that right now. It has used AI to create an ideal presidential candidate. They've named him George Jefferson. Or maybe it's Thomas Washington, I can't remember which it is. They believe their candidate will make an excellent president. Far better than either of our last two.

The Court: You could be right about that. But let's get back to your client's position. I don't see any basis for dismissing the case against Boogle at this point.

Mr. Thyme: Your Honor, Boogle only provides information and data to its customers. It's not responsible for what the customers do with that information. Boogle is selling a lawful product and cannot be liable for any misuse of that product by its customer.

The Court: Well, I rather suspect that's the core issue in this case. And I think it will ultimately be up to the jury to make that determination. Now, if you want to file a motion to dismiss, I can't stop you. But I want any such motion filed quickly. We'll set a schedule before we leave here today.

Now let's hear from counsel for Take America Back. Mr. Waters?

Mr. Waters: Thank you, Your Honor. I think the prosecution of this case will have a chilling effect on free speech. Take America Back is entitled to funnel money to the campaigns of candidates of its choosing. Whether those candidates are good or bad, honest or dishonest, or whether they are always truthful or only sometimes truthful, is irrelevant. My client has a First Amendment right to provide financial support to them. This lawsuit threatens that right and it must therefore be dismissed.

The Court: As I told Mr. Thyme, you can make your motion but you'll have to do it on the timetable that we'll set here today. Now, that leaves Mr. ....

Mr. Waters: I wasn't finished, Your Honor. We also intend to file a cross-motion against Boogle. In the event there's a judgment against Take America Back, we believe the underlying liability should rest with Boogle. They're the ones who created the phony bio and the phony speeches and campaign statements. Take America Back relied on those materials in deciding to spend money on Mr. Sandoza's campaign.

The Court: Okay, I understand your position. Now let's hear from you, Mr. Badd.

Mr. Goode: I'm Mr. Goode, Mr. Badd is back there (pointing). Lots of people get us confused. That's until they see Mr. Badd in action, then there's never any confusion.

The Court: I'm sorry for the confusion, I'm sure I'll get it straight as the case proceeds. In any event, I suppose you'll pursue the same strategy as Take America Back. You plan to argue that Democracy Now had a right to support Mr. Sandoza whatever his faults or lies.

I understand that argument. But for the life of me, I can't figure out why Democracy Now – which, insofar as I know, only backs liberal and left-wing candidates – decided to back Gregory Sandoza. Perhaps you'll enlighten me on that that at some point in the litigation.

Mr. Goode: I'll leave my client's motive for another day. But yes, our position is the same as Take America Back's position: the case against us should be dismissed on First Amendment grounds. If it's not dismissed, we will also pursue a cross-claim against Boogle for generating the false information Democracy Now relied on.

The Court: Okay, we need to wrap this up. Here's what we're going to do.

First, any defendant wishing to pursue a motion to dismiss must do so in the next thirty days. Plaintiffs can respond to the motions separately or all at once, but the responses will be due twenty days after the last motion is filed.

Second, defendants may take the deposition of the proposed class representatives within the next ninety days.

Third, plaintiffs may take the deposition of Take America Back and Democracy Now any time after the plaintiffs have been deposed. Beau, have I covered everything?

Mr. Garte: What about the cross-claims against Boogle? I think both Super PACs want to make cross-claims.

The Court: Yes, thanks for reminding me. Anyone who wants to file a cross-claim may do so within the next thirty days. However, I plan to sever the cross-claims and set them aside for separate discovery and trial after the main part of the case, the class action, has been completed.

Oh, and Mr. Peters, let us know if you are successful in working out some sort of asset freeze with defendants. If you can't work it out, please submit a motion along with a proposed Order and we'll schedule a hearing on the matter.

I think that's all for today. Mr. Garte will be in touch with a date for oral argument on the motions to dismiss. We're adjourned.

Mr. Garte: All rise.

Pap looked at Pup and Melissa and smiled. "This was a good day. We couldn't have done any better."

When Pup picked up his briefcase and made a step toward the courtroom door, Pap took his arm and held him in place.

"Pup, lets take our time here, mingle with our adversaries. Maybe speak with the court reporter. After everyone's departed, we'll go down and meet with the press in front of the courthouse. "Melissa, you need to tell those folks from the press to hang around until Pup and I come down. Tell them we can't speak with them in the courtroom but we're happy to do so outside."

Chapter 13

BRIDGET

"Hey, Bridget, are you there?"

"Sure, Mister Lester, I's right here. How are you'se to-nite?"

"Bridget, please stop calling me Lester. You know I hate that name. Call me Les, that's what all my friends call me."

"Why sure, Mister Les. I'll tries to 'member that."

"It's easy to remember, Bridget. Just remember my motto: Les is always more."

"Tha's funny, Mister Les. I's sure I kin 'member that."

"You see, my last name is Moore. That's the word more but with two o's. But in my motto, it's just plain more. Only one 'o.'"

"Tha's kinda confusin' Mister Les. Why don' I jus' call you Les and we's kin fergit 'bout this more stuff."

"Sure, Bridget, I was just trying to make it easy for you."

"So now Les, wat's you doin' tonight?"

"Working late, as usual."

"I see's it's 'bout ten o'clock. Wat you'se workin' on?"

"Another deal. We're trying to get it closed by the end of the month."

"So wat's the deal? Are you'se buyin' or sellin' this time?"

"Bridget, you know I can't tell you that. Our deals are confidential until they're publicly announced."

"But ever-thing we says here is confidenshall. You knows that."

"Yes, I know that Bridget. But the firm is really strict about confidentiality."

"Okay, Les, I don' wan' you'se to lose yur job with that there firm, 'Golden Smack' I think you calls it."

"Golden Slacks. Jesus, Bridget, I tell you the firm's name every time we talk. Why can't you remember it?"

"I's sure sorry, Les. I'll tries to 'member it next time."

"Bridget, let's talk about something besides my job. I didn't call you to talk about my work."

"Why sure, Les, we's kin talk 'bout anythin' you'se like. Are you'se feelin' lonely to-nite?"

"To tell you the truth, Bridget, I am. There's only a couple of us still here at the office. And there's no one home at the apartment. Chloe and the kids are at our summer place on Shelter Island. I only see 'em on Saturday night and Sunday."

"Speakin' 'bout that there island, do you'se go to that kinky bakery I been hearin' 'bout?"

"You mean Eiffel's Tower Bakery?"

"Yeah. The one wear the owner does all that kinky stuff. Spanks his employees if they's do some-pin wrong. Gropes and pokes the lady cust-mers."

"We sometimes go there for brunch. It's a great place. I've never been groped or poked. Or spanked for that matter."

"I's heard that some of the ladies has been spanked with celery."

"Well, I've never . . . . "

"Les, we's could do that next time if you'se like. I wou-nut mind if you'se spanked me before we's make love. That could be real fun."

"Bridget, you know I don't go in for that kinky stuff."

"Then whys you keep on goin' to that there kinky bakery?"

"I told you I've never seen anything kinky going on there. Some disgruntled employee probably started that rumor."

"Wat you mean dis-grunted employee?"

"Someone who got reprimanded or fired. But listen, let's change the subject. I called you because I was feeling lonely and wanted to hear your voice."

"Les, you'se no need to feel lonely now, I's right here."

"Frankly, I wish you were here with me."

"Well, I wish I wuz there too, We cud have us a real nice time. Specially since Chloe is out on that there island."

"What do you have in mind?"

"Les, you knows wat I has in mind. It's wat I has in mind ever time I hears from you."

"That's more like it, Bridget. I'm getting excited just sitting here thinking about it."

"I's thinkin' 'bout it too, Les. Specially when we's not together. I loves lyin' in yur nice big arms. And I loves that special thing you does on my tummy."

"And I love the way you purr like a kitten. And that special name you call me."

"You mean sweetypie?"

"No, no, I've told you that's what Chloe calls me. I've never liked it, it's not at all romantic."

"Sure, Les, I's sorry. I think it's sweetheart you'se like, not sweetypie. At least I's got the sweet part rite."

"Right, Bridget. And now here's a good way for you to remember it. I'm your sweet heart. And you're my sweet tart."

"Tha's clever, Les. Tha's why I likes you'se so much. You'se clever and witty, not like all them other guys."

"What other guys? Are you two-timing me?"

"Why no Les, you knows you'se the only one for me. I just meant those other guys I knew a'fore I mets you."

"So, Bridget, do you only like me because I'm clever and witty?"

"Why no . . . . "

"Don't you also like me because I'm a great lover? Didn't you say that the last time we were together?"

"Why sure, Les, you'se a great lover. In fact, Les, you'se the best. Maybe you should change that there slogan."

"You mean change it to Les is the best?"

"Yes-siree. You know, Les, I's never forget that first time we's made love. It was sure sumpin.'"

"Yeah, Bridget, you really exhausted me. I could hardly stand up afterward."

"Les, we's cud do that again to-nite if you likes."

"I'd sure like that, Bridget. But look, it's almost eleven now and I've got another hour or so of work. So I'm afraid I'll have to take a rain check."

"Well, you'se kin cash in that there rain check any time you likes. You knows how to git in touch with me."

"I do. Now I'm afraid I'd better get back to work. We really have to get this deal done. I think my bonus depends on it. So listen, I'm gonna sign off now. Bridget, I'll be thinking of you. You take care now."

"Sure, Les, I'll takes care. You get that there work done and then git some sleep. Go-nite, sweetypie."

* * * *

Chip turned off the recording. He couldn't believe what he had just heard. That was Lydia! Pretending to be Bridget! Her voice was unmistakable. He would know her voice anywhere, he had spent hundreds of hours with her.

They had spent time together in the office. And in the many courtrooms where her cases landed. And of course in bed. Sometimes at her old apartment. Sometimes at her new apartment down in Soho. Sometimes at his apartment, back in the days before Francoise moved in. And once or twice in the Worry Room. And even once in the manager's office at the Rainbow Room, during the firm's Christmas party last year.

Jesus, was Pap ever steamed about that. Lydia was supposed to appear on stage in front of all their clients in the Rainbow Room. The firm was hosting a Holiday Party to celebrate its fifth anniversary and Pap had regaled the attendees with accounts of the firm's cases.

Lydia was their most famous client. Everyone was anxious to get a look at her as Pap recounted the many cases they had successfully brought on her behalf. But Lydia was nowhere to be found. Instead of being on stage with Pap, she was climbing all over Chip in the manager's office.

So Chip absolutely knew that voice.

And Les! Les Moore! Les was an up-and-coming banker at Golden Slacks and he and Chip had recently become friends. Chip and Francoise had met Les and his wife Chloe last summer on Shelter Island.

The two of them had stayed in touch back in the city; they tried to have lunch once a month, usually at Les's club, the University Club on Fifth Avenue. Chip liked Les. But what he particularly relished was a contact with the most prestigious investment bank in New York City. You never knew when such a contact might pay off.

At their most recent lunch, Chip had told Les about the firm's interest in artificial intelligence, and told him about their work on the Sandoza case. He had also told Les about the numerous people who, because of the publicity the firm received from the Sandoza case, were now calling the firm to seek its help on AI matters. There seemed to be no end to the weird uses to which AI was being put.

That's when Les had proceeded to tell Chip about chatbots. They were really the latest thing. Especially the celebrity chatbots. Well-known celebrities were selling their image and voice to AI companies, who then used the images and voices to create virtual characters.

For example, Les continued, the retired football player Lom Grady - who had been paid over fifty million dollars by the disgraced founder of a cryptocurrency company to promote the company's now worthless crypto – had recently been paid five million dollars by an AI company for the use of his image and voice to create a virtual character. In this case, the character was a wisecracking sportscaster featured on one of those call-in radio shows.

"I know all about Lom Grady and his promotion of crypto currency" said Chip. "Our firm brought a class action case against Grady and the other celebrities who were pitching the crypto currency of that company FUX, which is now bankrupt. We sued Grady, his ex-wife Gazelle Munchkin, and the actors Batt Gamon and Harry Mavid.

"We knew there was little money to be had by suing Conman-Steele and FUX. But we also knew that Grady and the other celebrities were incredibly wealthy and that they would have considerable personal liability insurance. So we sued them on behalf of people who had invested in FUX crypto."

"How'd the case turn out?" asked Les.

"Well, they all hired expensive lawyers and tried every angle to get out of the case. But after the court ruled that the case could proceed as a class action and that it would go to trial in front of a jury, they settled. Big time."

"How much was the settlement?"

"One hundred and forty-five million. It was a class action so the settlement covered tens of thousands of individual investors."

Chip wanted Les to know he was part of a dynamic firm that was a major player in the legal world. So he decided to expand on his answer.

"There were close to a million people who had invested in FUX crypto tokens – which, by the way, were called FU's. Those people had invested close to sixteen billion in FUs. Of course we didn't expect to get anything close to sixteen billion for the class. But with the one hundred-forty-five million we received, we were able to pay the investors an average of one-hundred-and-forty-five thousand dollars each.

"The funny thing is, Les, not everyone wanted their money in dollars. Some of the class members were professional investors. They wanted their share to be paid in crypto. Can you believe that?"

"I hope you didn't give them back that FU crypto."

"Of course not, it was worthless by then. But we set aside part of the settlement money for class members who wanted to be paid in crypto."

Les was impressed. "You guys seem to be at the cutting edge of things. First the FUX case and now the Sandoza AI case."

After a long pause, Les continued. "Speaking of AI, you guys should take a look at some of the illegal stuff going on with these programs. Particularly the various chatbot programs."

"What's going on that's illegal? You said Lom Grady was being paid for the use of his voice and likeness. I assume other celebrities are also doing the same."

"Oh, sure. People like Soupy Dog, the rapper. And Paris Zilton, the self-proclaimed celebrity. I'm sure dozens more have agreed to allow their likeness to be exploited. But there's been a proliferation of chatbot programs in just the past few months. I'll bet some of them are using images and voices of famous people without their knowledge or consent."

"Such as?"

"Well, such as a program I use. It's called Lulu. It's put out by an AI company called Replicon. It's an App you access on your cell phone. The App provides virtual characters you can talk with."

"You use this program?"

"Sure. I'm always working late. Really late, frequently eleven or twelve o'clock. It gets lonely at the office then. So I signed up to chat with a lovely creature named Bridget. I call her once or twice a week when I'm working late and need a little break. We have a really nice relationship. She's more understanding than Chloe."

"Jesus, Les, that sounds kind of kinky. You've got a fantastic job, you make tons of money, and you've got a beautiful wife and three lovely kids. Why are you chatting with a female bot late at night?"

"Look. Chloe's at the house on Shelter Island all summer. I never see her and the kids except on weekends. It gets boring at the office after ten o'clock. Bridget is a nice pick-me-up, she helps me get through those long nights."

"So where does this company get the voices from to create the chatbots?"

"I don't know. It's possible they have some program that generates lots of different voices from scratch. But I doubt it. It's more likely they've recorded real voices from real people and then used them to generate different chatbots. Like Bridget, her voice could be that of a real person for all I know."

"And maybe Replicon didn't pay that real person for the use of her voice" said Chip.

"I don't really know one way or the other. But there's a chance not everyone is being paid. So there could be a lawsuit just waiting to happen."

"That would make for a terrific lawsuit. Maybe I should try to find this company – Replicon, I think you called it - and sign up for a female companion and see what happens."

"You don't need to do that. Why don't you start by listening to one of my conversations with Bridget. I could send you an audio transcription."

"You record your chats with Bridget? Jesus, Les, why do you do that?"

"I get a kick out of listening to them. I have an App on my cell called Audacity. It allows me to record any audio I receive."

"But what would Chloe say if she heard one of those chats?"

"She'll never know. I do it on my cell, there's no way she could access it."

"What about your firm? What if they found out you're talking with a chatbot in the office at eleven o'clock at night?"

"I doubt they'd do anything. Half the guys on my floor have a chatbot they talk to at night. We sometimes compare notes about our chats, some of the guys have really raunchy chats. Talking about our chats is good for morale. As long as we get our work done, the firm doesn't care."

"I guess investment banks are different from law firms."

"Listen, Chip, here's what I'll do. I'll send you the recording from my most recent chat with Bridget. There's nothing too raunchy on it. It'll give you an idea how this thing works. But look, if this thing ever leads to a lawsuit, leave me out of it. I'm happy to give you the recording as background, but that's as far as I'm willing to go."

"Of course, Les. I'll just listen to it. To get an idea what this is all about. If it happens to lead to a lawsuit, our conversation never happened. You can count on that."

"Great, Chip. We've got a deal. Now I've got to get back to the office. Otherwise I'll be there until midnight again."

"Yeah, but you can talk with Bridget tonight. I'm sure she'll cheer you up."

"Right. She always does. We'll try for lunch again next month. See ya."

Chapter 14

THE BATHHOUSE

Chip and Lydia were sitting on a wooden bench in the sauna of the Flatiron Bathhouse, a new luxury spa on 22nd Street in the Flatiron District. Chip had left the office at four, telling everyone he had a meeting with a witness.

Located in a building that until recently served as a parking garage, the Flatiron Bathhouse was a luxurious 35,000 square-foot complex spread over several floors. It offered no less than six thermal pools. There were two hot pools, two cold pools, a neutral pool and a saltwater pool.

The facility also offered a steam room, a dry sauna, an infrared sauna and it had a bevy of message therapists who offered a variety of messages and body scrubs. The bathhouse was extremely modern. With its dimly lighted and futuristic interior, it felt like a stylish nightclub.

But perhaps the most striking feature of the Flatiron Bathhouse was its clientele. Charging $75 for a day visit - $85 on weekends – the bathhouse catered to a young, upscale crowd of fit, toned and beautiful people. Customers went from one amenity to another clad in their underwear or bathing suits. It appeared to Chip that anyone without a perfect body who managed to get into the place would slink away in disgrace once they got a look at the other customers.

In fact, the people who ran the Flatiron Bathhouse deliberately cultivated the facility's reputation as a haven for beautiful young professionals. The Spa's motto, proudly displayed at the entrance and on its website was:

"A Home for People Like You
   Where You Can Look And Feel Your Very Best
   And Strut Your Stuff."

Chip was wearing his navy blue swimming trunks. Lydia was wearing a tiny blue bikini that left little to the imagination. Of course, Chip didn't need to use his imagination when it came to Lydia's marvelous body. He was intimately familiar with every square inch of it, having endlessly explored it during their many times together.

Lydia looked so fetching that Chip didn't even notice the constant parade of scantily clad young ladies that came and went from the sauna. The two of them were in the Dry Sauna, an 800 square-foot room heated to exactly 185 degrees Fahrenheit. Lydia had suggested they meet there, where they could talk. Later, they could take a swim in one of the pools, she liked the saltwater one best.

"How did you know about this place?" asked Chip.

"Why, I comes here all the time. My friend Honey told me 'bout it. You 'member Honey Combe, she worked with me at that there Bottoms Up club where we's first met. It's only 'bout fifteen minutes from my 'partment."

"It seems pretty new. Has it been here long?"

"I think it's new. Honey says they's also one in Brooklyn. But I ain't goin' all the way to Brooklyn just to sit an' sweat. Anyways, it's sure better than them there gyms. You goes there an' all you'se do is push and pull and grunt and groan with some guy who says he's helpin' you gits in shape. But he's really jus' tryin' to git in your pants.

"This place is diff-rent. You'se kin just sit here an' relax, or you'se kin go fur a swim. Or if you'se really wanna sweat, they's a steam room."

"But look at all those guys strutting around trying to look like Arnold Schwarzenegger. Don't they try to hit on you?"

"No. I don' wear this skimpy thing when I comes here alone. I's only wearin' it for you. Anyways, they's lots of other girls for 'em to hit on, that's why all them girls comes here in the first place."

Lydia took Chip's hand and gave him a big smile. "I's glad you called, Chip, you don' call me as much as you use to."

"Well, Lydia, I'm really glad to see you too. And I must say you look particularly delicious in that little blue bikini. But I do have something I need to ask you about."

"You mean we comes here on 'count a' business? I thought maybe you'se just wanted to see me."

"Well, I did want to see you. You know how much I love being with you. But first, I have to ask you a question that pertains to business."

"Sure, go 'head an' ask. And then maybe we can gits down to havin' some fun."

"Lydia, look. I need to ask you about Bridget. Who is she?"

"Bridget? I don' know no-one named Bridget. But tha's sure a sexy name. Wat's her last name?"

"This Bridget doesn't have a last name. In fact, she's not a real person. She's just a voice on an AI platform."

"Lookie here, Chip. If this here Bridget ain't no real person, how wud I knows her? And wat's AI?"

"AI stands for artificial intelligence. Computer companies can do almost anything with artificial intelligence. Including creating virtual persons."

"Wat's a vir-tul person? Seems to me you'se either a person or you'se not a person."

"A virtual person's someone who's not real but only exists on an AI platform."

"Wat's an AI platform? Is that wear all them there virtual persons stand?"

"Yeah, you can think of it that way. If you want to chat with some virtual person, you do it on your computer or maybe on your smartphone. You access the AI service and you can chat with that virtual person."

"You'se not makin' any sense, Chip. Why wud anyone wants to go on they's computer an' talk with someone who's not a real person? And how can that person, who's not a real person, talk with the real person who's tryin' to talk with 'em? And if they's not a real person, they's cou-nut say nothin' anyways. And besides, even if they's cud talk, they wu-nut know wat to say."

"Lydia, that's where computer programming comes in. The computer geeks who create these things can program the nonperson to talk. The nonperson who talks is called a chatbot. There are dozens, maybe even hundreds, of chatbots around and they do all kinds of strange things."

"Chip, why you'se tellin' me all this? I don't know no chatbots and I ain't never tried to talk to one of 'em. Why wud I want to do that anyways?"

"Well, Lydia, lots of guys like to talk with female chatbots. Maybe not the guys around here – it looks like they can score at will with these babes. But lonely guys, guys without girl friends or any hope of finding one, they might want to talk with a female chatbot."

"I still don' see wat all this gots to do with me."

"It's because of Bridget. Some AI company created a female chatbot named Bridget. And Bridget talks to those lonely guys who need a girl friend."

"Tha's certainly nice a' Bridget to do that."

"Right. But guess what? Bridget uses your voice to talk with those guys."

"Chip, you'se confusin' me again. How can this here Bridget use my voice? I don' even knows her. And how cud I since you'se just said she's not a real person?"

"Lydia, the AI geeks stole your voice. They probably had a tape of one of the press conferences where you spoke. Remember, those press conferences always generated lots of TV coverage."

"But I wasn't talkin' to no lonely guys at them there press things. I wuz talkin' 'bout our cases."

"Lydia, once they have a recording of your voice, they can program the bot to sound like you when it speaks. Whatever Bridget says, like when she's talking dirty to one of the guys, she says it in your voice."

"You mean I's talkin' dirty to those guys who's talkin' to Bridget?"

"I'm afraid so. Sometimes it's just everyday banter – like what are you doing right now or how are you feeling – that kind of thing. But sometimes it's very intimate, stuff you wouldn't want anyone to hear you saying."

"Why thas' outrageous. How kin they's do that? Maybe we should sue 'em. Like we did them there folks that made me an aviator in that Bunny Hop thing." Lydia had never understood that the Bunny Hop game used her and others as avatars, not aviators.

"Right" said Chip. "And just like last year, when we sued that company that was using your image on its nonfungible tokens. Just as those companies couldn't use your visual image without your permission, these computer guys can't use your voice without getting your permission."

"Chip, I swear, I's never given nobody permission to use my voice. 'Ticularly for a woman who ain't a real woman and who talks dirty to a bunch a' lonely guys."

"That's what I hoped you would say. I'll tell Pap and Pup we've got another great case to bring on your behalf. And on behalf of all the other ladies whose voices are being used without their permission. It'll be another class action. And as you know, we always win when you're our plaintiff."

"Yeah, Chip, you'se sure done a good job a' takin' care a' me. Seems like someone's always tryin' to take advantage a' me and you'se always there to per-tect me."

"And we always will be. We're very loyal to our clients. If they need help, we're always there to provide it."

"Tha's real good, Chip. Now we's got that there Bridget thing straightened out, maybe we kin git some-pin else straightened out."

And with that Lydia took her right hand and placed it on the inside of Chip's left thigh. Chip flinched, then looked at Lydia.

"Lydia, what . . . . "

Lydia slowly moved her hand up the inside of Chip's thigh. His whole body was tingling.

"Jesus, Lydia, not here. What will people think?"

"I know wat they's will think" she said, her hand now touching the bottom of Chip's swim trunks.

"Come on Lydia, stop it. This isn't the place . . . ."

"Maybe this is the place" she said as she started to move her fingers under his swim trunks.

Chip grabbed her arm and pulled it away. "Now look what you've done. Anyone who comes by will notice."

"Maybe we's should cover it up" she said with a mischievous smile. And in one lightening quick move, she swung herself onto Chip's lap, her knees bent underneath her so that she was now directly facing him.

"Lydia, for God's sake, this isn't helping."

"It sure is helpin' me" she said as she pressed herself against him.

"Lydia, for heaven's sake, you gotta get off. We can't be doing this in here."

Lydia reluctantly moved off of his lap. His excitement was noticeable.

"Why don't you go and get me a towel" he suggested. "I'll put it around my waist and then we can leave."

"Okay, Chip, whatever you says. I'll go getcha a towel."

Chip was suddenly alone on the bench. He tried to look like nothing was amiss.

Just then a stunning brunette in a two-piece suit walked by. "Hey handsome, what's up there? I'm Suzanne. Would you like me to join you?"

Chip tried to think of something to say. He had been trying to take his mind off the problem by thinking about his cases at the office. But that immediately caused him to think about their new client, Holly Gonightly, and boy she was really something. Thinking about the office wasn't helping. It only exacerbated the situation.

"No thanks" he finally said to the brunette named Suzanne. "I'm about to go take a swim."

"In that condition? You better be careful."

Half a minute later a nice looking blonde walked by. Chip had always been fond of blondes, they always seemed to have more fun.

"Hey, big guy, what's going on there? Do you need a hand?"

But Chip was ready this time. "No thanks. I'm waiting for my wife. When she gets back, we're going up to the saltwater pool for a swim."

"Well, if you go up, you won't find it. That pool's down one level from here. But I hope you and your wife realize that you married folks are ruining the reputation of this place."

Despite the reprimand, the interchange with the blonde had not helped his situation. Jesus, what a place, Chip said to himself. The bathhouse seemed to be sex city.

After two more agonizing minutes, during which several other young ladies offered their assistance, Lydia finally returned, towel in hand.

"It sure took you long enough, what were you doing?"

"Well, you sees, I thought the towels was downstairs, so I goes down but they wasn't any towels there. So I had to go up a couple a' floors before I found 'em. Then I had to comes back down here. I hope you dint think I left."

Chip rose and quickly wrapped the towel around his waist. "You should have brought one for yourself" he said as he tried not to stare at Lydia's fabulous body. "You should be covered up."

"Oh, I's all right" she said. "They's got plenty a' towels in the dressing rooms. Besides, I like it when you looks at me like that."

With one hand securing the towel around his waist and another hand on Lydia's arm, he guided them out of the sauna and up toward the locker rooms.

"How far from here did you say your apartment is?" he asked.

"'Bout fifteen minutes if you walks. But if you'se get us a cab, or one of them there Uver things, we kin be there in five minutes."

"I'll call Uber now" Chip said as he disappeared into the dressing room.

Chapter 15

SUE THE BOTS

The Monday after Chip's encounter with Lydia at the Flatiron Bathhouse, the lawyers assembled for their regular weekly meeting. Without waiting for Pap to open the discussion, Chip announced he had some important news.

"Remember that actress named Autumn Sleaves that Pup mentioned a couple of weeks ago?"

"Sure" said Melissa. "The one who said her voice was being used by a female chatbot who talks dirty to lonely guys. And you agreed to look for the app that was using her voice and see what you could learn about it."

"Right" said Chip. "Well, I never found anything on my computer. Well, actually I didn't look. I didn't want some AI company to have my email address and think I was a lonely guy who needed female companionship."

"So that's your news?"

"It turned out I didn't need to go online to find out about it. The answer fell right into my lap. You see, I discovered that Lydia's voice is being used by a chatbot named Bridget."

"You mean you discovered this when Lydia was on your lap?" asked Helen.

"Maybe" said Brandon "he means he discovered it when Bridget was on his lap."

"I think it was Lydia who was on his lap" said Melissa. "Probably after the two of them had a very expensive lunch at Le Bernardin. At the firm's expense."

"Melissa, you're dead wrong. This only cost the firm one hundred fifty dollars. That was the price for two one-day passes at the Flatiron Bathhouse."

"Why were you having a client meeting at a bathhouse?" asked Brandon.

"Because when I asked Lydia if we could meet, she suggested the Flatiron Bathhouse. Said she always spends Thursday afternoon there."

"Do people go around undressed?" asked Brandon. He'd never been to a bathhouse.

"Well, everyone is either in a bathing suit or their underwear. The object seems to be to show off your body. Everyone there was young, tanned and very fit."

"Were any of them fat?" asked Helen.

"Of course not. If you were fat you'd feel really out of place."

"Well" said Helen, "once the new city ordinance takes effect, they'll have to let fat people in."

"What ordinance is that?"

"Don't you read the papers, Chip? Our enlightened City Council just passed an amendment to the City's Administrative Code. It makes discrimination on the basis of height, weight, shape or body size illegal in employment, housing and public accommodations.

"It seems the ordinance was proposed by a council member who had gained forty pounds during the Covid lockdown. She got angry because all her friends were making fun of her. This legislation was her revenge."

"You think this bill applies to bathhouses?" asked Brandon.

"I'm sure it does" replied Helen. "A bathhouse would qualify as a public accommodation, just like a hotel or bus or restaurant."

"Well" said Chip, "based on my two hours there, I think a fat person would feel totally out of place. And they'd probably be shamed by the staff and the other customers."

"Maybe they could have a safe space for fat people" said Melissa, who had always been thin as a rail. "Safe spaces are all the rage these days."

"All right" said Pap. "Now that we know the City is protecting all our short and fat people, I think we should let Chip tell us what he learned from Lydia. While they were sitting around with no clothes on in a bathhouse. For which the firm has apparently reimbursed him one hundred and fifty dollars."

"It all started with my good friend Les Moore" Chip began. "He's a banker at Golden Slacks. We have lunch once a month . . . ."

"Don't tell me the firm is . . . . " said Pap.

"No, the firm isn't paying for it. We always have lunch at the University Club, Les belongs there. His firm pays for all its young bankers to join a . . . . "

"We're not paying dues for you guys to join some high-fallutin' club in the city" said Pap emphatically.

"I'm not suggesting you should" said Chip. "I'd rather have lunch at Le Bernardin and charge it to the firm.

"Anyway, Les was telling me how, during the summer, he's always at the office late at night while his wife and kids are at their vacation place on Shelter Island. He gets lonely. So, once or twice a week he dials up an app on his cell phone and talks to Bridget. Bridget consoles him, says she wishes she could be there with him."

"What's Bridget got to do with Lydia?" asked Brandon.

"Bridget *is* Lydia. Well, Bridget's voice is Lydia's voice. That's what that Autumn Sleaves lady was talking about when she called Pup."

"Pup" asked Pap, "did Autumn console you when she called? Maybe suggest she'd like to be sitting on your lap, or . . . ."

"That's ridiculous. You know her call was all business. Besides, she's not the one who talks flirty. It's her stolen voice that talks flirty."

"Same with Lydia" said Chip. "It's her voice, speaking as Bridget, that sometimes talks flirty."

"Does Lydia ever talk flirty with you?" asked Melissa.

"Or dirty?" chimed in Brandon. "Flirty or dirty?"

"Look" Chip protested, "I'm trying to get the firm a new case. Can we just focus on the case and knock off all the innuendo?"

"Okay" said Brandon. "But how did your friend Les know it was Lydia's voice that Bridget was using?"

"He didn't. I only discovered it when I listened to a recording of one of his late night chats with Bridget."

Melissa was astonished. "There's a recording? Why would anyone talk with a chatbot if their conversation's being recorded?"

"It wasn't the AI company that made the recording. It was Les. He sometimes records their conversations. That way he can play them back on evenings when he doesn't want to bother having a new conversation."

"This is getting really kinky" said Helen. "You've got a friend who records his dirty conversations with a virtual girlfriend and then you talk about those conversations with Lydia while sitting around in a bathhouse with no clothes on."

"We were in our bathing suits" Chip insisted. "I wouldn't talk business with a client with no clothes on."

"I assume" said Melissa, "that Lydia said she had no idea her voice was being used and never gave anyone permission to use it."

"Exactly."

Pap realized this had the makings of a terrific new case. "It sounds like the firm's one hundred fifty dollars was well-spent. Lydia has confirmed what Autumn Sleaves told Pup: someone is using the voice of female actresses and celebrities for chatbots that lonely guys can access via an AI platform.

"That company is stealing those ladies' likeness just as Erotic Arts stole the likeness of Lydia and other *Playboy* Centerfolds for their Bunny Hop video game. It's a misappropriation of the ladies' right of publicity."

"Does it matter that they're only using the ladies' voices but not their visual images?" asked Brandon.

"Absolutely not" said Melissa. "A celebrity's voice is just as much a part of their identity as their visual image. And don't forget, we know that many celebs, such as Lom Grady, have sold their voice to AI companies for use in creating virtual persons."

"Melissa's right" said Pup. "So if this AI company is using the voices of Autumn and Lydia for its chatbots, it must be using the voices of numerous others. We need to find some other women who've been victimized by this. But I doubt Lydia would know any other victims."

"Autumn might" said Pap. "She's an aspiring actress. Probably has tons of women friends who are trying to break into theater or TV. I think we should start by meeting with her."

"I'll be happy to meet with her" said Chip.

"If she's an actress" said Melissa, "she's probably good looking. This could lead to an addition to our Wall of Fame."

"But here's the thing" said Pup. "If we proceed, this case – along with the Sandoza case – would certainly put us at the forefront of AI law. But we need to realize this could get sordid. I suspect a lot of the conversations will be more than merely suggestive. Some will probably be downright smutty."

"Smutty never stopped us before" said Melissa. "We've sued on behalf of strippers in strip clubs. Naked centerfolds from *Playboy*. Dirty images in video games. We're up to our ears in smut."

"Melissa's right" said Chip. "Apes, bots, smut – Peters and Peters goes where the action is."

"Right" said Pap. "But what's more important, we now know that AI is being used to exploit innocent young ladies who are being turned into dirty-talking chatbots without their knowledge or consent. That's not right. Someone needs to put a stop to it, why not us?"

"I guess you're right" said Pup. "Except the part about innocent young ladies. I don't know about Autumn but I certainly don't think of Lydia as innocent. At least not in the virginal sense."

"Who's talking about virgins?" said Pap. "We're talking about a class action. I doubt there's enough virgins in New York City to form a plaintiffs class. But you won't have to be a virgin to get into this class."

"It doesn't hurt that all these young ladies are likely to be beautiful" said Melissa. "A whole class of beautiful young women."

"I can't think of a better class of plaintiffs" said Chip.

"Okay" said Pap. "It sounds like we all agree we should proceed. Now, there are several things we need to do right away.

"First, we need to meet with Autumn Sleaves and see if she can come up with some other victims. We might as well let Chip do that, he's gonna make sure he's the one who works with her no matter who first interviews her.

"Next . . . ."

Melissa interrupted, she had an idea. "Pup, what about that lady writer who contacted you about material in her books being stolen by some AI program?"

"She was complaining about the theft of her written work, not her voice" said Pup.

"But if her books are popular, I'll bet there are audio versions of them. That would make it easy for someone to steal her voice."

"That's a great idea, Melissa" said Pap. "Chip, it's another lady, you want to contact her as well?"

"If she's a writer, she's probably not attractive. Someone else should meet with her, maybe Brandon."

"Good idea" said Pap. "Brandon, here's your chance. Even if she's not pretty, we could still put her photo up on the Wall of Fame. That would give you one to Chip's ten."

Before Brandon could protest, Pap continued.

"And here's something else you can do, Brandon. We need to find out more about this company that runs the chatbots. I think someone said its name is Replicon. Why don't you start digging into them. Find out if they're financially sound. If not, find out who's behind the company, we might have to sue them if Replicon's just a shell.

"Now here's the final thing we need to do. We know we can sue them under common law privacy and publicity laws, just like we did in the other cases. But in this case, the violation is being carried out by the use of AI.

"There are lots of fairly new laws governing internet misuse and theft. Helen, take a look at them. I think most of them are criminal laws, but see if any of them allow for civil lawsuits. And even if they don't, see if what Replicon is doing amounts to a cyber crime. We can hold that over their head if they're reluctant to settle."

* * * *

Pap paused for a moment to collect his thoughts.

"Okay, we need to talk about the lawsuit involving the professor and the heiress. Helen, what did you find out about suing the auction houses?"

"You want the short answer or the long answer?"

"I want the short answer. But Pup will undoubtedly want the long answer, so you might as well give us both."

"Okay, the short answer is that we can sue the auction houses. Our basic claim would be that they failed to use due diligence in ascertaining ownership of the jewelry they obtained from Gray. I think that claim would withstand a motion to dismiss."

"Great, that's all we need. But for Pup's benefit, you may as well give us the long answer. Pup went to Yale, you know, they like long answers there. Especially if they involve ambiguity and nuance."

"Okay. Most of the cases against auction houses involve claims by the ultimate buyer who bought something that had been stolen. In those cases, there's a big distinction between a dealer and an auction house.

"A dealer buys the item from the seller and then arranges a private sale. Because the dealer owns the goods at the time of the resale, it has an obligation to convey good title to the buyer. If the goods are stolen, the dealer can't convey good title and so is liable to the buyer.

"Auction houses typically take the goods on consignment. Since they don't own them, they have no obligation to see that the buyer obtains good title."

"Helen, I'm sure Pup is beside himself with excitement at this legal discourse, but we could care less about the rights of the buyers. It's the rights of the original owners we care about. They're the ones who'll be suing the auction houses."

"Well, there's not much case law on that issue. But we can use the law I just described to shape our argument.

"For example, if any of the auction houses acted as dealers, they are clearly liable to the original owner. They had a duty to ensure that Gray had good title when he conveyed the goods to them.

"On the other hand, if they merely took the goods on consignment, we can still argue that they had a duty to see that the consignor – Gray –

had a right to consign them. They might not be liable to the ultimate buyer, but they should still be liable to the original owner. They were essentially taking possession of stolen goods and reselling them.

"So we can assert three causes of action: failure to exercise due diligence, conversion of goods belonging to another, and wrongful possession and sale of stolen merchandise."

"Beautiful" said Pap. "Lets lead with possession and sale of stolen merchandise. That's a criminal violation in every state. That will give us enormous leverage. The auction houses will beg us not to sue.

"Now, we need to see which of the victims are willing to sign on as plaintiffs. If the auction houses see there are several plaintiffs, and that all of them are wealthy high society types, they'll settle. They won't want the bad publicity.

"As you know, the press loves stories about stolen goods being sold by fancy auction houses. Those cases usually involve paintings and artworks, but there's no reason to think the press wouldn't have the same interest in stolen jewelry.

"Especially here, where the culprits are a gentleman professor with impeccable manners and a Swiss heiress who's not an heiress at all but a grifter who wormed her way into the top echelons of society. The press will eat this up."

"You sound like you're already working on your press conference speech" said Melissa. "But I thought the plan was to get them to settle without having to file a lawsuit - using DA Braggert's press conference and the criminal indictment as leverage."

"That's exactly the plan. Our leverage with the auction houses is the threat of filing the complaint – which of course we will show them as a courtesy. If they won't settle, we go ahead and file. And hold our own press conference outlining everything. But I don't think the auction houses will let that happen."

"The firm won't get any publicity if the case gets settled without our filing the lawsuit" said Melissa. "You'd have to promise the auction houses there would be no publicity."

"But there would be money. We like money as much as we like publicity. And remember, our clients are all wealthy members of the upper class, they won't want publicity either. They'll appreciate that we got a settlement without spreading their names around in the tabloids."

"So Braggert will be the only one getting publicity?" asked Brandon.

"Initially, that's correct. But at some point I'm sure it will slip out that Peters and Peters, New York City's leading class action law firm, put together the investigation that Braggert used to go after Gray and Borokin."

"I wonder how that would ever slip out" said Melissa.

Chapter 16

MARTHA AND MOE

Three days later, Pap was sitting in the Bridgeport courtroom of Judge Orville Rite. Judge Rite was just finishing an arraignment of two teenagers for attempted robbery.

Sheriff Ryder was the arresting officer and had accompanied prosecutor Belle Towles to the arraignment. When it was over, Ryder nodded to Pap and took a seat in the second row of the spectator section. Judge Rite's bailiff, Virgil Trucks, called the case of State versus Mona Lott et al.

Transcript of Proceedings:

The Court: Good morning everyone. I think we should start with .... Virgil, there's only a couple of people at the defense table. What happened to all those other people we had last time? Weren't there twenty or so?

Mr. Trucks: Twenty-three. We started with twenty-three defendants. But three of them were the balloon pilots and you dismissed the charges against them. Four of them were young kids, you also dismissed the charges against them.

That left sixteen. At that point you asked Ms. Towles to choose one of the remaining sixteen as a representative defendant. She chose Mrs. Lott, that lady there (pointing).

(Defendant smiles and waves to the Court.)

You then dismissed the charges against the other fifteen without prejudice.

The Court: Yes, I remember now. So we have just one defendant, not twenty-three. But the number of attorneys seems to have doubled. We had two the last time and now we seem to have four. I guess we better start by getting your appearances.

Mr. Snake: Good morning, Your Honor. I'm Sam Snake from Snake and Rolle. As you know we used to be Snake, Rabble and Rolle but we had to let Mr. Rabble go. We recently filed a Notice of Appearance to represent Mrs. Lott.

The Court: It's always nice to see you Mr. Snake. And I'm glad you got rid of that Rabble guy, he was a real troublemaker.

Mr. Snake: Your Honor, I'm only here to assist my good friend Mr. Peters as local counsel. Mr. Peters and I started out together in the Manhattan DA's office in New York. After we left that office, he stayed in New York to practice. I couldn't get a job in New York so I came up here.

The Court: That's New York's loss and Connecticut's gain. Now Mr. Peters, I assume you will be doing the speaking on behalf of Mrs. Lott?

Mr. Peters: Yes. You may recall you granted Mr. Snake's motion for my admission pro haec vice. As Mrs. Lott is a neighbor of mine and I've represented her in prior matters, she asked me if I would take the lead. And by the way, it's not that Sam couldn't get a job in New York. He had plenty of offers but wanted to come back to his home town to practice.

The Court: I was sure that was the case. Mr. Snake has an excellent reputation among the judges here. Now, I see that Ms. Towles will continue to represent the State in this matter?

Ms. Towles: Yes, Your Honor. But I'll be assisted on this motion by counsel for the Town of Westport. May I introduce Herman Hahn of the Westport firm of Hahn and Hoff.

The Court: Good morning, Mr. Hahn. I noticed that both you and Mr. Hoff filed notices of appearance. Will Mr. Hoff be with us today?

Mr. Hahn: No, Your Honor, Mr. Hoff is off dealing with an emergency for the Town of Fairfield. A large Chinese developer has bought up thirty acres of land just above the town beach. He wants to build a shopping center there.

The Court: The Chinese want to build a shopping center above the town beach in Fairfield?

Mr. Hahn: That's correct, Your Honor. But it's believed the Chinese really want to use the property to keep an eye on Navy ships coming down the Sound toward New York City.

The Court: The Navy has ships coming down the Sound on their way to New York City?

Mr. Hahn: Well, not yet. But there's a big submarine base at New London. At some point the Navy might want to send one of them down toward New York City. And you know the Chinese, they're always looking ten and twenty years ahead. By the time the Navy decides to send a sub down the Sound toward New York, the Chinese will be ready.

The Court: You might want to alert the Navy to this. Anyway, we're happy to have you with us today, Mr. Hahn.

(Court studies papers in front of him)

Okay, this is a hearing on defendant's motion for a restraining order suspending enforcement of two Westport zoning regulations Mrs. Lott is accused of violating. I was hoping you folks could resolve this matter without taking up any more of the court's time. But obviously you couldn't. So here we are.

I've read the papers submitted by the parties. I'll give each side an opportunity to briefly argue their respective positions. Mr. Peters, would you like to proceed?

Mr. Peters: Thank you, Your Honor. I'm sorry we have to burden you with this hearing. I reached out to Ms. Towles after our hearing in June. She consulted with the attorneys for the town and they were not interested in pursuing a resolution. So we had no choice but to file the motion for a restraining order.

Let me start with the regulation prohibiting all lawn mowing in May, the so-called "No Mow May" ordinance. As set forth in our brief, this regulation is unconstitutional. It's unconstitutional because it impinges on Mrs. Lott's right of free expression under the First Amendment. There are numerous cases, in Connecticut and elsewhere, holding that a zoning ordinance that inhibits free speech is unconstitutional.

Ms. Towles: Your Honor, this entire argument is irrelevant. No one is trying to restrict Mrs. Lott's speech. She can say whatever she wants.

Mr. Peters: Well, no one except Ms. Towles is trying to restrict Mrs. Lott's speech. Perhaps she's forgotten that she's prosecuting Mrs. Lott for exercising her right of free speech on the Staples High School football field. Of course, that's a different issue, her arrest for that incident is not before the Court today.

What is before the Court today is that the State is prosecuting Mrs. Lott for violating the "No Mow May" regulation. Now, we admit that Mrs. Lott has violated that regulation. In fact, she mowed her lawn on two separate weekends in May.

But why did she do that? She did it because she likes to keep her lawn – and in fact her entire property – neat and tidy. That's her way of expressing her love of beauty. Her love of beauty and harmony. Some people may like a lawn with weeds and grass five feet tall, which is what you get if you don't mow your lawn the entire month of May. But that's not the aesthetic Mrs. Lott wants.

In support of this argument, we've submitted an affidavit from Martha Stewart, one of the foremost experts in the country on gardening and property beautification. Ms. Stewart has spent her entire career helping people create aesthetically pleasing homes and gardens. In her affidavit, Ms. Stewart explains that the aesthetic appeal of a lawn or garden is a reflection of the artistic vision of the owner.

Ms. Towles: I object to Martha Stewart's affidavit and move that it be stricken from the record.

The Court: On what grounds?

Ms. Towles: Martha Stewart no longer lives in Westport. She did at one time but she long ago vacated Westport for tonier places, like Bedford, New York, and East Hampton.

The Court: What does it matter where she lives?

Ms. Towles: If she doesn't live in Westport she can't speak for the aesthetic views of the Westport community – as reflected in the lawn mowing regulation.

Mr. Peters: I'm afraid Ms. Towles is a bit confused. The question here is not whether the aesthetic views of the Westport community – as reflected in the May mowing ban – are good or bad. The question is whether the regulation inhibits Mrs. Lott's right to express her own aesthetic preference – a preference for a neat and tidy lawn.

The Court: I think Mr. Peters is right. Is there any other basis on which you object to Ms. Stewart's affidavit?

Ms. Towles: Yes. She's an ex-con. She spent more than a year in jail.

The Court: Ms. Towles, Martha Stewart only spent five months in jail, not a year. And her conviction had to do with her statements to investigators about an alleged insider trading scheme. It had nothing to do with gardening or landscaping, so it has no bearing on her expertise on that subject.

Ms. Towles: I don't think this case should be decided on the basis of testimony by an ex-con.

The Court: Ms. Towles, you need to stop calling her that. You should know that the legal theory on which she was investigated has been the subject of intense criticism by legal scholars. You should also know that, while she was incarcerated, she performed exemplary service by working with underprivileged inmates.

And everyone knows that, since being released from prison, she has resumed a full and productive life and is once again a respected member of the community. As a prosecutor, you should applaud that, not denigrate it.

(Ms. Towles sulks.)

So, Mr. Peters, I'm inclined to grant your motion with respect to the May mowing ban. Do you want to address the other ordinance at issue?

Mr. Peters: Yes, Your Honor. The regulation banning mowing on Saturday afternoons and all day Sunday has two legal infirmities.

First, it is unduly burdensome on property owners and thus amounts to an unlawful taking of property in violation of the Fifth and Fourteenth Amendments.

Second, it is economically discriminatory and has a disproportionate impact on lower income residents of Westport. Those residents, most of whom are blue collar workers, can't afford to hire someone to mow their lawn. They have to mow it themselves. But they work all week and so the only time they can mow their grass is on weekends.

As you know, Your Honor, Westport is a very wealthy town; in fact, it's one of the richest towns in the state. The average income is over $237,000. For the town's wealthy residents, the mowing regulation is not a problem - they can hire a lawn mowing service to mow their lawn during the week. The burden of the regulation falls only on lower income residents. They are disproportionately affected by the weekend mowing ban.

In support of this argument we've submitted the affidavit of Mr. Moe Downes. Mr. Downes is president of the Shady Lane Homeowners Association. As Mr. Downes explains in his affidavit, all residents in the Shady Lane neighborhood are blue collar workers who work all week and can only mow their lawn on weekends.

Ms. Towles: Your Honor, before you admit this affidavit, I would like to cross-examine Mr. Downes. I believe he's here in court now. That's him sitting next to Sheriff Ryder. I don't know why Sheriff Ryder's here, he always ducks out of court as soon as he can.

The Court: I believe Sheriff Ryder is acquainted with Mr. Peters. They became friends the last time Mrs. Lott was unjustly arrested. Now, you want to cross-examine Mr. Downes?

Ms. Towles: Yes. If you're going to admit his affidavit I have a right to cross-examine him.

The Court: Okay, here's what we'll do. I'm admitting Mr. Downes' affidavit and we will consider that to be his direct testimony. You may cross-examine him. Mr. Downes, will you please take the seat here on my left and Mr. Trucks will swear you in.

(Witness is sworn in)

Cross-Examination by Ms. Towles:

Q: Mr. Downes, you say in your affidavit that you cannot mow your lawn during the week?

A: That's correct.

Q: And that's because you work every day during the week?

A: That's correct.

Q: What day is today?

A: I believe it's Thursday.

Q: So you could mow your lawn today when you get home?

A: Yes.

Q: So you lied when you said you couldn't mow your lawn during the week?

A: I get two week's vacation. I took this week as one of them. If I wasn't on vacation I couldn't mow my lawn today.

Q: Where do you work?

A: At Staples High School in Westport. I'm the head groundskeeper. I spend most of the week mowing the lawns around the school. And also the football field, that's a real bear. I sure wish they'd put in artificial grass like other schools.

Q: Staples High School is a public high school?

A: Yes.

Q: Supported by the town of Westport?

A: I assume so but I don't know how this budget stuff works.

Q: But your salary is paid by the town of Westport?

A: Yes.

Q: Does the town know you submitted an affidavit in support of Mrs. Lott's challenge to a town zoning regulation?

A: I've no idea.

Q: So you get paid by the town but you're now testifying against the town in this case?

A: I'm testifying on behalf of my neighborhood association. I don't see the problem.

Q: Now, I understand you spend most of your workday mowing grass at the high school. You must be pretty efficient at lawn mowing?

A: I've never had any complaints about my work.

Q: How big is the lawn at your house?

A: It's pretty small. Almost all the houses in the Shady Lane neighborhood are on small lots, maybe just a quarter acre or so.

Q: And you're efficient at mowing grass, you do it all week long?

A: In the spring and summer, yes. We don't have to mow in the winter, especially if there's snow on the ground.

Q: So how long does it take you to mow your small lawn?

A: Including trimming – I use a gasoline-powered weed whacker, those electric ones are no good – I can do it in an hour.

Q: So all you need is an hour on Saturday to mow and trim your lawn?

A: Yes.

Q: And you've got from, say, eight a.m. to two o'clock to do it?

A: Yes but I'm never home then.

Q: You're away every Saturday from April to October? You have a vacation home somewhere?

A: On a school groundkeeper's salary? You must be kidding.

Q: So where are you every Saturday that you can't take an hour to mow your grass?

A: Fishing. My neighbor, Trout Bass and I, go fishing every Saturday.

Q: Where do you fish?

A: Anywhere there's water.

Q: Could you be more specific?

A: The Aspetuck River, it's the closest. But also Long Island Sound. The Housatonic River upstate, it's one of our favorite places. There are dozens of lakes and streams in Connecticut that are good for fishing.

Q: But isn't fishing limited to six weeks or so in March and early April? That would be well before your grass even starts to grow.

A: Only trout fishing is limited to that time frame. You can do most other fishing year-round in Connecticut.

Q: So when do you mow your lawn?

A: On Sundays.

Q: But there's no mowing all day on Sunday in Westport.

A: There is in the Shady Lane neighborhood.

Q: Don't your neighbors complain?

A: Why would they? They're all mowing their lawns then.

Q: How many times have you received a citation for mowing on Sunday?

A: None. I think that only happens in the rich neighborhoods. In the Shady Lane neighborhood, we all just mind our own business.

Q: How many households are there in this association?

A: I believe we have eighteen families in the association.

Q: And they all mow their lawns on Sunday?

A: Well, a few of them mow on Saturday afternoon, after they've finished their errands and chores.

Q: So, all eighteen families in the Shady Lane Homeowners Association are deliberately violating the law every week?

A: Yes, they have no choice. They're all working class families and one or both of the parents work all week. Like my neighbor, Trout Bass. He's the custodian at Coleytown Elementary School, works all week like me.

Q: But like you, Mr. Trout prefers to go fishing on Saturday morning when he could be mowing his lawn?

A: It's Mr. Bass. Trout's his first name.

Q: But you both choose to go fishing on Saturday morning rather than stay home and mow your grass so that you're in compliance with your town's lawn mowing regulations?

A: We would rather fish than be in compliance with the town's lawn mowing regulations.

Q: Mr. Downes, there are other ways you and your neighbors could deal with this matter, are there not?

A: Such as?

Q: Such as by going in and meeting with the Planning and Zoning Commission and explaining your dilemma.

A: We did that. All eighteen families turned out for the meeting when the weekend mowing regulation was discussed. But they weren't interested in hearing from us. They only allowed one of us to speak.

Q: But you were allowed to speak on behalf of the association?

A: Yes. For one minute. The folks who spoke in favor of the regulation were allowed to speak as long as they wanted. I was only allowed to speak for one minute.

Q: Mr. Downes, you are speaking on behalf of eighteen families, is that correct?

A: Yes.

Q: And Westport has over 28,000 residents. Surely you understand you're in a very small minority?

A: I'm sure there are more than eighteen families in Westport who own small homes and work all week and can't afford to hire a service to mow their lawn.

Q: But surely you recognize that you're in the minority on this issue?

A: Maybe so, but I don't see why those residents wealthy enough to pay someone to mow their lawn should be entitled to tell the rest of us when we can and can't mow our lawns.

Ms. Towles: Your Honor, I have no further questions. But I fail to see the relevance of Mr. Downes' testimony.

The Court: If you didn't think it was relevant, why did you spend more than half an hour cross-examining him? Mr. Peters, do you have any redirect?

Mr. Peters: No, Your Honor.

The Court: Ms. Towles, do you have anything further to present?

Ms. Towles: No, Your Honor.

The Court: Very well. I find the arguments made by Mr. Peters in court and in his brief compelling. I will shortly be issuing an opinion granting the motion for a restraining order. That order will suspend enforcement of the lawn mowing regulations in question pending a final ruling on the merits. That will be all for now.

Oh, I almost forgot. Mr. Peters, I assume you are in regular contact with Ms. Stewart with regard to this case?

Mr. Peters: Yes I am. She has been very pleasant to work with.

The Court: You see, my wife is a big fan of hers. In fact she has Ms. Stewart's first gardening book, I believe it's called Martha Stewart's Gardening Book. I have it in my chambers. Do you think you could ask Ms. Stewart to autograph it for my wife?

Mr. Peters: I'm sure Ms. Stewart would be happy to do so.

The Court: Virgil, will you see that Mr. Peters gets the book before he leaves?

Okay, that will be all. We're adjourned.

Chapter 17

THE LEDGER

On the Monday after the hearing in Bridgeport, everyone convened in Pap's office for their weekly meeting.

"Helen" Pap began, "you and Chip did a terrific job on the papers in Mona's case. Judge Rite granted the restraining order. And he admitted both the Martha Stewart and the Moe Downes affidavits. The prosecutor, Belle Towles, cross-examined Downes. Didn't lay a glove on him. You might say he mowed her down."

Following a collective groan, Pap continued. "Towles tried to exclude Ms. Stewart's affidavit, but to no avail. It turns out Judge Rite's wife is a big Martha Stewart fan. He asked me if I could get Ms. Stewart to autograph one of her gardening books, he gave me the book at the end of the hearing.

"Chip, you got Ms. Stewart to agree to submit the affidavit, could you meet with her and ask her to inscribe the book for the judge's wife? Maybe a nice warm personal message?"

"Sure."

"Will we be adding Martha Stewart's photo to the Wall of Fame?" asked Melissa.

"I draw the line at older women" said Chip.

"Still" said Melissa, "it was clever of Pap to have Chip go in person to visit Ms. Stewart and get her to sign the affidavit."

"On the subject of female witnesses that Chip is, ah, working with" said Brandon, "what about that actress whose voice is being used as a chatbot?"

"You mean Autumn Sleaves?" said Chip. "She contacted Pup first. Maybe he should put her picture on the wall in his office."

"All I did was speak with her over the phone" said Pup. "Chip's the one who's going to meet with her and see if she'll serve as a plaintiff."

"Yes, I'm meeting with her on Wednesday."

"Her photo will be on the Wall of Fame by Friday" said Melissa. "And the firm will have reimbursed Chip for a lavish lunch, probably at Le Bernardin."

"No, we're meeting at the Blue Water Grill on Union Square. I think Autumn's a downtown kind of girl. Le Bernardin would be too uptown for her."

"If you can get her to be a plaintiff for us, you can put in for reimbursement" said Pap. "But only if she says yes."

"I'll do my best" said Chip. Everyone knew that Chip doing his best would lead to the recruitment of another plaintiff and another photo for the Wall of Fame.

* * * *

"Okay" said Pap, "let's move on. We need to talk about the Prey/Borokin case. We just received Rollie's report. It's extremely thorough.

"Rollie managed to speak with all the victims. They all offered reasons why Prey was the likely thief. Unfortunately, only one of them – besides Urbacher – is willing to be named as a plaintiff.

"But the good news is that Rollie was able to determine where all the jewelry wound up. And almost all of it wound up at one of the three major auction houses in New York."

"How could he determine that?" asked Melissa. "Wouldn't he have to talk with Prey and Borokin to find that out?"

"Well, the police reports for two of the thefts traced the jewelry to Boyle Auctioneers here in New York City. As for the rest, Rollie had to use his ingenuity."

"What do you mean, his ingenuity?" asked Melissa, not liking where this was going.

"I've told you before, Rollie's really good. I've used him before to get information that's not available by ordinary methods."

"What kind of methods . . . . "

"What Pap means" said Pup, "is that Rollie can get into places we can't. He managed to find his way into Borokin's DC apartment. It was late July, so she and Prey were at her place in East Hampton."

"And guess what?" said Pap. "Borokin kept a ledger of all the stolen pieces: where they were stolen, who they were stolen from and where they were sold. She probably felt they needed to keep track so they could spread the items around to different buyers."

"You're saying Rollie made a copy of this ledger?" asked Brandon.

"Of course. That's why he broke into her apartment."

"But isn't that illegal?" Brandon insisted. "We could never use the ledger as evidence, it was unlawfully obtained."

"Who's talking about using it as evidence? We're just using it as a reference so we know we have some deep-pocket defendants to sue. A lawsuit against just Prey and Borokin wouldn't be worth bringing. We need to know we have some defendants who can afford to pay a king's ransom to get rid of the case."

"Besides" Helen said, "after Braggert issues an indictment, we'll be able to take their depositions. We can make them tell us what they did with all the jewelry."

"And" added Melissa, "if they claim they can't recall how they disposed of it, we can use the ledger to refresh their recollection."

"That's exactly the plan" said Pap. "Now, Pup's gone through Rollie's report with a fine tooth comb. Pup, why don't you take us through his findings."

"Sure. I'll go through the list on the basis of where the various items wound up. First of all, we have four items that wound up at Boyle.

"The first item is the platinum, diamond and sapphire brooch stolen from the Harrington's in Newport. Unfortunately, contrary to what

Urbacher expected, Harrington won't allow his name to be used in a lawsuit. He told Rollie his reputation as a savvy diplomat would be tarnished, and that it would be embarrassing if his European friends learned that he was a party to a class action lawsuit.

"The second item that wound up at Boyle was a ring from Van Cleef and Arpels. Its worth only a few thousand dollars, but it's one of the items the New York City police were able to trace to Boyle. The good news is that the victims – John and Jane Doe – are happy to have their names used in the complaint. Most of the plaintiffs will be listed as John Doe number 1, John Doe number 2, etc., so nobody will know it's actually them.

"The third item that wound up at Boyle was an expensive Patek Philippe watch. It was taken from the Georgetown townhouse of Jack and Keri Hines Carey. Carey works in the State Department on the Monaco desk. My friend in the State Department says that they put him there because they don't trust him to work on any country that's important. Anyway, Carey won't allow his name to be used in the lawsuit, he feels it could hurt his reputation, not that he has much of one anyway.

"The last items to wind up at Boyle were stolen from Thelma and Louise, sisters who live together in Manhattan. Between them they had twelve pieces of jewelry with a combined value of seventy or eighty thousand dollars. This is the other theft the police were able to trace to Boyle. Because the sisters live alone, they don't want their names to show up in the newspapers. In fact, they refused to give the police their last name, said their friends just referred to them as Thelma and Louise and that should be good enough for the police.

"So now let's turn to Krispies. They purchased four items. The first two were a Buccellati brooch and a pair of Buccellati earrings. They were stolen, perhaps at separate times, from an Upper West Side couple, Albert and Alba Tross. They refused to participate in the lawsuit. They don't want it known that they spend that kind of money on jewelry, it wouldn't sit well with their liberal friends.

"The third Krispies item is really interesting. It's a very expensive Verdura brooch. It was stolen from Dorothy and Rick Tracy, who live in lower Manhattan. Tracy's an army veteran, he was a career intelligence officer. He now runs a detective agency.

"But here's the rub. The original Verdura brooch is not the one that was stolen. What Prey stole was an imitation of the original. Tracy had a jeweler in the Diamond District – he wouldn't disclose the jeweler's name – make a perfect fake. And that's what Prey took."

"We can't sue for damages for the real brooch if it wasn't what was stolen" said Brandon.

"Why not?" said Pap. "Insofar as Prey knew, he was stealing a genuine Verdura brooch. And insofar as Krispies knew, that's what they were buying. It's their fault for not doing proper due diligence when they bought the brooch. They don't deserve a break."

Pup resumed. "The last item that wound up at Krispies was a Richard Mille watch. It was stolen from Floria Vanderbank's home in Newport. Her home is actually a mansion but in Newport they call mansions 'cottages.' The watch could be worth as much as a million dollars. But of course Ms. Vanderbank doesn't want her name used in a lawsuit. She knows the lawsuit would get lots of publicity and she doesn't like seeing her name in the papers.

"Now we get to the third auction house, Motheby. They bought three items and they're all big-ticket items.

"First is the collection if heirloom jewelry stolen from Urbacher's East Hampton home during his daughter's wedding. He told Pap this stuff was worth over fifty thousand dollars.

"The second item is a platinum sapphire ring. It was taken from Jack and Mary Aster's townhouse on the Upper East Side. The Asters also want to keep their names out of the papers.

"The final item that wound up at Motheby is a Himalayan Birkin bag, worth anywhere from fifty to eighty thousand dollars. It belonged to Katherine Cabot, she's married to that retired politician, Harry Cabot. The bag was taken from their home in Newport. Needless to say, the Cabots don't want it known that Katherine had spent that kind of money on a handbag.

"There's also one item that wound up at that place in the Diamond District, Diamond's Best Friend. They bought an enormous diamond ring that had been stolen from Dr. and Mauguerite Faust in Georgetown."

"Thanks, Pup" said Pap. "Now the next step is to take Rollie's report and organize it the way Pup just did. We should provide a reference to the police report for each incident. Helen, can you do this? When you're done, I'll make an appointment with Braggert and give him the report and our proposal.

"The next step would be taking the depositions of Prey and Borokin. However, you can't take a deposition before the complaint is filed unless you have a court order. So we'll go in, ex parte, to our friend Justice Leghetti and ask him to allow the depositions. Brandon, will you prepare a motion that we can submit to him?"

"Why can't we just file the complaint?" asked Brandon. "That would avoid the need for a court order."

"Brandon, we don't want to file a complaint against the auction houses. If we did that, we'd lose our leverage. Our leverage is the *threat* of filing a complaint. We need the auction houses to beg to settle with us in order to avoid being named as defendants in a class action lawsuit.

"They'll also want to avoid having every media outlet in the Metropolitan area cover our press conference the day we file the lawsuit. They'll know that, at the press conference, we would name all the prominent society people whose stolen jewelry was bought by the auction houses and then resold. They won't want that kind of publicity."

"I thought Pup just told us most of the victims won't allow us to use their names in the complaint" said Brandon. "How could we use their names at the press conference?"

"Brandon, we're not going to tell the auction houses that the victims won't allow us to use their names. We're going to tell them all the victims have allowed us to us their names."

"But that wouldn't be truthful."

"Why does what we tell the auction houses have to be truthful?"

"Well . . . . "

"All's fair in love and war" said Helen.

"And also in class action litigation" said Melissa.

Chapter 18

HOLLY NAILS IT

On the last Tuesday in August, Pup, Chip and Holly appeared at the office of Omar Sadly in Garden City for Holly's deposition in the Sandoza case.

As they entered the conference room, all conversation stopped and everyone's eyes went immediately to the stunning Holly Gonightly.

Sadly was the first to speak up, greeting all three and thanking Pup for agreeing to do the deposition at his office. Shaking Holly's hand longer than necessary, he offered to fetch her a cup of coffee or tea. If there was anything else she needed, she should just ask him.

Rosemary, a partner in Boogle's counsel Sage, Rosemary and Thyme approached and introduced herself. She explained that everyone should just refer to her as "Rosemary."

Addressing Chip who, as always, looked as if he had just stepped out of the pages of *Vanity Fair*, she asked "Are you Ms. Gonightly's husband? I'm sorry, but third parties aren't allowed to be present at a deposition."

"I'm with Mr. Peters" Chip replied evenly. "I'm flattered you think I might be Ms. Gonightly's husband, but I'm afraid I'm just one of her lawyers."

Walt Waters of Underbridge and Waters, counsel for Take America Back, introduced himself next. He kept his eyes glued on Holly, never once looking at Pup or Chip. He was going to have a hard time concentrating during the deposition, thank goodness Rosemary was going to do most of the questioning.

Finally, Barry Badd of Goode and Badd, introduced himself and stated that he was counsel for Democracy Now.

"What happened to Mister Goode?" asked Pup. "He seemed to be doing all the talking when we were in Judge Spade's courtroom."

"Oh, Mister Goode only gets involved when we're in court and we want to make a good impression on the judge."

After everyone was seated, the court reporter started up the video recorder, swore in Holly and the deposition commenced.

Questions by Rosemary:

Q: Good morning, Ms. Gonightly. I'm Rosemary. I represent defendant Boogle and I'll be asking you some questions on behalf of all the defendants. If there's any question you don't understand, or if you need any clarification, please feel free to ask me to repeat or clarify it. Otherwise, we'll assume you fully understand the question. Is that satisfactory?

A: Yes. They told me you would probably say that.

Q: Who's "they?"

A: Mr. Peters and Mr. Pierpont, the one you thought was my husband.

Q: Did you meet with them to prepare for this deposition?

A: Yes, of course.

Q: How many times?

A: Well, we had one day-long session at their office in the City.

Q: Who was there?

A: Mr. Peters and Mr. Pierpont.

Q: Anyone else?

A: Well, the other Mr. Peters stopped in just to say hello.

Q: The other Mr. Peters is the one who looks like this Mr. Peters?

A: Yes. I think they're twins.

Q: What did you talk about at this meeting?

A: We talked about the case. They explained what the case was about and what happens at a deposition.

Q: What did they tell you the case was about?

Mr. Peters: Rosemary, you know that's privileged. Ms. Gonightly is our client and the substance of our conversations with her are privileged. You're only entitled to ask about where and when we met.

Q: Okay. Now were there any other prep sessions with your lawyers other than the one you just told us about?

A: Well, there were a few supplemental sessions.

Q: What do you mean "supplemental sessions?"

A: Well, after that first meeting I met a couple of times with Mr. Pierpont.

Q: Where did those meetings occur?

A: In Garden City.

Q: Where in Garden City?

A: The Garden City Hotel. We had lunch in their restaurant – the Red Salt Room, I think it's called - a couple of times.

Q: And you talked about the case over lunch in the Red Salt Room at the Garden City Hotel?

A: A little bit.

Q: What did you talk about "a little bit" regarding the case?

Mr. Peters: That's privileged, we just went through that.

Q: Okay, when you weren't talking about the case, what did you talk about?

Mr. Peters: Anything they talked about not relating to the case would be irrelevant.

Rosemary: Are you directing her not to answer what she and Mr. Pierpont talked about at all those lunches?

Mr. Peters: Yes, I'm directing her not to answer. If they talked about the case, that's privileged. If they talked about something else, that's none of your business. Why don't you ask her some questions that are relevant.

Rosemary: Well, it may or may not be legally relevant. But it's certainly interesting that your Mr. Pierpont seems to have been wining and dining your star witness. No wonder I thought he was her husband.

Ms. Gonightly: He wasn't wining and dining me. In fact, we never had wine. We just had lunch.

Q: Okay. Now, Ms. Gonightly, let me move on to something that is patently relevant. How did you happen to become a plaintiff in this case?

A: I was asked by the Peters firm.

Q: Who in that firm asked you?

A: Mr. Pierpont.

Q: Where were you when he asked you?

A: In the restaurant at the Garden City Hotel.

Q: You just had lunch, right? No wine?

A: That's correct.

Q: What about dessert? Did you have dessert?

A: We probably did. Mr. Pierpont loves dessert.

Q: What led to Mr. Pierpont having lunch with you – no wine but probably dessert – at the Red Salt Room in the Garden City Hotel?

A: My friend Candy Lande gave my name to the Peters firm. That's Land with an "e" on the end.

Q: Who's Candy Lande?

A: She's a writer for an online newsletter about the tech industry. "TechTok" I think it's called. Candy and I grew up together in Oyster Bay.

Q: Does Candy Lande have some connection with the Peters law firm?

A: Well, she was a plaintiff in their case against Godiva.

Q: They sued Godiva, the Belgian Chocolate company?

A: Yes. The chocolates were called Belgian Chocolates but they were actually made somewhere in Pennsylvania.

Q: How did your friend Ms. Lande come to be a plaintiff in the Godiva case?

A: I believe she was recruited by the Peters firm.

Q: Do you know who in the firm recruited her?

A: Mr. Pierpont. Candy said he told her about the case and then helped her get through her deposition and also the trial.

Q: Mr. Pierpont sure seems to get around.

Mr. Peters: That's not a question.

Rosemary: No, but it's an observation. There seems to be an interesting pattern here.

Mr. Peters: You can speculate all you want. But I suggest you move on to something relevant.

Q: Ms. Gonightly, tell us about your education.

A: I went to public schools in Oyster Bay, that's where I grew up. Then I went to NYU and received a degree in theater performance.

Q: So, you're a professional actress?

A: Well, yes and no. All actresses would like to be on stage or in movies. But sometimes you have to start out doing advertising. That's what I've done so far.

Q: What kind of advertising?

A: TV commercials.

Q: For what products?

A: My first two commercials, a few years ago, were for Uncle Ben's Rice. I appeared in the commercials as Mildred, a housewife who always served her family Uncle Ben's Rice.

Q: Have you continued making commercials for Uncle Ben's Rice?

A: No. They had to change the name of the product. People were claiming it was racist. Now it's just "Ben's Original" rice. They had to drop the picture of Uncle Ben. He was a very handsome and well-dressed Black. For some reason they thought it was racist to portray Uncle Ben as a handsome, well-dressed Black.

Q: And so they dropped you from the commercials?

A: Yes, they said they needed to take the advertising in a whole new direction.

Q: Have you been in any other commercials?

A: Yes. I was in several commercials for TIDE laundry detergent and CLOROX bleach.

Q: What did you do in those commercials?

151

A: I was a frumpy, middle class housewife who liked to get her laundry really clean.

Q: My dear, you hardly look like a frumpy middle class housewife.

A: You'd be amazed what they can do with makeup.

Q: Any other commercials?

A: I told them I didn't want to do any more commercials for laundry products. So they asked if I would do one for CASCADE, the dishwasher liquid. I needed the money so I agreed.

Q: Were you another frumpy middle class housewife?

A: I was more of an upscale housewife in that commercial. The kitchen it was filmed in was really nice. But that was my last commercial, I wanted out of that business.

Q: So what did you do then?

A: I decided to try modeling. That was my mother's career until she married my dad. So I signed a contract with a modeling agency.

Q: Which agency is that?

A: The Big Top Modeling Agency.

Q: And did they find any modeling jobs for you?

A: Yes. I was in several shots used by L.L. Bean in their catalog.

Q: What did you model?

A: Pajamas. Bulky pajamas, sometimes flannel ones.

Q: Anything else?

A: Yes. The company liked the way I looked so they moved me up to underwear. Long underwear.

Q: So you're still doing the frumpy housewife thing?

A: Yes. But L.L. Bean also sells bathing suits, so I asked them if I could be in some of their bathing suit pictures.

Q: And?

A: They said no. Said I was too attractive, and also too thin, to be in their bathing suit ads.

Q: So that was the end of your modeling career?

A: No. The agency finally came through for me.

Q: In what way?

A: I'm going to be one of the models in Forbes Magazine's new "Trimsuit" issue. It's a special issue of the magazine they plan to publish every summer. Actually, late summer, when their circulation always tanks because all their readers are away on vacation.

Q: So, you'll finally get to model in a bathing suit?

A: Oh no. Forbes is a business magazine. We'll all be wearing the latest in women's business suits. It'll be like the Sports Illustrated Swimsuit edition except all of us will be in business suits.

(Long Pause)

Q: Let's move on. Ms. Gonightly, did you vote in the election last Fall?

A: Certainly.

Q: Did you vote for a Congressional candidate?

A: Yes, of course.

Q: And did you vote for Mr. Sandoza?

A: Yes.

Q: Why did you vote for him?

A: Well, like my parents I'm a Republican. And from what I heard about him, he seemed like a great candidate.

Q: What did you hear or read about him that made you think he was a great candidate?

A: Pretty much everything. Starting with his education – he supposedly was in the top five percent of his class at Baruch College. Then he got an MBA from NYU's Stern School of Business. I went to NYU myself, so I know the Stern School has an excellent reputation.

Also, he seemed to have a great background in the financial world. Citibank and Golden Slacks. Everyone knows they only hire the top people. Then there was his family background. His grandparents being caught up in the Holocaust, then his mother being in the North Tower of the World Trade Center on nine-eleven. That was all very compelling.

Q: Anything else?

A: Well, he was a Latino. The Republican party needs to attract more Hispanic and minority voters. So a Republican Latino candidate was a great thing for the party.

Q: Did anything about his politics attract you?

A: I don't recall him talking much about the issues. But the one thing I do remember is his concern about China. Its threat to the U.S. I believe he gave a speech about it.

Q: That was after he was already elected. He gave it on the floor of the House. So that couldn't have been a reason you voted for him.

A: Okay, but it's a reason I liked him after he was elected. China's a big problem for us. So I was very glad to hear him speak out about it.

Q: Did you ever worry that everything you heard about Mr. Sandoza was too good to be true?

A: No. Why would I think that?

Q: But surely you were just a little bit skeptical about everything you were hearing? Grandparents disappearing during the Holocaust and then his mother having a terminal illness due to being in the World Trade Center on nine-eleven? How likely was it that both of those things were true?

A: Why couldn't they be true? If anything wasn't true it would have been discovered long before the election. Every candidate has researchers who scan the background of the opposition candidate with a fine tooth comb. They look for a discrepancy they can exploit, then feed it to the media.

Q: So you're saying it's the fault of the media for failing to discover that nothing about him was true?

A: No. The fault lies with Mr. Sandoza and Boogle. Mr. Sandoza knew that everything he was saying and writing about himself was not true. And Boogle knew that everything he said or wrote came straight from their AI program.

Q: Ms. Gonightly, you're a lifelong Republican, are you not?

A: Yes.

Q: And you really wanted a Republican to be elected to Congress from your District?

A: Sure.

Q: And you would have voted for Mr. Sandoza even if you had known that not everything about him was true?

A: That's not correct. Maybe if I had known that he exaggerated a little, say he was only in the middle of his class at Baruch, not the top five percent, that might not have bothered me. Lots of politicians exaggerate that kind of thing. Like the president saying his uncle was eaten by cannibals when his plane crashed in New Guinea during World War II.

But had I known that everything about Sandoza was a total fabrication, I certainly would not have voted for him. Why would anyone, Republican or Democrat, vote for someone who used AI to fabricate their background?

Q: How are you injured by all this?

A: I voted for a candidate who wasn't real. Nothing about him was real. Why would I waste my vote on someone who isn't real.

Q: Any other way you've been injured?

A: Sure. Sandoza's probably going to get thrown out of Congress. At that point, voters in the Third District will no longer have a Republican representing them.

Q: But if he gets expelled, there would have to be a special election to replace him. Another Republican could well be elected.

A: That's unlikely. I think it will be several years before voters in the Third District trust another Republican candidate.

Q: But you would agree that none of this has had any effect on your career?

A: But it has. As you know this case has received lots of publicity. And the publicity sometimes mentions that I'm one of the plaintiffs. When the Big Top agency heard that I was a Republican and that I had voted for Sandoza, they dropped me like a hot potato. So now I've got to find a new agency to represent me.

Q: But Forbes hasn't dropped you?

A: No, the spread for the Trimsuit issue was shot and put to bed before news of the lawsuit came out. But I'm worried they won't want me for next year's Trimsuit issue.

Rosemary: Thank you, Ms. Gonightly, that's all I have. I think my colleagues may have some questions.

Mr. Peters: Why don't we take a short break. I'm sure the court reporter would appreciate it.

(Deposition resumes at 12:10 p.m.)

Questions by Mr. Waters:

Q: Ms. Gonightly, I assume from your testimony this morning that Take America Back's support for Mr. Sandoza's campaign played no role in your decision to vote for him?

A: But it did. Take America Back is one of the leading PACs supporting Republican candidates. Knowing that they were supporting Mr. Sandoza – in fact, spending money on his campaign – was very important to me. It confirmed my view that he was a solid candidate that I could support.

Mr. Waters: I have no further questions.

Questions by Mr. Badd:

Q: Ms. Gonightly, I suppose you're going to tell us that Democracy Now's support for Mr. Sandoza's campaign was also important to your decision to vote for him?

A: Yes, of course. How did you know that?

Q: It's obvious from all your answers here today that you've been very well coached by your counsel. You always give exactly the answer that supports their argument in this case.

A: Mr. Badd, I'm sorry to hear you say that. Now it's true that, when I was doing those commercials for TIDE and CLOROX, they told me what to say. After all, I grew up in Oyster Bay – what did I know about the best detergent or bleach to use in your laundry, we had a lady who did all that stuff for us. But nobody had to tell me what to say in this deposition.

Q: Then why did you have to meet so many times with Mr. Pierpont? At that fancy restaurant in the Garden City Hotel?

A: As I told her (pointing), it was partly business and partly social.

Q: So you have a social relationship with one of your lawyers? I'm sure the Bar Association would be interested to hear about that.

A: No, we had a business relationship. It's just that sometimes we talked about more than business. What's wrong with that?

Q: We'll ask the Bar Association what's wrong with it. I'm sure they....

Mr. Peters: Mr. Badd, this line of questioning has nothing to do with the issues in this case. If you have any more questions that are relevant, now's the time to ask them. If not, we'll terminate the deposition now.

Mr. Badd: Well, I'm sure Mr. Pierpont is anxious to end the deposition so that he can take the witness to lunch at the Garden City Hotel. It's only a block or so away.

Mr. Peters: Okay, that's it....

Mr. Badd: Hold on, I'm not done. I have a few more questions.

Q: Ms. Gonightly, you said your decision to vote for Mr. Sandoza was influenced by Democracy Now's support of his campaign.

A: Yes.

Q: But I assume it wasn't as important as Take America Back's support for his campaign?

A: On the contrary, Mr. Badd, your client's support was more important to me. Everyone knows Democracy Now is a very liberal PAC and that it always supports liberal candidates. So it seemed to me that, if Democracy Now was supporting a Republican, he must be a really fine candidate. Why else would they support him?

Mr. Badd: I've no further questions.

Chapter 19

MOW ON

The following Tuesday – Monday having been Labor Day – everyone assembled in Pap's office for their weekly meeting.

"How did Holly Gonightly's deposition go?" asked Helen.

"She was terrific" said Pup. "She knocked every question out of the box. Even managed to say that her vote for Sandoza had been influenced by the two Super PACs – Take America Back and Democracy Now. Even though, when Chip and I met with her, she told us she'd never heard of them."

"You mean she lied about it?" asked Brandon.

"She really didn't lie" said Chip. "When I worked with her after the meeting with Pup and me, I refreshed her recollection that she really had heard of them and that their support of Sandoza had helped convince her to vote for him."

"I'll admit that does substantially help the case" said Pup. "But look, Chip, your incessant meetings with our witnesses are causing us a lot of headaches. They spent half the deposition asking about your lunches with Holly at the Garden City Hotel."

"I thought Chip only met with her there once" said Melissa. "The first time he met her."

"Well" Pup responded, "Holly was forced to admit that she and Chip had met there for lunch a few times. She wasn't specific as to the precise number of times."

"It was five" said Chip. "Six if you include the initial meeting when I was sounding her out about the case."

"You mean the firm paid for six lunches for you and Holly at the Garden City Hotel restaurant?" said Melissa.

"Yes. But I billed my time to the case on all six occasions."

"He billed five hours of time for each lunch" said Pup.

"How did you know that?" said a surprised Chip.

"I review the billing records every month. I like to see how hard everyone's working."

Brandon was astonished. "Chip, you say you spent five hours with her on six different occasions? What on earth were you doing?"

"Talking about the case. That's proven by the entries in my billing report. Five hours talking about the case each time."

"We don't normally spend that much time with our witnesses" said Brandon.

"Brandon, Pap's always telling us to be sure we maximize our billable hours; they're the starting point when we file our fee applications."

"I hope the two of you had a good time at all those lunches where you talked about the case for five hours" said Melissa.

"Melissa" Chip protested, "we didn't even have wine. Holly made that clear in her deposition."

"But you always had dessert" said Pup. "Holly also made that clear in her deposition."

"I wonder what kind of dessert you two had" said Melissa.

"And where you had it" added Helen.

"Look" said Chip, "the proof is in the pudding. You just heard Pup say Holly was a fabulous witness. That's the important thing."

"Chip's right" said Pap. "He seems to work magic on our female witnesses, they always come through for us in court. So the firm is happy to reimburse him for all his lunches and dinners with witnesses. It's money well spent.

"I love my job" said Chip.

"Right. So let's . . . ."

"I think we could have a new AI case in the making" interrupted Helen. "Against Boogle."

"We've got rather a full plate right now" said Pup, "but if it's AI, tell us about it."

"Well, according to Saturday's *New York Post* . . . . "

"You read the *New York Post*?" asked an astonished Melissa.

"Sure. Keith subscribes to it. He says he likes their sports coverage. But I think he really likes it because of all the girly pictures.

"Anyway, Keith says all his banker colleagues look at it every day. If they've been out to a fancy opening or gala with their wives, they want to see if their picture's in the paper. And if they've got something going on the side, they want to make sure their picture's not in the paper."

"Will you please tell us about the potential AI case" said Pup.

"Well" Helen began, "it seems that Boogle's BotsUp? app has a new feature that allows it to spit out pictures of famous historical figures really fast. You don't have to go looking through books or spend lots of time searching the Internet, you just tell BotsUp? who's photo you want and the app immediately sends it to you."

"Sounds like that could be really useful" said Melissa.

"It could. But it seems you don't get what you asked for. For some reason, BotsUp? has been programmed to turn out what might be called politically correct photos instead of the real photos."

"Such as?"

"Such as a picture of the Pope. Instead of a picture of Pope Francis or any of his more than two hundred predecessors, you get a picture of either a Southeast Asian woman or a black man. Both of them wearing Pope-like vestments and crowns.

"Or George Washington. You ask for a picture of 'the father of our country' and you get a picture of a handsome black man in a white wig and an army uniform. There's also the famous Vermeer painting 'Girl with a Pearl Earring.' You get a picture of a young black woman with a large pearl earring in her left ear.

"Then there's the Vikings, the notorious Scandinavian warriors. They're depicted as a group of diverse warriors of all colors and sexes. There's a shirtless black man with dreadlocks, a young black woman and also an Asian man standing in a desert."

"Sounds like Boogle has gone totally woke" said Melissa.

"Oh, they admit they have" said Helen. "They even boast about it. One of their executives was quoted as saying that Boogle wanted to provide a quote 'more accurate and inclusive representation of the historical context of these people.'"

"Maybe we could get the heirs of George Washington to agree to sue" suggested Brandon.

"And also Vermeer's heirs" said Melissa. "But I'm not sure where we'd go to look for them. Maybe they're still in Holland."

"Okay" said Pap. "You three can work on a new case against Boogle. But do it in your spare time. Maybe you could count it toward your pro bono obligation. In the meantime, we need to talk about our cases."

* * * *

"So, Mona's case has finally settled" he began. "After Judge Rite granted the restraining order, I contacted Bess Chance, Westport's First Selectman, and asked if I could come in and talk with her.

"So last week I met with her and the town's outside attorneys, Hahn and Hoff. Both of them were there even though only Hahn had been at the hearing before Judge Rite.

"I told Bess it was obvious Judge Rite would make the restraining order permanent once we had a full trial on the merits. I explained how that would be bad for the town, not just in the immediate case but in the future.

"For example, it would encourage Westport residents to file more lawsuits regarding zoning matters. Today it's just restrictions on lawn mowing. Next time it could be something really important to the town, such as acreage levels or setback requirements.

"I told Bess the town's best chance to resolve the case was now, when the injunction was only temporary; once it becomes final the town will be in a much tougher position.

"Hahn came on quite strong. He told Bess he thought they could eventually win the case on appeal. He even suggested they take an immediate appeal of the restraining order.

"But Hoff was much more cautious, he pretty much agreed with everything I had said. He thought there was no way an appellate court would intervene at this juncture in the case. And he thought the chance of a reversal once there was a final decision in our favor was extremely low.

"Chance wasn't happy to see them disagree. She asked why they couldn't come up with a single recommendation that they both agreed on. Hoff told her she should think of it as getting two opinions for the price of one.

"Chance ultimately sided with Hoff. She was pretty sure they couldn't get the order reversed at this point. And the town couldn't afford to continue spending money on the case in the hope that, after two more years of litigation, the ruling might be reversed.

"So I gave her our proposal. If the town would agree to rescind the ban on May mowing, and the partial ban on Saturday mowing, we would agree to a restriction on Sunday morning mowing. After some back and forth, we agreed that Sunday mowing would be banned until two in the afternoon.

"Chance agreed to take that proposal back to the zoning commission. She'll take Hoff with her. She was confident they could get the Commission to agree to the changes. We won't know for sure for a couple of weeks but I think it's a done deal."

"That's a great result" said Melissa. "But what does the firm get out of this?"

"What the firm gets out of the case is that Pup and I, and our wives and children, don't get prosecuted for trespassing and engaging in an unlawful demonstration. What would you guys do if Pup and I were sitting around in jail for a year?"

"I don't think they put people in jail for a year for trespassing" said Chip. "Maybe two or three months but not a year."

"We do most of the work around here anyway" said Melissa. "So the cases would continue being worked on. If one if you had an idea for a new case, you could send us a note and one if us would come and visit you."

"By the way" asked Brandon, "where is the state prison in Connecticut anyway?"

"I'm glad you're all having fun with this" said Pap. "At least Helen took the case seriously, she prepared the papers that got us the restraining order."

"I helped her" said Chip.

"Right. You worked with her in her apartment the week her husband was in Japan. Thanks for reminding me."

* * * *

"We need to get back on track" said Pup. "We should go over our plans for the next couple of weeks."

"Okay" said Pap, "let's start with the Prey/Borokin case.

"The first thing is our meeting with Braggert's office. Helen pulled together everything we need to give them and it's ready to go. I contacted my old friend Witt Clinton. He's a career prosecutor in the DA's office. We were friends when I worked there. He's set up a meeting for Pup and me with himself and Braggert for Thursday afternoon.

"Assuming Braggert goes along with our plan, the next thing we'll need is an order permitting depositions. Brandon, how are you coming on that motion?"

"It'll be ready by the end of the week."

"Great. We'll take it straight to Justice Leghetti. That's the beauty of an ex parte motion. You get to choose which judge you want to take it to. Justice Leghetti knows us, I'm sure he'll sign the order."

"I thought they had an emergency motion judge assigned to deal with stuff like this" said Helen. "Isn't a new one designated every week or so?"

"This isn't an emergency motion" said Pap. "This is a let's-take-it-to-Justice-Leghetti motion. We don't want to deal with whatever hack is in the motion part that day.

"Now, Melissa, you were going to start thinking about the Prey and Borokin depositions. I think you and Helen should take them. They'll let down their guard when they see its just two young female associates asking the questions."

"Are you saying we don't look professional enough to take a deposition from a significant witness?" said Helen.

"No, I'm saying . . . . Look, you all know exactly what I mean, I'm not going to take time to explain it.

"The other immediate priority is the Sandoza case. The depositions of the two Super PACs are scheduled for a week from Thursday. Since they insisted on taking Gonightly's deposition at their office, we insisted they bring their witnesses to our office. We've scheduled Take America Back for the morning and Democracy Now for the afternoon. Chip, you need to work with Pup, he'll be taking both depositions.

"But I need the two of you to stick around after we finish. I have a couple of ideas. I want us to have a nice surprise for defendants and their counsel.

"Okay, anything we haven't addressed?"

"Who's gonna draw up the new complaint against Boogle for the woke AI photos?" asked Brandon. "And how are we supposed to contact George Washington's heirs to get their permission to file the lawsuit? Do you think they still live down in Mt. Vernon?"

"Helen, you figure this out. You're the one who called the matter to our attention."

Chapter 20

PAC MEN

On Thursday September 14th, all the lawyers in the Sandoza case appeared at the office of Peters and Peters for depositions of the two Super PAC defendants. The deposition of Take America Back would start at ten o'clock while the deposition of Democracy Now was scheduled for two o'clock.

Pap had instructed his secretary Vera Pesky, who also served as the firm's receptionist, to keep all the lawyers and witnesses in the waiting area just inside the door until Pup was ready to start the first deposition. Under no circumstances was she to allow anyone into the conference room until Pup gave her the signal.

At a few minutes past ten, Ms. Pesky invited the lawyers and their clients to enter the conference room where Pup, Chip and the court reporter Ruby Redd had already assembled.

As they entered the conference room, everyone stopped and stared in amazement. Every inch of wall space was covered with posters from the Sandoza campaign. With bright red lettering on a white background, the posters featured a photo of a smiling Sandoza. Just above the photo was the headline:

"The RIGHT Candidate For The Right's Moment"

A television had been placed at the far end of the conference room. It was playing and replaying a recording of a Sandoza commercial that had been broadcast extensively on Fox News. Against background music of John Philip Sousa's "Stars and Stripes Forever," an announcer with a deep baritone voice intoned:

"Gregory Sandoza, a First Generation American. The Right Candidate For The Right's Moment."

The two-minute-long commercial displayed a smiling Sandoza with his wife and two young children as the announcer listed highlights from his career: Graduate of Baruch College and the NYU Stern School of Business. Wall Street veteran. Founder of Pet Friends, an animal rescue center. It ended with the statement:

"As a young man who has faced the adversity of grandparents who perished during the Holocaust and a mother who contacted a fatal illness while in the North Tower of the World Trade Center on nine-eleven, Gregory Sandoza understands pain and grief. He will always have empathy for the less fortunate members of our community."

At the end of the commercial, the following statement was displayed:

"Paid for by Take America Back, a Political Action Committee not associated with the Gregory Sandoza campaign."

When the lawyers looked for an appropriate seat at the long conference table, they discovered that each place sported a trim note pad with "Gregory Sandoza 2022" at the bottom, a pair of plastic buttons saying "Sandoza 2022," and a four-by-four-inch rubber jar opener bearing the legend:

"Gregory Sandoza 2022
  Opening up Congress to new ideas"

Rosemary, Boogle's attorney, was the first to speak. "Isn't this somewhat irregular?"

"Not really" said Pup. "We redecorate our conference room every few weeks. Otherwise the décor gets a little stale."

"How do you expect the witnesses to be able to concentrate?" said Omar Sadly, counsel for Sandoza and Goldstone Strategies.

"We'll turn down the volume on the television once we start" Pup assured him.

"You're free to take the note pads, buttons and jar openers with you when you leave" said Chip. "We don't want anyone to leave empty-handed."

"This is an outrage" said an angry Barry Badd, Democracy Now's counsel. "The witnesses shouldn't have to testify in this environment."

"What's wrong with the environment?" said Dusty Rhodes. Rhodes had made his fortune in road building and was the founder of Take America Back. To Pap and Pup's surprise, he had been designated by that PAC to appear as its spokesman at the deposition.

"This room is a tribute to Congressman Sandoza" Rhodes added. "We all helped him get elected. We should be proud, not angry, at this tribute."

Badd shot daggers at Walt Waters, counsel for Take America Back, and said: "Walter, I suggest you instruct your client not to speak until the deposition starts. We don't need off-the-record statements coming back to haunt us."

"I wouldn't worry about this being off the record" said Pup. "The court reporter has had her audio and video equipment on since you all came into the conference room."

"That's unethical!" Badd was now virtually shouting. "Wait until Judge Spade finds out about this."

Ignoring Badd, Pup calmly said "Why don't we start the deposition. Ms. Redd, would you swear in Mr. Rhodes."

(Transcript of Deposition of Dusty Rhodes)

Questions by Mr. Prescott Peters:

Q: Mr. Rhodes, you are the founder of Take America Back?

A: Yes.

Q: And Take America Back is a Political Action Committee that mainly supports conservative Republican candidates?

A: We only support conservative Republican candidates.

Q: Take America back is actually a Super PAC, is it not?

A: That's correct.

Q: And as a Super PAC, you cannot donate money directly to a candidate's campaign; rather, you must spend the money yourself, such as running print ads or generating commercials and paying for them to run?

A: That's correct.

Q: Now, it appears that in the last election cycle, the 2022 midterm elections, Take America Back raised around $82 million and disbursed about $79 million?

A: That sounds about right.

Q: And about $2 million of that $79 million was spent in support of Mr. Sandoza?

A: That's right.

Q: Was most of that spent on television advertising?

A: Yes. We produced the commercial you've been running on that television over there. But we also ran a few print ads, mainly in the *New York Post* and *Newsday*.

Q: Why did your PAC spend $2 million on Mr. Sandoza's campaign?

A: He was a great candidate. Conservative. Family man. And he's a Hispanic. That was a real plus. The Republican party needs more Hispanic candidates.

Q: Do you think voters in the Third Congressional District were influenced to vote for Mr. Sandoza by the commercials and ads your PAC sponsored?

A: I certainly hope so. They're great.

Q: Did you or anyone at Take America Back conduct any investigation or make and inquiries into Mr. Sandoza's background?

A: Why would we do that?

Q: Well, to make sure that what he said about himself was true?

A: He's a conservative Republican. If you can't trust a conservative Republican, who can you trust?

Q: So you have no idea whether he graduated from Baruch College in the top five percent of his class or whether he has an MBA from NYU's Stern School of Business?

A: He said he did, that was good enough for us.

Q: And you have no idea whether or not he had a successful career with Citibank and Golden Slacks?

A: We had no reason to doubt that.

Q: And the same would be true about his work with the Florida investment firm, Harbor Capital, and the Long Island business development company, Landbridge Investments?

A: Correct.

Q: Did you look into whether his grandparents were caught up in the Holocaust and whether his mother died from an illness she suffered while in the North Tower on nine-eleven?

A: Why would we look into that? Who would make that stuff up?

Q: So, was it a surprise to you when Newsday broke the story that his entire background and career were bogus? That there was no truth to any of it?

A: Yes, it was a complete surprise.

Q: Had you known at the time you decided to back Mr. Sandoza what you know now – that everything about Mr. Sandoza had been made up, in fact made up by an artificial intelligence program – would Take America Back have spent $2 million on his campaign?

A: I don't see why not. He was still a great candidate. We're really pleased he got elected.

Q: Even though everything he claimed about himself is false?

A: Sure. He was the right candidate. And the 2022 midterm election was our moment. Just like all those beautiful posters on your wall say, he was the right candidate for the right's moment.

Mr. Peters: I've no further questions.

Mr. Waters: I've no questions.

(Deposition adjourns at 11:35 a.m.)

* * * *

At two o'clock, the lawyers returned to the conference room for the deposition of Leo Givenchy, an executive with the Super PAC Democracy Now.

All of the Sandoza campaign materials remained in place. But a different commercial was playing on the television. It was a thirty-second commercial that had appeared frequently on CNN and MSNBC. The Commercial carried the headline:

"A New Republican for a New Congress"

It went on to say "The Third District needs Gregory Sandoza." After a shot of Sandoza and his family, the announcer states:

"Join the thousands of Queens and Nassau County voters who have discovered the inspiring story of Gregory Sandoza. Husband, father, businessman and not-for-profit leader."

The commercial ends with the command "Vote for Gregory Sandoza." The following statement then appeared on screen:

"Paid for by Democracy Now, a Political Action Committee not associated with the Sandoza campaign."

"This is all highly improper" complained Barry Badd. "We're doing this deposition under protest."

"Under protest? What does that mean?" asked Pup.

"It means that we object to your attempt to intimidate the witness with this display. And we will move to preclude your use of the deposition at trial."

173

"We're merely displaying materials that were used in Mr. Sandoza's campaign" said Pup. "Including a commercial that your client paid for. So I don't see any intimidation here. Now, I think we're ready to begin. Ms. Redd, will you swear in Mr. Givenchy."

(Transcript of Deposition of Leo Givenchy)

Questions by Mr. Prescott Peters:

Q: Mr. Givenchy, you're an executive with the Super PAC Democracy Now?

A: Yes.

Q: What are your duties?

A: I'm Directer of Candidate Funding for the Tri-State Area, New York, New Jersey and Connecticut.

Q: And in that position you're responsible for deciding which campaigns in those states Democracy Now will support?

A: Yes.

Q: Democracy Now typically supports liberal candidates, does it not?

A: Yes. That's why Mr. Taurus set up the PAC. We support liberal candidates who will fight to preserve democracy.

Q: It's not just liberal candidates you support, but most often you support candidates you consider to be "woke"?

A: Yes.

Q: You even say on your website and in all your communications: "If it ain't woke, you gotta fix it."

A: That's correct.

Q: Now, in the 2022 election cycle, Democracy Now spent over $125 million to support various progressive candidates?

A: Yes, I believe that is correct.

Q: And you spent a little over $3 million to support the Sandoza campaign?

A: Yes.

Q: Were you the one who made the decision to spend $3 million to support Mr. Sandoza?

A: I made the recommendation. All spending has to be approved by Democracy Now's president, Alex Taurus.

Q: He's the son of your founder, George Taurus?

A: Yes.

Q: You were aware Mr. Sandoza is a Republican?

A: Yes.

Q: And that he was running as a conservative Republican?

A: Yes.

Q: So why did you recommend that Democracy Now spend over $3 million on the campaign of a conservative Republican?

A: I thought – and Alex agreed – that the Republicans could benefit from having a Hispanic in Congress. The diversity would be good for them and, ultimately, for the country as well.

Q: And you didn't mind that this Hispanic Republican was also a conservative Republican?

A: We thought he was a responsible conservative. Believe it or not, there are a few of them. One or two at least.

Q: Any other reason why you supported the Sandoza campaign?

A: Yes, the backstory about his family. Grandparents wiped out in the Holocaust. Mother fatally ill as a result of being in the World Trade Center on nine-eleven. We thought that would give him considerable empathy for less fortunate members of the community.

Q: During the time Democracy Now was spending money on the Sandoza campaign, did you become aware that some or all of his claimed background, education and professional career were not true?

A: No, we had no idea any of it was untrue.

Q: Mr. Givenchy, I remind you that you're under oath. I ask you again: At any time during the 2022 campaign did you become aware that some or all of Mr. Sandoza's claimed background, education and professional career were untrue?

Mr. Badd: Asked and answered. He just answered that.

Mr. Peters: Yes, and I just reminded him that he's under oath and might want to reconsider his answer.

Mr. Badd: Of course he's under oath, every deposition's under oath.

Mr. Peters: I frequently find it useful to remind witnesses of that.

Q: Now, Mr. Givenchy, please answer my question: At any time during the 2022 election campaign did you become aware that some or all of Mr. Sandoza's claimed background, education and professional career were untrue?

A: As I said before, no.

Q: If you had become aware that some or all of his background, education and professional career were not as he claimed, would you have continued your financial support of him?

A: Of course not. Democracy Now is not in the habit of supporting candidates with phony backgrounds and records.

Q: But you now know that the entirety of Mr. Sandoza's background, education and professional career were totally fabricated?

A: Yes, we know that now.

Q: But you didn't know it at the time you spent $3 million to support his candidacy?

A: That's correct.

Q: And had you known it, you would not have spent $3 million on his campaign?

A: That's correct.

Q: Mr. Givenchy, I remind you that you are under oath. I ask you . . . .

Mr. Badd: You keep saying that. Mr. Givenchy knows he's under oath, so you can stop reminding him.

Mr. Peters: I won't stop reminding him until he admits he's lying.

Mr. Badd: You've no right to say that. You have absolutely no basis to say that Mr. Givenchy is lying.

Mr. Peters: I believe I do.

Mr. Badd: Then you'd better prove that right now. Otherwise I'm going to terminate the deposition.

Mr. Peters: I'm glad you suggested I prove that your client is lying. I ask the court reporter to mark this document as Plaintiffs' Exhibit A.

(Document marked as Plaintiffs' Exhibit A)

Q: Mr. Givenchy, I show you Plaintiffs' Exhibit A. It's a memorandum labeled "Personal and Confidential" from you to Alex Taurus. It's dated January 18, 2022.

Mr. Badd: Where did you get this document? It's not part of Democracy Now's document production.

Mr. Peters: That's the interesting part. Perhaps you can explain why it was not part of Democracy Now's document production.

Mr. Badd: There's no proof this is an authentic document.

Mr. Peters: Why don't we ask the witness.

Q: Mr. Givenchy, reminding you that you are under oath, and that lying under oath constitutes perjury, a federal crime punishable by several years in prison, do you recognize this document?

A: Yes.

Q: And is it a copy of a memorandum you sent to Mr. Alex Taurus on January 18, 2022?

A: Yes.

Mr. Badd: Whether or not this document is authentic, I object to its use at this deposition unless you tell us how you obtained it.

Mr. Peters: Perhaps we should start with your telling us why it was deliberately withheld from your document production.

Mr. Badd: We'll take this up with Judge Spade. I'm sure he'll want to know how you managed to obtain it.

Mr. Peters: I'm sure he'll be even more interested in why you deliberately withheld it. Now, let's get back to the witness.

Q: Mr. Givenchy, you were the author of this document?

A: Yes.

Q: And you sent it to Mr. Taurus on January 18, 2022?

A: Yes.

Q: And you sent it in the normal course of business, in your capacity as Director of Candidate Funding for the Tri-State Area?

A: Yes.

Q: Would you please read the memorandum into the record.

Mr. Badd: He doesn't have to do that. The document says whatever it says.

Mr. Peters: Okay, if Mr. Givenchy won't read it, I'll have Mr. Pierpont do so. Chip, would you read this memorandum into the record.

(Mr. Pierpont reads Plaintiffs' Exhibit A into the Record)

January 18, 2022
Personal and Confidential
From: Leo Givenchy
To: Alex Taurus

We have an incredible opportunity to play a unique role in the 2022 midterms. The candidate for New York's Third Congressional District – which covers Nassau County and part of Queens - is Gregory Sandoza. He's a Hispanic running as a conservative Republican. He is likely to be a very appealing candidate to voters in that district.

He's a graduate of Baruch College and has an MBA from NYU's Stern School of Business. He worked on Wall Street with Citibank and Golden Slacks. He also founded a not-for-profit that rescues dogs and cats. His grandparents were killed during the Holocaust and his mother died from an illness she suffered when she was in the North Tower of the World Trade Center on nine-eleven. He has an attractive wife and two young children.

But here's the rub. We have it from a reliable source that much, if not most of this, may not be true. Our source believes it will eventually be discovered that most of Sandoza's story has been fabricated. But he doesn't believe this will be uncovered until after the election when there will be an extensive focus on the winner.

If it comes out after the election that Sandoza's story has been fabricated, it would be a big black eye, not just for him but for all Republicans. And not just in Nassau County but across the country, as the story would likely receive national coverage. Once it's known that this Republican was elected on the basis of a phony bio, people will begin having doubts about all Republican candidates. And in New York's Third District, it could result in Democrats holding onto this seat indefinitely.

I therefore recommend that we begin supporting this campaign. We can start slowly, so that if the truth starts coming out, we can pull back our support and say we were duped like everyone else. But if nothing comes out during the campaign, we can step up our support in the last few weeks prior to the election, such as by saturating CNN and MSNBC with commercials.

If we spend our usual amount - $2 to $3 million – on this campaign, we will have an impact not only on the immediate race but on future Congressional races across the country. Please let me know if you concur.

(Questioning Resumes)

Q: Those were your words, Mr. Givenchy?

A: Yes.

Q: And Mr. Alex Taurus sent you a "Personal and Confidential" response a few days later, did he not?

A: Yes.

Mr. Peters: I ask the court reporter to mark this document as Plaintiffs' Exhibit B.

(Plaintiffs' Exhibit B is marked)

Q: Mr. Givenchy, did you receive Plaintiffs' Exhibit B on or about January 25th?

A: Yes.

Mr. Peters: I won't ask the witness to read it into the record, I'll do so myself. It's quite short.

(Mr. Peters reads Plaintiffs' Exhibit B into the Record)

Personal and Confidential
January 25, 2022
From: Alex Taurus
To: Leo Givenchy

Regarding your memorandum of January 18th, please proceed as you suggest.

P.S. I cleared it with the big guy.

Q: The "big guy" Alex Taurus was referring to was his father, George Taurus?

A: Yes.

Q: And did you proceed as you had proposed in your memorandum of January 18th?

A: Yes.

Q: And all the money you spent on the Sandoza campaign was spent after January 25th?

A: Yes.

Q: And much of the money you spent on Sandoza's campaign was spent on producing and then running the commercial that was playing on the television when we entered the room?

A: Yes.

Q: That's the commercial that begins "Join the thousands of Queens and Long Island voters who have discovered the inspiring story of Gregory Sandoza"?

A: Yes.

Q: That commercial was run extensively on CNN and MSNBC in the run-up to the 2022 election?

A: Yes.

Mr. Peters: Thank you, Mr. Givenchy. I have no further questions.

Mr. Badd: I have no questions at this time. But we'll be moving to exclude this deposition and your exhibits from trial. And we'll also be asking Judge Spade to impose sanctions on you and your firm.

Mr. Peters: We look forward to your motion.

Mr. Pierpont: When everyone leaves, don't forget to take the notepads, buttons and jar openers in front of you. Mr. Badd, you may take them too. We have enough for everyone.

Chapter 21

EX PARTE

It was four-thirty on Thursday afternoon in late September. Pap had arranged for an ex parte meeting with their old friend Justice Louis Leghetti who, because there was no adverse party present, was meeting with them in his chambers.

Justice Leghetti had presided over the firm's first case for Lydia, a class action on behalf of lap dancers in three gentlemen's clubs in New York. The clubs had been cheating the girls by characterizing them as independent contractors rather than employees, thereby allowing them to evade New York's minimum wage laws. They were also stealing the girls' tips.

As the class representative, Lydia had been required to testify in support of the settlement agreement. Justice Leghetti and his bailiff, Tony Romo, had been smitten with her. They admired not only her beauty but also her practice of making a hash of the English language.

And so, whenever Lydia was involved in another case, even if it was in the federal courthouse next door, they always managed to show up to watch her testify. She always waved to them when she took the witness stand.

"We were hoping we'd get to see Lydia today" said Justice Leghetti amiably. "Whenever you two show up in court she always seems to be with you."

"Well, Lydia sends you and Mister Romo her greetings" said Pap. "You'll be glad to know we're working on another case on her behalf. Some AI company has taken the voices of models and actresses and used them as chatbots who talk dirty to lonely guys. They never bothered to get the consent of the ladies whose voices they use. It's an amusing case. We'll be sure to let Tony know when Lydia testifies."

"Great" said Leghetti. "Now, I understand you want me to sign an order for a deposition in a case that hasn't been filed yet."

"That's correct. CPLR Section 3102(c) permits a plaintiff, upon court order, to take a deposition before the complaint is filed in order to – and I quote: 'To locate the whereabouts of chattels sought to be replevined.' And that's the purpose of the two depositions we seek.

"Let me add a little more detail. I'm sure you're aware of District Attorney Braggert's press conference on Monday. He announced the indictment of two grifters for stealing extremely valuable jewelry from a string of high society victims."

"Yes, I read the account of his press conference. What an incredible story."

"It certainly is" said Pap. "The two of them hung out in Manhattan, the Hamptons, and Georgetown. Even Newport. And every time they attended some high society event – wedding, dinner or cocktail party – they walked away with one or more pieces of expensive jewelry. If someone made up a story like that, nobody would believe it."

"Unfortunately" said Leghetti, "I doubt those two will ever see the inside of a jail. Braggert doesn't like putting people in jail.

"But look, what's your firm's involvement in this matter?"

"We've been retained by several of the victims to see if we can get their jewelry back. Or, if we can't, to get compensation from whoever profited from buying and then reselling it.

"Now, the only way we can do that is to find out what happened to the jewelry after it was stolen. And we can only find that out by talking directly to the culprits, Gray and Borokin."

"They won't tell you anything" said Leghetti. "They'll take the Fifth."

"Actually" said Pap, "I think they won't. You see, we spoke with Braggert long before his press conference. We offered to provide him with the information we had collected about the thefts. We told him he could take credit for the investigation. All we wanted was for him to enter into a plea deal that required Gray and Borokin to cooperate with us in our civil case.

"We were pretty sure that, even with the information we gave him, Braggert wouldn't want to waste his office's time on a trial. He'd just want to do some sort of plea deal. And there was no reason a deal couldn't include a requirement that they cooperate with us - by giving a full account of the thefts and what they did with the stolen goods. So, if you authorize the depositions, I'm sure Gray and Borokin will be quite willing to cooperate."

"Hot damn" said Justice Leghetti. "That's a clever scheme you've concocted. What do you say, Tony?"

"It's brilliant, Judge. These two are always coming up with creative ideas. Like the settlement they arranged in the case for Lydia and the other strippers . . . . "

"They weren't strippers" said Pap, "they were lap dancers. Our firm doesn't represent strippers."

"Right, the lap dancers case" said Tony. "But remember, judge, how instead of getting money for the ladies, they arranged for all those really weird benefits? Like subscriptions to The New York Review of Books. Can you imagine, a bunch of strippers reading The New York Review of Books? I don't even read it myself." After a pause, he added "nor does my wife."

"The one I remember" said Leghetti "is the gift pack of Godiva chocolates. Your client said they were quite valuable because the girls could stuff them in their panties for the customers – Joes, I think she called them – to find."

"Those weren't wealthy defendants we were suing" Pap explained. "There was a limit to how much money the clubs could pay in a settlement, so we had to come up with some creative class benefits."

"Right" Leghetti agreed. "I approved the settlement so I guess you could say it passed muster. Now, let's get back to the case at hand."

"Okay. Here's a copy of the complaint we plan to eventually file" said Pap as he handed it to Leghetti. "Right now the plaintiffs are John Doe, John Doe number 2 and John Doe number three."

"Shouldn't the first John Doe be referred to as John Doe number one?" asked Romo.

"No, its John Doe. That's his name. His wife is Jane Doe. They live in Manhattan. Gray stole a Van Cleef and Arpels ring worth about thirty-five-hundred dollars from them. The police were able to trace the ring to Boyle Auctioneers, the big auction house up on eighty-seventh street. That leads us to believe that many of the other stolen items may have been sold to auction houses as well.

"Now, at this point, the defendants are just Gray, the professor, and Gladys Delray, the real name of the fake heiress who called herself Ava Borokin."

"How did someone from New Jersey named Gladys manage to con all those high society people in Manhattan, Georgetown and Newport?" asked Romo.

"Beats me" said Pap.

"I think it was her alleged Swiss ancestry" said Pup. "Trust fund set up by her wealthy father, money in secret Swiss bank accounts, it all sounds kind of exotic. Delray knew what would resonate with the high society types she was exploiting."

"Okay" said Leghetti, "let's get back to your application. I assume that once you take the depositions and find out where all the jewelry wound up, you'll sue them? And you believe most of them will be auction houses like Doyle?"

"Exactly. If they still have the jewelry, we'll recover it by replevin. If they've sold it to a third party, we'll seek for damages for conversion."

"You plan to make this a class action?"

"Sure. We've identified twelve victims so far. And I'm sure we'll find others as the case proceeds."

"But your real objective is to find out if other major auction houses were involved?"

"Right."

"And then you'll sue them for big bucks?"

"Exactly" said Pap. "If auction houses bought all this stuff from Gray and Borokin without conducting proper due diligence, they deserve to pay up big time."

"What do you plan to do with Gray and Borokin after you take their depositions?"

"If they're totally forthcoming, we'll leave them in the case as nominal defendants. But they will have fulfilled their principal purpose. What happens to them next is up to Braggert."

"All right" said Leghetti, "I'll sign your order for a deposition. But look, when you file the real complaint, with the auction houses added as defendants, I'm not sure the case would be assigned to me. I think it would go into the wheel for random assignment."

"We'll speak with Sal Marino" said Pap, "the clerk for the Commercial Part. We might be able to convince him that, since you've already taken action in the case, it should stay with you."

Pap paused and then continued. "Tony, I'll let you know when we file the complaint. Maybe you could also have a chat with Marino, tell him Justice Leghetti believes the case should stay with him."

"Sure" said Romo. "I'll be happy to do that. Just don't forget to let us know when Lydia will be testifying."

Chapter 22

BADD LUCK

Two weeks later the lawyers in the Sandoza case filed into the courtroom of Judge Samuel Spade in Central Islip. It quickly became apparent that Judge Spade was not in a good mood.

Transcript of Proceedings:

The Court: I'm very distressed at having to interrupt my busy docket to hold a hearing regarding disputes arising at a deposition. I generally refer discovery disputes to a magistrate. But the issues you've raised warrant my personal attention. I hope this will be the last time I have to deal with such disputes.

We'll start with the motion filed by Democracy Now. Who's here on behalf of Democracy Now?

Mr. Goode: I am, Your Honor. Gordon Goode of Goode and Badd in New York City.

The Court: You may proceed, Mr. Goode.

Mr. Goode: Your Honor, our motion seeks to preclude plaintiffs' use at trial of the deposition of Mr. Givenchy as well as Exhibits A and B from his deposition. I'll start with the reason to exclude the deposition. As we explained in our brief . . . .

The Court: Your brief has been stricken.

Mr. Goode: Stricken?

The Court: That's right, it's been stricken from the record. I'll be sanctioning your firm for filing a frivolous brief that cites cases having nothing to do with the issues raised by your motion.

Mr. Goode: What do you mean? We cited cases that show Mr. Givenchy's deposition cannot be used at trial because . . . .

The Court: Well, let's see about that. On page six of your brief, you cite the case of Burns v. Allen, allegedly decided by Judge John E. Carson of the Central District of California.

On that same page you cite the case of Nick v. Nora, allegedly decided by Judge Felix Frank Ferter – that's middle name Frank, last name Ferter, F-E-R-T-E-R – of the District of Massachusetts.

And on page seven, you cite the case of Ruth v. Gehrig decided by Judge Kenesaw Mountain Landis of the Southern District of New York.

Mr. Goode: You don't think those cases support our position?

The Court: Mr. Goode, those cases don't exist. And aside from the late Judge Landis, none of those judges ever existed. Where did you get the material you used in your brief?

Mr. Goode: Mr. Badd was in charge of the brief, he's the one who represented Mr. Givenchy at the deposition.

The Court: Where's Mr. Badd, we need to hear from him.

Mr. Goode: He couldn't be here today, Your Honor.

The Court: Why not?

Mr. Goode: He has a cold.

The Court: Maybe I should send him a get well card.

Mr. Goode: I'm sure he'd appreciate that, Your Honor.

The Court: Well then, Mr. Goode, since Mr. Badd isn't here, I'm afraid it's your bad luck to have to explain how your firm could submit a brief that contains citations to cases that do not exist and allegedly decided by judges, two of whom never existed and one of whom has been dead for over 50 years.

Mr. Goode: Well, Mr. Badd told me he had spoken with Rosemary after the deposition. And she suggested that, in preparing the brief, he check out an AI program put out by Boogle. As I understand it, the program uses AI to assist lawyers with the preparation of briefs and legal memos.

The Court: Ms. Rosemary, is what Mr. Goode just said true?

Rosemary: Your Honor, it's not Ms. Rosemary. It's just plain Rosemary.

The Court: Okay, just plain Rosemary. Is what Mr. Goode just said true?

Rosemary: Well, it's not bad. In fact I'd say it's good.

The Court: I don't care if it's good or bad, I just want to know if it's true.

Rosemary: Yes, what Mr. Goode said Mr. Badd said I told him is true. Boogle is developing several new AI programs and one is a program to assist busy lawyers. It's called "Briefly Speaking." I don't believe Boogle's had any problems with it so far.

The Court: If it spits out cases that don't exist, decided by judges that don't exist, I would say there's a problem.

Rosemary: Your Honor, it's not Boogle's fault that Mr. Badd, or someone in his firm, didn't check to see if the case citations were appropriate. We would expect the attorneys who . . . .

The Court: It seems that nothing is ever Boogle's fault. Well, it is. Boogle has no business offering an AI program that provides fictional legal cases to its users. What if one of my law clerks hadn't spotted the problem when she read that brief? Or what if the brief had been submitted to a busy state court judge in Brooklyn who doesn't have a law clerk to help him check out all the cited cases?

Rosemary: It's not Boogle's fault if New York doesn't adequately fund its court system.

The Court: Right, nothing is ever Boogle's fault. Well, your client has no business offering an AI program that provides fictional cases to its users. Frankly, I don't think Boogle or anyone else has any business peddling legal briefs generated by AI, but that's beyond my jurisdiction.

What is within my jurisdiction is any such brief submitted to this Court. I find the brief generated by your client, and submitted by Mr. Goode on behalf of his client, irrelevant and offensive. That's why I've stricken it. And that's why I will be imposing sanctions on both of your firms. I'll issue an order after today's hearing setting the amount of the sanction.

Now, Mr. Goode, if you have anything to say in support of your motion, you may do so now.

Mr. Goode: Your Honor, plaintiffs should not be permitted to use Mr. Givenchy's deposition at trial. It was taken in an atmosphere of coercion and intimidation.

The Court: You mean the Gregory Sandoza campaign posters that were mounted on the walls? And the Sandoza campaign commercial that was playing on the television?

Mr. Goode: Yes, Your Honor, that was a blatant attempt to distract and intimidate Mr. Givenchy. It . . . .

The Court: The posters and TV commercial didn't seem to bother the other witness, the one from Take America Back.

Mr. Goode: Well, it certainly intimidated Mr. Givenchy . . . .

The Court: That's ridiculous. How could Mr. Givenchy – who seems to have made the recommendation that Democracy Now spend $3 million on the Sandoza campaign – be intimidated by the display of materials used in his campaign?

Mr. Goode: Because . . . .

The Court: I've heard enough. Your motion regarding the use of Mr. Givenchy's deposition is denied. Now, do you want to say anything regarding your motion to exclude the two exhibits?

Mr. Goode: Yes. Those exhibits were not part of the record in the case. Mr. Peters – that's the other Mr. Peters (pointing), he's the one who took the deposition – sprung them on the witness.

The Court: I don't believe there's any law against springing documents on witnesses.

Mr. Goode: But we're entitled to know where the exhibits came from. When we asked Mr. Peters where they came from, he refused to answer. So . . . .

The Court: The documents clearly came from your client's files. How Mr. Peters got them is neither here nor there. The question here is why your client failed to produce them in discovery.

Mr. Goode: But Mr. Peters must have used some nefarious method to obtain them. If he obtained them unlawfully, we need to know that.

The Court: If Mr. Peters did use some nefarious method to obtain them, he only did so because your client failed to produce them. It's good that Mr. Peters was successful in obtaining them, they will help me and the jury get to the bottom of things.

Now, Mr. Goode, please tell me why these documents were not produced by your client.

Mr. Goode: Well, Mr, Badd was in charge of our document production. He must have overlooked them.

The Court: Perhaps we should ask Mr. Badd why they weren't produced.

Mr. Goode: He's not here. As I said earlier, he has a cold.

The Court: I can see why he didn't want to be here. In any event, the exhibits were authenticated by Mr. Givenchy so there is no basis to preclude their use at trial.

Mr. Goode, I'm appalled that your firm withheld important – maybe even crucial – documents from your document production. I will be sanctioning your firm, and perhaps your client as well. I'll include the sanctions in the order I plan to issue after the hearing.

Furthermore, if in the future I find myself required to issue another sanction against your firm, you will be disqualified from continuing in the case.

Mr. Goode: Disqualified?

The Court: That's right. Three strikes and you're out. And please tell Mr. Badd I hope he's feeling better.

We'll take a short recess, I have to deal with anther matter.

* * * *

(Hearing Resumes at 11:20 a.m.)

The Court: Okay, now we'll take up plaintiffs' motion regarding the Aaron Durr deposition. Mr. Peters, please proceed.

Mr. Peters: Thank you, Your Honor. Two weeks ago, we commenced the deposition of Aaron Durr, Boogle's vice-president in charge of its BotsUp? division. We succeeded in obtaining his name, educational background and his position and duties.

But when we got into the heart of the deposition, we were only successful in obtaining a general description of BotsUp? – nothing we couldn't have learned from Boogle's marketing materials. When we tried to go beyond that, we got nothing. With your permission, I'd like to read the final two minutes of the deposition.

The Court: Yes, you may do so.

Rosemary: I object, Your Honor. Those pages are attached to Mr. Peters' motion. I don't see why they have to be read out loud now. He only wants to embarrass me.

The Court: If your conduct at the deposition was proper, I don't see why you would be embarrassed. You may proceed Mr. Peters.

(Mr. Patrick Peters reads from the deposition of Aaron Durr, taken by Mr. Prescott Peters)

Q: Did Boogle, through its BotsUp? app, provide biographical materials to Mr. Sandoza or someone acting on his behalf?

A: Boogle provided biographical materials to a customer.

Q: To whom did Boogle provide those materials?

Rosemary: Objection, confidential. The names of Boogle's BotsUp? users are confidential.

Mr. Peters: It's fine with me if you want to designate this portion of the deposition as Confidential.

Rosemary: That doesn't solve the problem. The problem is that Boogle promises the customers who use BotsUp? that it won't disclose their identity.

Mr. Peters: Are you directing Mr. Durr not to answer the question?

Rosemary: Yes, I direct him not to answer.

Q: Mr. Durr, this person you will not identify, what did he or she ask the BotsUp? app to provide?

Rosemary: Objection, that's confidential. The interaction between the BotsUp? App and Boogle's customer is confidential.

Mr. Peters: Are you directing him not to answer?

Rosemary: That's correct.

Q: Mr. Durr, did anyone at Boogle know that Mr. Sandoza was using information obtained from BotsUp? for purposes of his Congressional campaign?

Rosemary: Same objection. I direct the witness not to answer.

Mr. Peters: Rosemary, perhaps you misunderstood my question. I wasn't asking about an interaction between BotsUp? and Boogle's customer. I was asking whether anyone at Boogle knew that the information it supplied to this unnamed customer was being used in the Sandoza campaign.

Rosemary: That's irrelevant. Boogle has no duty to ascertain how its customers use information and data supplied by BotsUp? Since Boogle has no such duty, then what it knew or didn't know is irrelevant.

Mr. Peters: You're directing him not to answer?

Rosemary: That's correct.

Q: Did anyone at Boogle know that everything Mr. Sandoza said during his campaign about his education and professional background had been generated by BotsUp?

Rosemary: Same objection and same instruction.

Q: Did anyone at Boogle know that the campaign speeches and other communications issued by Mr. Sandoza had been generated by BotsUp?

Rosemary: Same objection and instruction.

(End of Deposition Reading)

Mr. Peters: As you see, Your Honor, Rosemary prevented us from learning anything of substance from Mr. Durr. The questions she directed him not to answer go to the core issues in this case.

The Court: I agree. Counsel (addressing Rosemary), I don't see any basis on which you are entitled to block Mr. Durr's testimony on those questions.

Rosemary: Your Honor, confidentiality goes to the heart of the business model for BotsUp? Boogle promises its users that it will keep their identity confidential. Otherwise, why would anyone use information it generates?

For example, many BotsUp? users are college students. BotsUp? can supply them with information for use in term papers or essays. If Boogle was required to tell the college that the paper was generated by AI, the user could get in trouble.

Or what if a PhD candidate used material supplied by BotsUp? for their dissertation? And someone questioned the integrity of the candidate's research? Disclosure of Boogle's role could ruin their academic career.

The Court: Perhaps there's a public interest in many situations that supersedes the user's interest in confidentiality. Such as the public interest in this case - knowing that Congressman Sandoza's entire persona was fabricated by artificial intelligence.

Rosemary: You seem to be prejudging the case. I think . . . .

The Court: I'm not prejudging the case but I am ruling on what is before me at the moment. And I find that the questions you blocked at

Mr. Durr's deposition were material and relevant. And that your objections to them were without merit.

Accordingly, when I issue my order on sanctions against Goode and Badd, I'll include sanctions against you and your firm as well.

Finally, I'm directing you to bring back Mr. Durr for the completion of his deposition. We'll do it here in the courtroom where I'll be able to rule immediately on any objections that arise.

Mr. Peters, my calendar is open next Tuesday morning. Would that be a convenient time to resume the deposition?

Mr. Peters: Certainly, Your Honor. Should we bring our court reporter to transcribe the deposition?

The Court: That's a good idea.

Rosemary: I'll contact Mr. Durr to see if he's free then.

The Court: I don't care if he's free or not, just make sure he's in this court next Tuesday at 10:00 a.m. We're adjourned.

Chapter 23

BAD BOOGLE

On the following Tuesday, the lawyers trudged back into the courtroom of the Honorable Sam Spade. Defendants' attorneys were depressed, things were not going well. And they feared things were about to get worse.

Transcript of Proceedings:

The Court: Okay, we're here today for the continuation of the deposition of Aaron Durr, an executive of defendant Boogle. Mr. Peters, I see that you've brought your own reporter.

Mr. Peters: Yes, Your Honor, this is Ms. Redd. Ruby Redd. She's an excellent reporter, fast and accurate.

The Court: Some of the ones who work for the Government are neither fast nor accurate.

Mr. Durr, please take the witness stand. I know you were sworn in prior to the earlier part of your deposition, but we'll ask Ms. Redd to swear you in again. That way, your counsel can't argue that you weren't under oath when you said whatever you're going to say today.

(Witness is sworn in)

Mr. Prescott Peters: Mr. Durr, I'll resume where we left off last time. Before your attorney began blocking your testimony.

Rosemary: I object, Your Honor, he's . . . .

The Court: Just sit down, Rosemary.

Q: Now, you previously confirmed that Boogle's BotsUp? app provided biographical materials to someone?

A: That's correct.

Q: To whom were those materials provided?

A: I wouldn't have been involved. I'm vice-president for the BotsUp? Division, I don't interact with customers.

Q: But Boogle has records showing who those materials were provided to?

A: Yes.

Q: And you have access to those records?

A: Yes.

Q: And you've reviewed those records as part of your preparation for this deposition?

A: Yes.

Q: Now please tell us who those records show was the recipient of these biographical materials?

A: Do I have to answer that?

The Court: Yes, that's why we're here today.

A: His name is Magic Thomson.

Q: Do your records show his address?

A: Only his email address.

Q: Okay, what is that address?

A: Magic at Gregory Sandoza for Congress dot com.

Q: So Magic Thomson worked for the Sandoza campaign?

A: It appears so.

Q: Did someone at Boogle ascertain what his position in the campaign was?

A: How would we do that?

Q: By going to the website shown by his email address: Gregory Sandoza for Congress dot com.

A: I believe someone did look at that.

Q: And what did that someone find?

A: He was listed as Campaign Manager.

Q: Were these biographical materials sent to anyone else besides Magic Thomson?

A: We have no record of sending them to anyone else.

Q: So Magic Thomson was the only one who received the biographical materials used in Mr. Sandoza's campaign?

A: He's the only one who received the materials. We wouldn't have known that he used them in the Sandoza campaign.

Q: Well, let's look at Mr. Thomson's initial interaction with your company. Showing you Plaintiffs' Exhibit C, isn't it true that, in this communication, Mr. Thomson asked BotsUp? to generate biographical materials for a hypothetical Congressman from Nassau County in New York?

A: Yes.

Q: Specifically, it asked for a biography reflecting a first-rate education in New York and professional experience on Wall Street?

A: Yes.

Q: So, the information regarding his graduation from Baruch College and an MBA from the Stern School of Business was generated by BotsUp?

A: Yes.

Q: And the information regarding his Wall Street career with Citibank and Golden Slacks was also generated by BotsUp?

A: Yes.

Q: And the information regarding his grandparents' death in the Holocaust and his mother's fatal illness as a result of being in the World Trade Center on nine-eleven was also generated by BotsUp?

A: Yes.

Q: It sounds like a very compelling biography for a politician. Was Mr. Thomson happy with it?

A: I have no way of knowing.

Q: Were you happy with it?

A: Yes, we were certainly happy with it. BotsUp? had created a perfect political biography for a candidate in the New York Metropolitan area. It showed the world what BotsUp? could do.

Q: Now Mr. Durr, these materials that BotsUp? generated and passed on to Magic Thomson, they were all used by Mr. Sandoza in his Congressional campaign, were they not?

A: You'd have to ask Mr. Thomson.

Q: Mr. Thomson isn't here today so I'm asking you. You knew that all of these materials had been supplied to Magic Thomson and that Magic was Mr. Sandoza's Campaign Manager. So you obviously knew the materials would be used in Mr. Sandoza's campaign?

A: We never ask our customers what they do with the materials we provide to them.

Q: I'm not asking whether Boogle asked Magic Thomson if the materials were being used in the Sandoza campaign. I'm asking whether Boogle in fact knew that the materials were being used in the campaign?

A: How would we know that?

Q: Someone at Boogle might have read about Sandoza's campaign in the newspaper or on TV or on social media. It was covered extensively in the media.

A: I told you we never track what our customers do with the material we provide them. We feel that's none of our business.

Q: So you deny that Boogle knew that Sandoza's campaign was using all the materials you had provided to Mr. Thomson?

A: Yes, I deny that.

Q: I remind you, you're under oath.

Rosemary: I think the witness knows that. He . . . .

The Court: He should, he's twice taken an oath to tell the truth. But he seems to have difficulty adhering to that oath.

Mr. Peters: I'll come back to this point in a few minutes. I want to first ask the witness about Mr. Sandoza's speeches.

Q: Mr. Durr, Mr. Sandoza gave over 300 speeches during the course of his campaign, did he not?

A: How would I know how many speeches he gave?

Q: Let me clarify my question. Mr. Sandoza gave one speech but he gave it over 300 times.

A: That could be the case.

Q: Now, did BotsUp? provide speech material to Magic Thomson?

A: Yes.

Q: Did it provide more than one set of speeches to Magic Thomson?

A: I believe we provided two or three proposed speeches. We would let his campaign use the speech they liked best.

Q: And so Boogle knew that Mr. Sandoza used one of the speeches you provided as the basis for his 300-plus speeches?

A: I have no idea.

Q: And what about his speech about China that he gave on the floor of the House after he was elected?

A: I have no idea whether Mr. Sandoza gave a speech about China on the floor of the House.

Q: Okay, but your BotsUp? app provided Magic Thomson with materials for a speech relating to the threat posed by China?

A: I believe so.

Q: But you continue to claim you have no idea whether Mr. Sandoza used that material when he gave his China speech?

A: Correct.

Q: So it's your testimony that you have no knowledge whether anything that the Sandoza campaign obtained from Boogle was used by Mr. Sandoza either in his campaign or in Congress?

A: That's correct.

Q: I remind you, Mr. Durr, you're under oath. Do you wish to change your answer?

Rosemary: Objection, that's repetitive and . . . .

The Court: The witness should answer. If I were him, I'd change my answer before it's too late.

A: I do not wish to change my answer. What I've told you is the truth.

Mr. Peters: I ask the reporter to mark this affidavit as Plaintiffs' Exhibit D.

Rosemary: Affidavit? I'm not aware of any affidavit in the record.

Mr. Peters: It's not in the record yet but it's about to be.

Q: Mr. Durr, I show you Plaintiffs' Exhibit D, an affidavit from Arnold Benedict dated August 22, 2023.

Rosemary: Objection. If Mr. Peters wants to use an affidavit that's not part of the record, he should have produced it earlier.

The Court: Why is that, Rosemary?

Rosemary: We should have had an opportunity to show it to the witness in advance so that we could help him figure out what's wrong with it.

The Court: Well, Mr. Durr has an opportunity to look at it now. If there's something wrong with it, he'll have to think of it without help from you.

Q: Mr. Durr, who is Arnold Benedict?

A: He's a dirty traitor.

Q: Why do you consider him a traitor?

A: He disclosed confidential company information to the press.

Q: By "the press" I assume you're referring to *Newsday*?

A: Yes.

Q: And the information he disclosed led to the series of stories they ran about Mr. Sandoza?

A: Yes.

Q: And those stories included the disclosure that everything about Mr. Sandoza had been generated by AI?

A: Yes.

Q: Specifically, AI generated by Boogle's BotsUp?

A: Yes.

Q: And because Arnold Benedict disclosed that to Newsday, Boogle fired him?

A: Yes.

Mr. Peters: Let's look at some of the things Mr. Benedict says in his affidavit. In paragraph three he says, and I quote:

"The company knew early on that Magic Thomson, the campaign manager for Gregory Sandoza, was using material generated by BotsUp? to provide Mr. Sandoza with an educational and professional background."

Q: That statement is true, is it not?

A: I believe so.

Mr. Peters: Now, in paragraph four, Mr. Benedict says this:

"At that point the company thought it would be interesting to see how Magic Thomson used this material to create a campaign biography for Mr. Sandoza, and then to see how voters reacted to it."

Q: That statement is true, is it not?

A: Yes.

Mr. Peters: Now, in paragraph five, Mr. Benedict states:

"As the Sandoza campaign moved along, and he began making speeches based on material furnished to him by BotsUp?, our internal discussions regarding this matter intensified. Some people, myself included, felt that things were going too far and we needed to pull the plug on the whole thing. Others, however, disagreed and wanted to see how everything turned out."

Q: That statement is true, is it not?

A: Yes.

Mr. Peters: Now I'll move to paragraph six, the next-to-last paragraph in the affidavit:

"In the month leading up to the election, it became more and more apparent that Mr. Sandoza was going to win. I and others argued that we needed to come clean then, before election day.

The matter went all the way up to the company's founder, Sergei Vain. Mr. Vain ultimately decided that going public then, right before the election, would do more harm than good. Not only would the company get a huge black eye, but it would   be unfair to Mr. Sandoza to disclose anything now. So Boogle   remained silent."

Q: Is that statement true?

A: Yes.

Mr. Peters: In the final paragraph of the affidavit, Mr. Benedict states that this silence is what caused him to leak the story to Newsday and that this in turn led to his being fired.

Q: So the leakage of the story to Newsday is what led the company to fire Mr. Benedict?

A: Yes.

Q: How did Boogle learn that Mr. Benedict had leaked the story to Newsday?.

A: We have programs that monitor everyone's email and phone calls. We have to be constantly on guard against our proprietary information getting leaked to our competitors.

Q: In other words, Boogle spies on its employees?

A: You could say that.

Q: So, Mr. Durr, we can agree that your previous answers to my questions about Boogle's knowledge of the BotsUp? materials being used by Mr. Sandoza and his campaign were not truthful?

A: They were truthful, but now Mr. Benedict's affidavit has reminded me of things I had forgotten.

Mr. Peters: We'll let the jury decide whether you had merely forgotten what happened or whether you lied about what happened.

Mr. Peters: I have no further questions.

The Court: Rosemary, do you have any questions for Mr. Durr?

Rosemary: No, Your Honor.

The Court: That's a good decision.

Now, if you will check with Mr. Garte tomorrow or Thursday, we'll have an order setting the amount of the sanctions I'm imposing on defendants' counsel for submitting a phony brief and obstructing Mr. Durr's deposition.

That's all, we're adjourned. Have a nice day.

Chapter 24

PIGCASSO

"We should start with a moment of silence for Pigcasso" said Melissa after everyone had sat down for their Monday morning meeting. "She died yesterday."

"Yesterday?" said Brandon. "Picasso died over fifty years ago. And everyone knows Picasso was a he, not a she."

"Maybe he transitioned late in life" suggested Chip.

"I think Melissa's talking about someone else" said Helen.

"That's right. I'm talking about Pig-casso, the pig who paints."

"Whoever heard of a pig that paints?" said Brandon.

"Brandon, you're just not au courant on the art world."

"What's au courant?"

"It's what you're not."

"Yes, but . . . ."

"Pigcasso" Melissa continued, "is the most successful non-human artist in the history of the world."

"You're kidding."

"I'm not kidding. Pigcasso lived in South Africa. She was rescued from the slaughterhouse by an animal rights activist when she was four weeks old. Four months later and she would have become bacon."

"I love bacon" said Chip. "I'm glad the pigs around here haven't all decided to become painters."

Ignoring Chip, Melissa continued. "The lady who rescued her is a South African named Lefson. Two years after the rescue, Lefson came up with the idea of attaching a paint brush to Pigcasso's mouth and standing her in front of a large blank canvas. The result was a series of random brush strokes on canvas, sort of like a Jackson Pollock painting."

"Sure" said Chip skeptically. "But Jackson Pollock's famous. And prolific."

"So's Pigcasso. She's the first animal to host a solo art exhibit. It was in Cape Town. Since then, she's had shows in the Netherlands, Germany and France.

"Her two most famous works are 'The Swine's View' and 'Wild and Free.' The latter sold for over twenty-five thousand dollars. That's the highest price ever paid for artwork created by an animal."

"But couldn't anyone take another animal, say a kangaroo, and have it splash paint on a canvas and say it's a Pigcasso?" asked Brandon.

"Maybe" said Melissa. "But that's why each painting is signed by Pigcasso with her trademark nose tip brush impression. And then the painting is countersigned by Lefson. Also, each painting comes with a certificate of authenticity guaranteeing that it was created by Pigcasso."

"How does this lady get Pigcasso to stand in front of a canvas and paint?" asked Chip.

"Apparently so long as Pigcasso is given plenty of food, she's willing to spend a few minutes splashing paint on the canvas. But she gets bored fairly quickly. So before they go off to paint, Lefson packs a large picnic basket with strawberries, guavas and caramel-coated popcorn. After Pigcasso pigs out on the food, she's willing to paint for a few minutes."

"And now she's gone?" said Chip.

"Yes. She's now in hog heaven."

* * * *

"Okay" said Pap. "Now that we know Pigcasso's no longer with us, would you mind if we talked about our cases?"

"Right" said Chip. "It's our cases that bring home the bacon."

Ignoring the laughter, Pap continued. "Given everything we've recently accomplished in the Sandoza case, I think it's time we moved to certify the class and for summary judgment as to liability. Obviously we can't seek summary judgment as to damages, that will be a matter for the jury.

"Chip, you and Pup defended the depositions of our two key witnesses – Holly and Ray Wray. You need to prepare a motion certifying the class and those two as the class representatives.

"As to summary judgment, Brandon and Melissa, you two need to pull together the documents and deposition testimony showing that all the essential facts as to liability have been conceded."

Melissa interrupted: "That evidence only shows what the defendants did and what they knew about the Sandoza campaign. But we also need to prove that members of the class relied on the materials generated by BotsUpn? when they voted."

"Sure" said Pap. "But look, the press always conducts exit polls on election day. Pull up the news reports from election night and the following day, I'm sure you'll find an exit poll. Any reason a voter gave for voting for Sandoza will likely be based on something generated by Boogle. That's our proof of voter reliance.

"Now Helen, you need to put all this into a brief. Make it clear that once the court grants our motion, the only thing left for trial will be damages. Judge Spade's a smart guy. He'll recognize that if defendants are facing a jury trial on damages, they'll be begging to settle."

"You think Judge Spade will award summary judgment?" asked Brandon.

"Of course" said Pup. "Just take a look at our recent sessions with him. He's really angry about their obstruction of the depositions.

"He's also furious that Democracy Now knew Sandoza's campaign bio was bogus and nevertheless supported him as a way to embarrass Republicans. And he's angry that Aaron Durr tried to deny that Boogle knew its BotsUp? material was the entire basis for Sandoza's campaign and did nothing to set the record straight.

"And he's not the least bit concerned that we had to use extra-judicial means to obtain those two key documents from Democracy

Now. He was only interested in why the documents hadn't been produced in discovery."

"So, how did we get those documents?" asked Brandon.

"We have our ways" said Pap.

"But what . . . ."

"Brandon, you're better off not knowing. If you don't know how we got them, nobody can ever criticize you for being involved."

* * * *

"Okay" said Pap. "Is there anything else we need to discuss?"

"The Prey and Borokin depositions" said Melissa. "They're coming up next week. Their counsel called and . . . ."

"Who's representing them?" asked Pap.

"Prey's represented by Frank Stein of Frank and Stein. They represented Madison Square Circle last year in the blacklist case. Borokin's represented by Gerry Mason of Mason and Dickson. He represented FiveStar Capital in the non-fungible tokens case."

"They're decent attorneys. But both of them will have a grudge against Pup and me from those cases – we forced both of their clients to settle on our terms. So it's good that you and Helen will be taking the depositions."

"You mean" said Helen, "you want no part of this and are hanging us out to dry."

"Would I do that?" said Pap.

"I wouldn't worry if I were you" said Pup. "Any lingering anger would be directed at Pap and me. I suspect they'll be on their best behavior, especially since their clients are required to cooperate with us."

"The immediate question" said Melissa "is where will the depositions take place. They want them to be taken at their offices."

"No way" said Pap. "We're doing them here. I want them to know that Pup or me will be available at a moment's notice if they give you a hard time.

"Tell them if they put up a fuss I'll contact Braggert and tell him their clients are not living up to the plea agreement. They know their clients got a sweetheart deal, they won't want to jeopardize it."

* * * *

Pap thought they were probably done. "Anything else?" he asked. "Yes, one more thing" said Pup.

"Miss Dropo came into my office this morning as soon as I arrived. Her brother Walter works for the VA in DC. Last Friday, a memorandum went out to all VA offices and hospitals directing them to take down the iconic photo of the V-J Day celebration in Times Square. Apparently it's on the walls of most VA offices and hospitals."

"What photo is that?" asked Brandon.

"Brandon, you must really live under a rock" said Chip. "It's a photo of a sailor in Times Square bending a nurse over and kissing her in celebration. It's called The Victory Kiss. It's famous. I use it as the background shot on my computer."

"Chip's right" said Melissa. "That photo's famous. But why is it being taken down?"

"According to Miss Dropo, who got the story from her brother, some woman undersecretary at VA headquarters said the photo no longer fit with the VA's values. Walter sent Eva a copy of the directive. I've got it right here.

"It says the sailor's kiss was, quote, 'inappropriate behavior' because it depicts a non-consensual act. It goes on to say that displaying the photo could be construed as a tacit endorsement of the inappropriate behavior it depicts.

"The directive concludes by stating that removal of the photo will, quote, 'foster a more trauma-informed environment' and that taking the photo down – now get this:

'Reflects our dedication to creating a respectful and safe workplace, and is in keeping with our broader efforts to promote a culture of inclusivity and awareness.'"

"Jesus Christ" said Pap. "Who the hell is the bureaucrat who wrote that?"

"According to Eva's brother, she's some fat lady who holds the title Fourth Assistant Undersecretary for Health and Wellness."

"She's probably angry she's never gotten a Victory Kiss from a sailor" said Chip.

"Either that or she's a lesbian" said Melissa.

"I've read about that picture" said Helen. "The sailor was there with his girl friend, who he eventually married. But they became separated in the huge crowd. All the sailors were excited, they were just kissing every woman they saw, particularly nurses. The nurses had recently helped rescue hundreds of sailors from the water when their ship was hit by kamikaze pilots. The sailor and the nurse in the photo actually became friends."

"Is Eva's brother a veteran?" asked Pap.

"I believe so" said Pup. "I think he was in the Marines in the nineteen nineties."

"Then tell Miss Dropo to call him and see if he'll agree to be a plaintiff in our case."

"What case is that?" asked Brandon.

"Our case against the VA and this idiot Fourth Assistant Undersecretary."

"We're suing the VA?" asked Melissa. "They would never agree to do more than simply rescind the directive. They certainly wouldn't agree to pay money to get rid of the case."

"Who said anything about money?" said Pap. "This will be the most high profile case we've ever brought. This will be in the news for weeks. I can see the headlines now: 'Peters and Peters gets iconic World War II photo reinstated.'

"But look. All those sleazy class action firms will be thinking the same thing. We've got to beat them to the punch. If Walter Dropo will agree to be the plaintiff, we could file suit in DC on Wednesday or Thursday. My old firm, Rogers and Autry, has an office there, I think I can get them to be local counsel."

"What's the legal claim?" asked Melissa.

"How would I know? I only just heard about this five minutes ago. All I know is we're going to sue and we're going to do it fast.

"Pup, you must have had something in mind when you brought this up?"

"I did. I don't think we can argue that the VA had no right to order the photos be taken down. They can put up whatever pictures they want in their offices and hospitals.

"But I think we can sue on the contents of the memorandum. It's defamatory of all veterans, especially all past and present sailors. Particularly World War Two sailors. So it would help if we could find a World War Two veteran, preferably one who was in the Navy."

"There's not many of them still alive" said Pap. "But look, Miss Dropo's brother works at VA headquarters. He should have access to their records. Tell Miss Dropo to have him go through the records and find a couple of World War Two Navy veterans who live in the DC area. One of us can go down and meet them, maybe even invite Walter to come with us."

"Miss Dropo's brother can't just rifle through VA files looking for potential plaintiffs" said Brandon.

"Why not?" said Pap.

"He probably doesn't have access to them as part of his job."

"So what? The records are there. Walter Dropo's there. I don't see the problem."

"What about all our other cases?" said Melissa. "You just told us to make a big push on summary judgment in the Sandoza case."

"For heaven's sake, all we need to do is get a complaint filed. Before someone else does. You guys ought to be able to write a Complaint in your sleep."

"Don't forget the press release for the press conference" said Chip. "Isn't that why we're filing the complaint anyway?"

"We'd never file a complaint just to get publicity."

"I can draft the complaint" said Pup. "It's not a big deal."

"And I'll do the press release" said Pap. "I've already got it composed in my head. It will be one of my best.

"But listen, this is the opportunity of a lifetime. This ridiculous directive from the VA will spark nationwide outrage. Everyone will want to know what's being done about it. And, of course, they'll want to know about the lawyers who stepped up to do something about it. We'll be doing our part to celebrate patriotism."

"And to celebrate the right of guys to kiss girls they've never met" said Chip. "That's what's really important here."

Chapter 25

PREY TELLS

On the last Wednesday in October, Frank Stein, of the New York City firm Frank and Stein, appeared at the offices of Peters and Peters with his client Barkley Prey. Melissa, who had participated in several of the firm's trials, was taking Prey's deposition. Ruby Redd swore in Prey and the deposition commenced.

Examination by Ms. Muffett:

Q: Mr. Prey, I understand you spent most of your career as a professor of political science at Georgetown University?

A: That's correct.

Q: When did you retire?

A: 2006. In the spring, at the end of the school year.

Q: Did you remain affiliated with the University as an adjunct or emeritus professor?

A: No.

Q: Do you have a pension from Georgetown?

A: Are you kidding? Professors don't get pensions when they retire. But we do get our names mentioned in an end-of-year message the president sends around to faculty and staff.

Q: So how did you support yourself when you retired?

A: By then I had met Jacqueline.

Q: Who's Jacqueline?

A: Jacqueline Quiller.

Q: Who's Jacqueline Quiller?

A: You've never heard of her? I thought everyone knew who Jacqueline Quiller was.

Q: I'm just a lawyer. You'll have to tell me who she was.

A: She was a wealthy socialite. Her grandfather was Alfred Lee Doomis, the legendary Wall Street tycoon.

Q: So she was wealthy?

A: Yes, extremely so.

Q: When did you meet her?

A: In early 2006, at an event at the University.

Q: Did you become friends?

A: We became more than friends.

Q: You had a romantic relationship with her?

A: Yes. It lasted for more than a decade.

Q: She didn't have a family of her own?

A: She was a divorcee. She had three grown sons.

Q: Did the two of you live together?

A: Yes. I moved in with her a month before my retirement.

Q: And you lived with her for over a decade?

A: Yes.

Q: Where?

A: In her townhouse in Washington DC. It was quite a step up from the apartment I had lived in during my teaching years.

Q: How did the two of you spend your time? I mean, aside from the romantic part, you don't have to tell me about that – unless, of course, you want to.

A: Jacqueline was a wealthy socialite. We spent our time doing what wealthy socialites do. We went to cocktail parties, dinner parties, art openings, classical music concerts, charity galas.

Q: So you had a taste of life in high society?

A: Yes.

Q: How did it compare to your life as a professor?

A: Ms. Muffett, it's obvious you've never set foot in high society circles. It's all quite pleasant. Especially if your significant other is paying for it.

Q: So this relationship lasted for a decade?

A: Yes.

Q: Did one of you end it?

A: Yes, she did.

Q: How did she end it?

A: She died.

Q: Please accept my condolences. Now, when did she die?

A: December of 2016. It was the saddest day of my life.

Q: Her death hit you hard?

A: Yes. Almost none of her society friends invited me to their Christmas parties that year. I had always looked forward to them.

Q: So where did you go after she died?

A: Nowhere. I stayed in her townhouse.

Q: How could you? Wasn't she the owner?

A: Yes, but all my stuff was there.

Q: How long did you stay on in her townhouse?

A: Until her sons evicted me. I believe I lived there about a year-and-a-half after she died.

Q: What did you live on?

A: Well, I had my IRA and some investments from my Georgetown days. But I knew I couldn't live on that forever.

Q: So what did you do?

A: Well, I started by packing up all of Jacqueline's clothing. You wouldn't believe the number of dresses and gowns she had. It was an incredible wardrobe.

Q: What did you do with all those clothes?

A: I took them to Le Caperie.

Q: What's Le Caperie?

A: It's a high-end consignment shop in Georgetown. They specialize in selling high-end used women's clothing, particularly evening gowns.

Q: Did they sell the clothing?

A: Yes.

Q: And gave you a percentage of the proceeds?

A: Yes. That helped me get through the first year.

Q: Did you take anything else that had belonged to Ms. Quiller?

Mr. Stein: Objection, this is irrelevant. Whatever Mr. Prey may have removed from Ms. Quiller's townhouse – and I'm sure its stuff she would have wanted him to have – isn't part of this case.

Ms. Muffett: I agree the clothing's not. But if he took jewelry and it wound up at one of the New York City auction houses, it most certainly is relevant.

Q: Mr. Prey, please answer the pending question: did you take anything else that had belonged to Ms. Quiller?

A: Yes. I took a few of her smaller paintings. She had so many I didn't think they'd be missed.

Q: What did you do with them?

A: I sold them to an auction house.

Q: What auction house was that?

A: Kotomac. That's Potomac but with a "K" instead of a "P." It's a reference to their location on K Street in DC.

Q: Did you ever take any of her jewelry?

A: Yes.

Q: What did you take?

A: Initially I just took a pair of diamond earrings. She always wore them when we were out together. I felt she would have wanted me to have them.

Q: What did you do with them?

A: I sold them to Kotomac.

Q: How much did you get for them?

A: $4,700 as I recall.

Q: Did you sell any more of Ms. Quiller's jewelry?

A: Well, that $4,700 didn't go very far. So a few months later I had to take another three sets of earrings.

Q: What did you do with them?

A: I took them to Boyle in New York City. Kotomac had just bought the paintings and the diamond earrings. I didn't want them to start asking questions.

Q: How much did Boyle pay you for the earrings?

A: About $5,700 as I recall.

Q: So that was the first time you sold anything to an auction house in New York City?

A: Yes.

Q: Did they ask how you came to be in possession of the earrings?

A: Well, when I took them in, I said they had been left to me by Ms. Quiller when she died. Jacqueline Quiller had an impeccable reputation, they weren't about to question me any further.

Q: Had you met Ms. Borokin at that point?

A: No, that didn't happen until 2018, more than a year after Jacqueline died.

Q: So how did you spend your time in 2017 and early 2018 – after Ms. Quiller died and before you met Ms. Borokin? I mean how did you spend it other than stealing Ms. Quiller's clothing and paintings and jewelry?

Mr. Stein: Ms. Muffett, please stop referring to Mr. Prey as a thief. I'm sure Mr. Prey believed in good faith that Ms. Quiller would have wanted him to have those things as mementos of their decade together.

Q: Mr. Prey, my question remains: how did you spend your time during the period following Ms. Quiller's death and your meeting Ms. Borokin?

A: Well, that's when I began to realize how easy it was to get an auction house to purchase jewelry that I had received elsewhere.

Q: You mean jewelry that you had stolen?

A: You could put it that way.

Q: So, are you saying that some of the thefts you and Ms. Borokin are charged with, thefts that occurred prior to your meeting her in 2018, were actually thefts you made on your own?

A: Yes.

Q: Okay. I think you're charged with three thefts in 2017. The first was a Van Cleef and Arpels ring that you took from John and Jane Doe in New York City?

A: Yes.

Q: Were the Does a couple you had met through Ms. Quiller?

A: Yes. They invited me to a dinner party at their apartment. I think they knew I was despondent over Jacqueline's death.

Q: You went up to New York City just for a dinner party?

A: Yes.

Q: Did you stay overnight?

A: Yes. I stayed at the Harvard Club. It only cost about $150 to stay there. But I got $3,500 for the ring at Boyle, so I came out ahead.

Q: When you took the ring to Boyle, did they ask how you came to have it?

A: No. Remember, I had taken three sets of Jacqueline's earrings there earlier. So another piece of jewelry that belonged to Jacqueline didn't raise any concern.

Q: But it hadn't belonged to Jacqueline, it had belonged to Jane Doe.

A: Why would I tell them that?

Q: The next item in 2017 was a Buccellati brooch that belonged to Albert and Alba Tross. I believe it was taken in New York City?

A: Yes. I had met the Trosses at the Does' dinner party. Alba Tross had asked if I'd be available to come to one of their dinner parties. She said they always needed a spare man, most of their women friends were widows. I enjoyed being a spare man.

Q: So when you were at the Trosses' Manhattan apartment for a dinner party, as a spare man, you pocketed the Buccellanti brooch?

A: Yes.

Q: Who did you sell it to?

A: I took it to Krispies in New York City the next day. I didn't want to keep going to Boyle every time I had an opportunity to sell some jewelry.

Q: Did Krispies ask how you had obtained the brooch?

A: No. Jacqueline Quiller's name opened a lot of doors.

Q: And they paid you $7,500 for the brooch?

A: Yes.

Ms. Muffett: I think our court reporter could use a break. Let's come back in ten minutes.

(Deposition resumes at 11:15 a.m.)

Q: Okay, Mr. Prey, we were talking about the jewelry that you, ah, removed from their rightful owners in 2017. I believe the third item taken during this time is the Patek Philipe watch?

A: Yes.

Q: And you took that from the Careys? Jack and Kerri Hines Carey in Georgetown?

A: Yes. I had met them with Jacqueline. They lived in Georgetown. As you know, Jack Carey worked for the State Department. They were having a cocktail party to celebrate President's Day and they invited me.

Q: How did you manage to steal a watch? Wasn't Mr. Carey wearing it?

A: Oh no, he has tons of watches. His wife's quite wealthy, you know. He had left the watch in his library on top of a stack of classified documents. I think he was using the watch as a paper weight.

Q: Weren't you worried that, once he went to his library, he'd realize the watch was missing?

A: Yes, I knew that. That's why I looked through his desk drawers until I found a real paperweight. It was all tarnished and beaten up, but you could still make out the legend on its face: "Careying for the Planet." So I put it on the stack of classified documents where the watch had been.

Q: Did you take any of the classified documents?

A: Heavens no. You could get in big trouble for that.

Q: Where did you dispose of the watch?

A: I took it to Boyle in New York City. I didn't want to take it to a DC auction house. If Carey had reported the matter to the police, a DC dealer would be on the lookout for it.

Q: What did you tell Boyle about the watch?

A: I told them my father had given it to me years ago when I got my Master's degree. But that I had stopped wearing it when I got my ROLEX.

Q: And they didn't ask any questions?

A: No.

Q: How did you come by a ROLEX?

A: Jacqueline gave it to me one year for Easter. She put it at the bottom of a little Easter Basket she had made up for me.

Q: Did she include some chocolates?

A: Yes, she put some nice chocolate truffles in the basket, they're my favorites. She also included several caramels, I never liked caramels. Besides, they stick to your teeth.

Q: Okay, let's move on. The takings that started in 2018, I think there were nine or ten of them listed in the indictment. Can I assume that all of them were taken by you and Ms. Borokin working together?

A: That's correct.

Q: So how did you meet Ms. Borokin?

A: I met her at the Carey's President's Day party that we just talked about. We were both there without partners, so we sort of gravitated toward each other.

Q: And the two of you hit it off?

A: Yes. She knew about my life with Jacqueline and our immersion in the Georgetown and New York City social scene.

Q: Did you know anything about her?

A: No, but she quickly told me. She said she was a Swiss heiress and that her father, some sort of banking or investment tycoon, had set up a large trust fund for her. Then she went through a long list of all the high society people she knew. It was an impressive list.

Q: Did that make her attractive to you.

A: It certainly helped. She was kind of plain looking, nowhere near as beautiful and elegant as Jacqueline.

Q: So you decided to settle for her?

A: Yes. She had a lot to offer.

Q: When did you become romantically involved with Ms. Borokin?

A: That night. She invited me for a nightcap in her suite at the Hay-Adams.

Q: You slept with her on your first date?

A: It wasn't really a date. We just met by chance at the Carey party.

Q: Did you ever wonder how Ms. Borokin could afford a suite at the Hay-Adams? It must have cost a small fortune.

A: Well, she'd just told me she was an heiress with a trust fund. If she wanted to spend her money on a suite at the Hay-Adams, who was I to complain?

Q: So you moved in with her after that first night?

A: Yes. I was about to be evicted from Jacqueline's townhouse where I had lived for almost twelve years. I needed somewhere to go.

Q: And you stayed with Ms. Borokin there until she moved to the Waldorf-Astoria?

A: Yes. The Hay-Adams was really nice but the Waldorf-Astoria was something else. I've never stayed in such a gorgeous place.

Q: Now, Mr. Prey, when did you and Ms. Borokin embark on your campaign of thefts?

A: That first night at the Hay-Adams.

Q: How did that come about?

A: Well, I had put Jack Carey's watch in the side pocket of my suit jacket, which I had draped around a chair in the bedroom. I had hung my suit trousers in her closet but then I couldn't find a second hanger so I had to put the jacket around the chair.

Q: Everyone says you always dress impeccably and take good care of your clothes.

A: Yes, that's important in my line of work. Anyway, when I woke up the next morning, Ava was standing at the foot of the bed holding the watch. She asked me what it was.

Q: What did you tell her?

A: Well, the first thing I did was ask her why she had been going through my jacket pockets.

Q: What did she say?

A: She said she always does that when she's with someone for the first time. She always worries that guys are just after her money and her jewelry.

Q: What did you tell her?

A: I told her I wasn't after her money or her jewelry. I said I was after other people's money and jewelry. And that I'd taken the watch from Mr. Carey's library the night before.

Q: What did she say to that?

A: She asked if I had ever stolen anything before that night.

Q: And . . . .

A: And I told her I had. I told her about the ring I had taken from the Does and the Buccellati brooch I'd taken from the Trosses.

Q: Did that bother her?

A: No, she seemed okay with that. But then she asked if I'd taken anything from Jacqueline.

Q: That must have presented a problem, what did you tell her?

A: I told her I had only taken a set of earrings after Jacqueline died. I told her Jacqueline always wore them when she was with me and wanted me to have them after she died.

Q: Did you tell her about the dresses and evening gowns and paintings you took from Ms. Quiller after she died?

A: Why would I tell her about all that?

Q: Right. But what was her reaction to all this? I wouldn't think she'd want a thief moving in with her.

A: Oh, she wasn't at all distressed. In fact, she wanted to know how much I'd been able to sell the jewelry for.

Q: And you told her?

A: Yes. I told her I got about $4,700 for the earrings Jacqueline wanted me to have, $3,500 for the Van Cleef and Arpels ring and $7,500 for the Buccellati brooch.

Q: What did she say to that?

A: She said that was small potatoes. She said I needed to think bigger. She said she knew scores of rich society people. And not just in Georgetown but also in New York and Newport. She said that, with her help, I could gain entree to numerous wealthy families. And that would open up a lot of opportunities to expand my business.

(Long Pause)

Ms. Muffett: This might be a good time to break for lunch. I've got a lot more to cover. Let's stop now and come back at 2:00.

(Deposition adjourns at 12:45 p.m.)

Chapter 26

FIFTY/FIFTY

Continued Examination by Ms. Muffett:

Q: Mr. Prey, before the lunch break you told us that Ms. Borokin encouraged you to quote "expand your business," is that correct?

A: Yes.

Q: And she suggested that she could help you do so by introducing you to wealthy families in Georgetown and New York?

A: Yes.

Q: And did she do so?

A: Oh yes. My social life with Ava picked up right where I had left off with Jacqueline, except that Ava spent lots of time in New York. And one summer she even took a house in Newport.

Q: Did she have a place in New York?

A: She had an apartment on Park Avenue. And she usually rented a house in the Hamptons in the summer.

Q: And you lived with her in each of those places?

A: Where else was I going to live?

Q: And she began introducing you to wealthy families you had not previously known?

A: That's correct.

Q: I'm going to go through the thefts the two of you committed, I believe there were at least nine. You must have taken jewelry from everyone you met.

A: Heavens no. I didn't want people to think I was a thief.

Q: You were never caught?

A: No, I was always careful. Besides, it was really Ava who committed most of the thefts during this time. I think that once she got started she became addicted to it.

Q: Okay, let's start with the first one. You took a diamond ring belonging to Marguerite Faust from her home in Georgetown?

A: No, Ava's the one who took it.

Q: Okay, but tell me about it.

A: Well, Ava introduced me to Dr. and Marguerite Faust at a cocktail party in Georgetown. She seemed to know them quite well.

Q: What's Dr. Faust's first name?

A: If he has one I'm not aware of it. He just goes by "Dr. Faust." Ava said he's the top anti-aging doctor in DC. She went to him all the time for BOTOX treatments.

Q: So Ava stole a diamond ring from her own doctor?

A: No, she stole it from Dr. Faust's wife.

Q: How did she steal it?

A: We were at a party in their DC townhouse. Marguerite was wearing a ring with a huge diamond. Ava pointed it out to me while we were sipping champagne, said it must be worth at least $25,000.

Q: If Marguerite was wearing the ring, how was Ms. Borokin able to take it?

A: She noticed that Marguerite left to go to the powder room and, when she returned, she wasn't wearing the ring. So Ava just went to the powder room and pocketed it. It had been left in plain sight next to the Estee Lauder moisturizing cream. Marguerite later told everyone she hadn't realized the ring was missing until that night when she went to take it off and discovered she didn't have it on.

Q: Where did you dispose of the ring?

A: Ava took it to that lady dealer in the Diamond District, I believe her name's Madonna. Madonna Barone. Her store's called Diamond's Best Friend, but she's more famous than the store. Smokes cigars constantly and refers to herself as "The Godmother of Diamonds."

Q: How much did you get for the ring?

A: Around $20,000.

Q: Did you split the money from the sale?

A: When we first discussed expanding my business, we agreed we would split everything fifty/fifty. But Ava always found a way to justify more for herself.

Q: So, in this case, how was the $20,000 split?

A: She took 90%. She said she was the one who carried out the theft, and also the one who knew Dr. Faust, he was her doctor. So she said she deserved 90%.

Q: Did you push back? Remind her of your prior agreement?

A: What could I do, she held all the cards. It was her homes and her friends. And besides, she's the one who walked out of the diamond store with the money.

Q: You mean this diamond lady paid for the ring in cash?

A: Yes. Madonna Barone wasn't known as "The Godmother of Diamonds" for nothing. You think those people do business in checks that can be traced?

Q: Did Ms. Borokin say whether the Godmother lady asked where the ring came from?

A: Since the Godmother lady paid for the ring in cash, I don't think she cared where it came from.

Q: Okay, let's move to the second item. The Buccellati earrings that were taken from Albert and Alba Tross. I believe you had previously taken a Buccellati brooch from the same couple?

A: Yes. As I said earlier, they had invited me to a dinner party at their New York apartment.

Q: And they invited you back even though a brooch had been stolen the first time you were there?

A: I don't think they realized anything had been taken that first time. Anyway, by then I had taken up with Ava and they wanted to meet her so they invited us for a cocktail party.

Q: How did you come to steal the earrings?

A: I wish you'd stop using the word "steal," it makes me sound like a thief.

Q: Would you feel better if I said "removed" or "took possession of"?

A: "Took possession of" would be a better way of putting it.

Q: Okay, so how did you manage to take possession of the earrings?

A: I told Ava that, the first time I had been there, Alba had been wearing a set of earrings that looked to be quite expensive. But she wasn't wearing them that night, they must be somewhere in her bedroom.

Q: So you snuck into her bedroom when nobody was looking and found them?

A: Ava's the one who snuck into the bedroom.

Q: And took possession of the earrings?

A: Yes. She found them in a large jewelry box with lots of other jewelry. That could explain why Mrs. Tross hadn't noticed the brooch was missing.

Q: Where did you dispose of the earrings?

A: Krispies. They had already bought the Buccellati brooch a few months earlier.

Q: Weren't they suspicious of you bringing in more Buccellati jewelry, particularly since you had moved on from Jacqueline to Ava?

A: That's why Ava handled the transaction.

Q: Did she say whether Krispies asked any questions?

A: They didn't. Ava told them the earrings had been a gift from her ex-husband and she didn't want to hang onto anything that would remind her of him.

Q: How much did she receive for the earrings?

A: Thirteen thousand.

Q: And how was it split?

A: She kept 90%. Said she's the one who carried out the operation.

Q: Even though you were the one who introduced her to the Trosses?

A: There was no reasoning with Ava.

Q: Okay, I believe the next item is another ring – a diamond sapphire ring owned by Jack and Mary Aster?

A: Yes. Ava knew the Asters and had attended several social functions with them. They invited us to a cocktail party at their brownstone in Manhattan.

Q: And what led to the two of you taking possession of the ring?

A: Ava said Mrs. Aster frequently wore a platinum sapphire ring, she was certain it was quite expensive. But she wasn't wearing it that night.

Q: So how was this transaction carried out?

A: We agreed that Ava would engage Mrs. Aster in conversation. Mrs. Aster is a big opera buff. So Ava asked her what she thought about all those ridiculous modern productions the Met keeps putting on. Rigoletto set in Las Vegas. Carmen set in Detroit. Macbeth set in Coney Island. Mrs. Aster ranted about those productions for over half an hour.

Q: While you went upstairs and took possession of the ring?

A: Yes.

Q: From her bedroom?

A: Yes. It was just sitting with some other jewelry on a silver tray on her dressing table.

Q: Where did you dispose of the ring?

A: Mothebys. We decided we needed to diversify the buyers, we couldn't always go to Boyle or Krispies.

Q: Did Motheby question the source of the ring?

A: No. Ava told them she had inherited it from her late mother who had lived in Switzerland. They had no reason to question her about it.

Q: I believe Motheby paid $18,000 for the ring?

A: Yes.

Q: And Ms. Borokin kept 90% of it?

A: Yes. She said I'd never have met the Asters if it wasn't for her.

Ms. Muffett: Let's take a short break. I still have a ways to go.

(Deposition resumes at 3:25 p.m.)

Q: Mr. Prey, I believe the next item is the Verdura brooch that belonged to Dorothy Tracy, the husband of Rick Tracy?

A: Yes.

Q: The Tracys were friends of Ava?

A: Yes. Of course I had heard of Mr. Tracy, he was a famous detective, but I'd never met him or his wife.

Q: And what led the two of you to take Mrs. Tracy's brooch?

A: Ava thought it would be great fun to steal something from a woman married to a detective.

Q: Who carried it out?

A: Ava insisted I do it. She said the Tracys didn't know me and so they wouldn't even notice if I went missing from the party for an hour.

Q: So what happened?

A: Well, Ava was right. It took me almost an hour and no one even noticed I had disappeared.

Q: Why did it take you an hour?

A: I had to go through dozens of drawers and cabinets before I finally found a jewelry box on the top shelf of their closet. I was getting really nervous, it was taking so long. So I just took the first thing I saw. It turned out to be the Verdura brooch.

Q: Where did you dispose of the brooch?

A: Krispies. They gave us $22,000 for it.

Q: Which of you dealt with Krispies?

A: I did. Ava had already sold two items to them so we thought I should deal with them this time.

Q: Did Krispies ask any questions about the brooch?

A: No. I explained that it had been left to me by Jacqueline, whose will had just been probated.

Q: How was the $22,000 split?

A: Ava said I could have 20% since I was the one who had spent an hour in the Tracy's bedroom and found the brooch.

Q: Okay, let's talk about the jewelry that belonged to those sisters, Thelma and Louise. First of all, how did you meet them? And what is their last name?

A: I've never heard their last name spoken. Everyone just calls them Thelma and Louise. Ava knew them, they were both active in the New York Historical Society.

Q: Ms. Borokin was active in the Historical Society?

A: Oh no, she hated history. But the society had sponsored some kind of party, maybe a fundraiser, at their headquarters which she had attended. She loved parties. And that's where she met Thelma and Louise.

Q: How was the transaction carried out?

A: This was the easiest one yet. Using my background as a professor of political science, I engaged the two of them in a long discussion of the temperance movement in the early twentieth century. They told me they had grown up in Ohio as Methodists, and they talked about the annual Temperance Sunday talk that someone from the WCTU always gave.

Q: What's the WCTU?

A: Women's Christian Temperance Union.

Q: This Temperance Union stuff was something you had lectured about at Georgetown?

A: Yes. None of my students at Georgetown had ever heard of the temperance movement, much less Temperance Sunday. They hated the very idea of temperance. And they hated Methodists, said they were merely Baptists who could read.

Q: So while you engaged Thelma and Louise with a discussion of the temperance movement, Ms. Borokin spent time in their bedroom?

A: Actually they had separate bedrooms so she went to both. It only took her about fifteen minutes to gather up all the pieces we walked out with.

Q: Where did you take this jewelry?

A: Boyle in New York City. Ava took it in.

Q: And Boyle paid $70,000 for it?

A: Yes.

Q: And Ms. Borokin kept 90% of the $70,000 because she was the one who actually took the jewelry?

A: Yes.

Q: Did Boyle ask Ms. Borokin how she happened to have all that jewelry?

A: No, they didn't ask any questions. Ava explained that each of the pieces had been given to her by a former husband or lover. I think she told them that six of the items were from ex-husbands.

Q: I believe the last New York transaction was the heirloom jewelry that went missing from the Urbachers following their daughter's wedding in East Hampton?

A: I really liked the Urbachers. I felt bad we took advantage of their hospitality.

Q: If they were such nice people, why did you target them?

A: Ava was miffed that some of the wedding guests had been invited to stay overnight after the reception the afternoon before the wedding and we hadn't been included.

Q: So she got her revenge by taking the jewelry?

A: Yes.

Q: And you took possession of it from Mrs. Urbacher's second floor bedroom?

A: Actually it was in her second floor dressing room, which was adjacent to her bedroom. But this was a really close call. One of the overnight guests saw me in the upstairs hallway just after I'd come out of the bedroom with the jewelry. He asked me what I was doing. I had to think fast. So I told him I was teaching a course in architecture and interior design and was observing how the Urbachers' architect had used the wainscoting and woodwork in the upstairs hallways.

Q: And he believed you?

A: Yes, but I felt bad lying about my interest in architecture.

Q: And where did you dispose of the jewelry?

A: Ava took it to Motheby. She told them it was another inheritance from her mother in Switzerland.

Q: And they asked no questions?

A: No, they just gave her $50,000 for it.

Q: And how much of that did you get?

A: The usual 10%.

Q: Even though you did all the work and almost got caught?

A: She said that was my fault, I should have looked to see if anyone was around when I came out of Mrs. Urbacher's room.

Ms. Muffett: Mr. Stein, it's a little after 5:00 and I've still got an hour or so more, I need to cover the three Newport episodes. Do you want to try to finish tonight or would you prefer to come back tomorrow?

The Witness: Let's keep going. I don't want to have to come back tomorrow, I understand Ava will be here then. I really don't want to be here when she's here.

Q: You've had a falling out with Ms. Borokin?

A: Yes, when I discovered she was a fraud. How would you like to be in a four-year relationship with someone and then find out they're not what they claimed to be?

Q: So you moved out of her suite at the Waldorf-Astoria?

A: She no longer had a suite at the Waldorf-Astoria. They evicted her and then sued her for ten months rent she hadn't paid.

Q: Where is she now?

A: A small apartment in Queens. I wasn't about to live in Queens.

Q: So where do you live?

A: I found an apartment in Arlington, just across the river from DC. But your DA insists I stay in New York until the case is over. Do you have any idea how much it costs me to stay at the Harvard Club for a month?

Ms. Muffett: I wouldn't know, I didn't go to Harvard.

The Witness: I can't keep paying for a place in Arlington and a room at the Harvard Club. Do you think you could get Mr. Braggert to allow me to stay in DC? I'll agree not to go anywhere else. I couldn't go anywhere anyway, I've got no money.

Mr. Stein: I have some friends in New York who have lots of money, I could introduce you to them. They might have some jewelry you could borrow.

Mr. Grey: Aren't you supposed to be my lawyer?

Ms. Muffett: I'll speak to Mr. Peters, he has a good relationship with Mr. Braggert. Maybe we can help you get back to DC, you've been very cooperative. Let's take a break.

Chapter 27

PRESS CONFERENCE

"Thank you all for coming. I believe most of you know me, I'm Patrick Peters of Peters and Peters and this is my brother Prescott Peters.

"We have just come from the Clerk's office where we've filed a complaint of enormous importance. After I tell you about it, I think you'll agree with me that the facts of this case are truly shocking.

"The villains in this story are three of the most prestigious auction houses in New York City, if not the world: Boyle, Krispies and Motheby. Our lawsuit will demonstrate that these institutions shamelessly betrayed the trust they have long enjoyed in the high-end auction world.

"The story starts with two con artists. By now you are undoubtedly aware of Barkley Prey, a retired professor of political science at Georgetown, and his Swiss heiress girl friend Ava Borokin. And by now I'm sure you're aware that Ms. Borokin is not a Swiss heiress and her name is not Ava Borokin. Ms. Borokin is actually Gladys Delray from Fort Lee.

"Now, a few weeks ago Mr. Prey and Ms. Delray were indicted by District Attorney Alvin Braggert for a series of jewel thefts that took place in homes from Georgetown to New York to Newport. This unsavory pair took advantage of Ms. Borokin's supposed status as a Swiss heiress to work their way into the highest reaches of society. The thefts they carried out are bad enough. But what happened next should shock the conscience of us all.

"These two grifters took the fruits of their thefts – jewelry, watches and the like - and turned them over to the auction houses that are the defendants in this case. Ignoring their duty to explore the source and origin of the jewelry, the defendants couldn't wait to pay lavish sums of money for every item Prey and Borokin offered them.

"And then, giving no thought to the possibility that they had no right to do so, they turned around and resold every single item either at auction or to a private buyer. We won't know how much they received for the stolen items until we complete discovery in the case. But I'm sure they profited handsomely from each sale.

"Of course the buyers who purchased the jewelry and other items from defendants will realize that they were cheated. After all, since the defendants had no legal right to any of these items, the buyers have no right to retain them. But that's a matter between defendants and their buyers. It's not the subject of our complaint.

"Our complaint centers on the unfortunate victims of the thefts. These victims were actually victimized twice. First by Prey and Borokin when they committed the thefts. And then by defendants when they purchased and then resold the stolen items.

"Let me tell you about some of the folks who were victimized by this scam. You will know many of them, they include prominent members of American society and professionals who have reached the peak of their profession. All of them have joined in as plaintiffs in this lawsuit.

"Some of them are leading public servants. For example, Averell Harrington, the former ambassador and presidential advisor. And Jack Carey, who holds a top State Department position where he works tirelessly to advance America's interests in the world. And the retired Senator Henry Cabot, respected and beloved on both sides of the aisle.

"Several plaintiffs are leading members of their profession. For example, Nick Urbacher, the first plaintiff listed in the complaint. Mr. Urbacher is one of the leading investment bankers in New York City. Another top professional is the world famous anti-aging specialist Dr.

Faust; Dr. Faust lives and works in Washington, DC but his reputation is worldwide.

"Of course, we also have several plaintiffs who come from the top echelons of society, such as Floria Vanderbank, Jack and Mary Aster and Albert and Alba Tross.

"Auction houses like Boyle, Krispies and Motheby have long catered to persons of this stature. And they once held the trust and respect of such customers. But that trust and respect has been betrayed. Betrayed in the interest of making a quick profit on the sale of goods they had no right to purchase, let alone resell. By this lawsuit, we will hold defendants to account for this betrayal of trust.

"I would be remiss if I did not add that this lawsuit is also brought in the interest of all future customers of these venerable institutions. What happened to our clients should never happen again. To anyone, regardless of their professional or social standing.

"We have copies of the Complaint for each of you. Our four associates standing over there can provide you with a copy. And if you have any questions, I'm sure they'll be happy to answer them.

"Thank you all for coming."

* * * *

Pap turned off the television and looked around the table in the firm's conference room. At the far left end were Trey Bears and Goldie Locke of Arnold and Hammer. Next to them was their client Lisa Silver, the General Counsel of Boyle.

In the middle of the table were Hortescue Horvath, IV and Shepperd Sherman, III of Oliver and Cromwell. Oliver and Cromwell was New York City's most prestigious law firm. Pup had been a partner there before Pap convinced him to leave the firm to start up Peters and Peters. Siting between them was Tiffany Jewel, General Counsel of Krispies.

At the far right end of the table were Elliott Hess and Jay Edward Hoover of Cravat, Swine and Hoare. They were accompanied by Leslie Gold, Motheby's General Counsel.

Pap and Pup had locked horns with each of these firms in prior cases. And each of them recognized that Pap and Pup were fearless - and occasionally reckless - but they never bluffed. If Pap said they would sue to evict your terminally ill grandmother from the only home she had ever lived in, they would do exactly that if their demands were not met.

Tiffany Jewel, Krispies' General Counsel, was well aware that Pap and Pup never bluffed. She experienced this first-hand when she was in-house litigation counsel for FiveStar capital. FiveStar had been the major investor in Sapper Labs, the non-fungible token company that had been caught in Peters and Peters' crosshairs for selling non-fungible tokens without the consent of the persons depicted on the tokens.

The deposition of FiveStar's main witness, Tyrone Power, had been a disaster. It included Tyrone's caught-on-camera flirtation with Lydia Lowlace, the lead plaintiff in the case, during a break in the deposition. The flirtation had led to an intimate dinner that evening followed by on-camera sexual hijinks between Tyrone and Lydia at her Soho apartment.

The videos had led to a disastrous settlement for FiveStar and left Tiffany looking for a new job. And now here she was again waiting for Pap and Pup to demand another enormous settlement from her employer.

* * * *

After giving everyone time to absorb the video, Pap began speaking.

"That's the speech I intend to give to the press next Monday on the courthouse steps after we file the complaint we're about to give you. We'll also give you a copy of the press release we'll be issuing to the national media. Pup, can you pass both documents around, there should be enough for everyone.

"I want to call your attention to two things in the complaint. First, you'll see that all of the victims are listed by name. There aren't enough of them to warrant a class action, so you'll be faced with claims by twelve different plaintiffs – eleven individuals or families and one estate, the estate of the late Jacqueline Quiller.

"I'm sure you'll quickly see that all the plaintiffs are extremely prominent people. The Urbachers, the Harringtons, the Careys, the Asters, Floria Vanderbank."

"I don't think John Doe is particularly prominent" said Lisa Silver. "In fact, it's not even a real name."

"I'm sorry, Ms. Silver, but you're wrong" Pap replied. "John Doe is alive and well and lives in New York City with his wife Jane. And he's so famous that Frank Capra made a movie about him."

Tiffany Jewel spoke up next. "I don't think anybody outside of law enforcement circles knows who Rick Tracy is."

"They will after this case is over" said Pap. "You see, Mr. Tracy made sure that his wife's Verdura brooch was never stolen. What was stolen was an imitation brooch that Tracy had someone at the Jewelry Exchange produce. Your client bought the fake brooch believing it was the real thing. That will make for a wonderful story: 'Krispies buys and then resells a fake Verdura brooch.'"

Pap paused, and then continued. "The other thing in the complaint I want you to notice is that it spells out the amount your clients paid Prey or Borokin for each stolen item. But it does not allege how much your clients received when they resold the items. We won't know that until we obtain discovery from your clients. But I'm certain we'll find that most if not all the items were sold for considerably more than your clients paid for them.

"Now, we're also giving you four DVDs. The first one has a video of DA Braggert's press conference where he announced the indictment of Prey and Borokin. There's probably nothing on there you don't already know. But I want you to notice that there was a large gathering of reporters at that event. Now, the story has died down considerably since Braggert's press conference. In fact, it was only in the news for a couple of days.

"But once we file the complaint and hold our own press conference, the story will spring back to life. And it won't die down in two or three days, like it did before. We'll make sure the press is kept informed of our progress on this extremely newsworthy case."

"That's blackmail" said Leslie Gold of Motheby.

"I'd prefer to call it legal transparency" said Pap. "As you know, transparency is very important these days.

"The second DVD is simply a video of the press conference we played for you at the start of the meeting. Your top executives may want to look at it when they contemplate our proposal.

"Now the other two DVDs are videos of the depositions of Barkley Prey and Ava Borokin. You will find that both of them were very forthcoming in their testimony. They didn't hold anything back. The details of each theft, and the subsequent sale of the stolen goods to your clients, are all disclosed in detail.

"Aside from your clients' total lack of due diligence, it's amusing to see how easily they were fooled by Prey and Borokin's stories of how they came by the stolen goods. That gullibility is scarcely what people expect from the foremost auction houses in the world. If I were you, I'd be worried about my standing in the auction world if this gets out."

"Look" said Elliott Hess, "I know you have a specific proposal you want to put to us. You didn't bring us here just to hit us over the head with how bad our clients will look if the case proceeds."

"Elliott, as always, you're absolutely right. And I appreciate your getting right to the point. We do have a specific proposal. In fact, we've prepared this one-page summary of the financial terms you will need to meet. It's quite simple, but let me walk you through it.

"As you can see, there's an entry for each defendant. The first is Boyle. Items from five of the thefts wound up there. The combined value of the items – based on what Boyle paid for them – comes to one hundred thousand dollars. Now, we didn't bring this lawsuit just to get that money back. So, as there were five victims who's jewelry wound up at Boyle, we've applied a multiplier of five. That brings Boyle's share up to five hundred thousand.

"Next is Krispies, which bought four stolen items. One of those is the Richard Mille watch, which is worth close to a million dollars. The total paid by Krispies for its acquisitions comes to a million and forty-two thousand dollars. To keep it simple, we've rounded that off to a straight million. With a multiple of four, that brings Krispies' share to four million.

"Motheby only bought three items. They had a cumulative value of about one hundred and fifty thousand dollars. Using a multiplier of three, Motheby's share comes to five hundred thousand."

"Three times one-hundred-and-fifty-thousand dollars is only four hundred and fifty thousand" said Leslie Gold. "Not five hundred thousand."

"Our computer rounded it up to five hundred thousand" said Pup. "It always rounds up to the nearest one hundred thousand."

"Now" said Pap, "we get to punitive damages. We . . . . "

"How can you include punitive damages?" demanded Lisa Silver. "The case hasn't even started and you're pretending you've already won."

"That's correct, Ms. Silver. We're presenting numbers to you based on having won a jury trial. If you believe Boyle could convince a jury to rule for it and not for our clients, you're free to reject our proposal.

"But I guarantee you that once the jury assesses monetary damages, it will also award punitive damages. We've been very conservative in our calculation."

"I wouldn't call two million dollars per defendant conservative" Lisa complained.

"I would" said Pap. "We'll be asking the jury to award far more than two million per defendant.

"Now, you can see near the bottom of the page, the total monetary recovery is eleven million. Five million in damages and six million in punitives."

"So you want us to pay a total of eleven million to settle this case?" said Tiffany Jewel.

"No. You will need to pay fourteen million to settle the case. There's three million in attorneys fees shown at the bottom. We're typically awarded thirty-three percent of the total monetary recovery. Thirty-three percent of eleven million is three-point-six million dollars.

"But to make it easier for you, we're willing to knock off the six hundred thousand and just make it a flat three million. We won't be so generous if you insist on taking the case to trial."

"Wasn't there a diamond ring taken from this Dr. Faust and then sold to a dealer in the Diamond District?" asked Lisa. "Where is that in here?"

"We've already settled with them" said Pup. "They paid us in cash. Your clients may prefer to pay by check or bank transfer."

"Now" said Pap, "if we can reach agreement on this proposal by the close of business on Friday, we will not file the complaint, hold a press conference, or issue a press release. The actual settlement agreement, which we can work out next week, will be strictly confidential and we will agree to reasonable terms regarding the number of copies we retain, how we store them and so forth.

"But if you don't wish to accept these terms, we will file the lawsuit Monday morning and hold a press conference immediately thereafter. It's now approximately twelve-thirty p.m., so you have forty-eight hours to let us know if we have a deal. Do not bother calling to ask if the terms can be changed. They cannot.

"But I assure you, the terms are quite fair and reasonable. Pup, wouldn't you agree that the terms are fair and reasonable?"

"Certainly. Our terms are always fair and reasonable."

"After you've had an opportunity to study the materials we've provided, I'm sure you'll agree with Pup and me that the terms are a fair and reasonable basis on which to resolve this unfortunate situation.

"Now, if there are no questions, I think everyone should go out and have a nice lunch. There's some good Italian restaurants a few blocks away on forty-fourth street, just west of Fifth Avenue. If you check with Ms. Pesky on the way out, she'll be happy to give you some specific recommendations."

Chapter 28

HAPPY THANKSGIVING

It was the Tuesday before Thanksgiving and Pap, Pup and Melissa were sitting at the counsel table in Judge Sam Spade's courtroom. Chip sat in the first row of the spectator section with Holly Gonightly. Brandon was next to them with Ray and Faye Wray while Helen was on the other side of them with Adam and Eve.

There were four attorneys at the defense table: Omar Sadly, counsel for Sandoza and Goldstone Strategies; Rosemary and Mark Thyme, counsel for Boogle; Walt Waters, counsel for Take America Back; and Gordon Goode, counsel for Democracy Now. Except for Omar, who was a sole practitioner, all of them were accompanied by an entourage of associates and paralegals, all of whom were sitting in the spectator section.

The entire courtroom was packed, there was scarcely an empty seat. Judge Spade and his courtroom deputy Beau Garte entered from the robing room and the hearing began.

Transcript of Proceedings:

The Court: Good morning, everyone. I hope we can complete this hearing today so that everyone can get back home for Thanksgiving.

We have two motions before us, both filed by plaintiffs. There's a motion to certify two groups of class action plaintiffs and a motion for partial summary judgment. We'll start with the motion for class certification. I'll hear first from defendants. Which one of you wants to tell me why I should not certify the two proposed classes?

(Counsel talk animatedly among themselves, pointing back and forth at each other.)

The Court: Ms. Rosemary, I see you've been selected to address this motion. Please proceed.

Rosemary: Don't you want to hear from plaintiffs first? It's their motion

The Court: They spelled out their position quite clearly in their brief. It's defendants' position I'm having trouble with.

Rosemary: Well, we also spelled out our position in our brief. As we said . . . .

The Court: You filed a 45-page brief, twenty pages over the limit that's specified in my standing rules. You should read them some time. And despite taking 45 pages to tell me what your position is, I can't figure out what you're saying. Frankly, the AI-generated brief you submitted the last time you were here was better.

Rosemary: I'm sorry, Your Honor, we . . . .

The Court: Let's do it this way. The first issue is whether to certify a class of donors who gave money to the Sandoza campaign without knowing that his entire persona was bogus. Please tell me why I shouldn't certify such a class.

Rosemary: Your Honor, so far they have only identified two couples who would be in the class. Mr. and Mrs. Wray and Mr. and Mrs. Eaves.

Mr. Peters: It's not Mrs. Eaves, it's Ms. Adams. Adam's wife's maiden name is Eve, Eve Adams. She's a professional writer and so she decided to keep her maiden name when she married Adam, otherwise her name would have been Eve Eaves. She loved Adam but she wasn't too keen on Eaves.

Rosemary: I don't see why people can't just have normal names.

Anyway, whatever her name is, she's one of two married couples, the Wrays and the Eaves – sorry, but I don't know how you're supposed to refer to a married couple with separate last names.

The Court: Why don't you just call them Adam and Eve, we'll all know who you're referring to.

Rosemary. Right. My point is these are just four people. And four people is not enough to justify a class action. There would have to be dozens of people in plaintiffs' shoes to warrant turning this into a class action.

The Court: But Rosemary, the class hasn't been certified yet. Once I certify a class of donors, I would expect scores of people to opt into the case as members of the class. Mr. Peters, isn't that the case?

Mr. Peters: Yes, Your Honor. We know that more than fifty people will immediately opt into the case. In fact, I believe at least half of them are here today. Perhaps we could have them stand?

The Court: That's a good idea. Anyone in the courtroom who donated money to Mr. Sandoza's campaign and would like to get their money back, could you please stand?

(All spectators on the left side of the courtroom stand.)

The Court: Beau, I counted twenty-seven, how about you?

Mr. Garte: I counted twenty-eight. Maybe we should have them do a roll call.

The Court: That won't be necessary, they're not prisoners. Twenty-seven or twenty-eight, either is more than enough to justify a class action.

Rosemary: Your Honor, we've not had an opportunity to depose any of these people. We only deposed the Wrays and the Eaves. How do we know that these people gave money to the Sandoza campaign because of information generated by Boogle's BotsUp? program? Maybe they would have given the money anyway.

The Court: Let's ask them. Will you folks please stand again?

(Everyone on left side of the spectator section again stands.)

The Court: At the request of Boogle's counsel, I'm posing this question to you: If you had known that Mr. Sandoza's background was totally bogus and had been generated by an artificial intelligence program, would you have nevertheless contributed money to his campaign? If your answer is "yes," please raise your hand.

(No hands are raised.)

In other words, had you known that Mr. Sandoza's purported background was bogus and had been generated by artificial intelligence, you would not have made a donation to his campaign. If your answer is "yes," please raise your hand.

(All hands are raised.)

The Court: So there's your answer, Rosemary. We have another twenty-seven plaintiffs right here in the courtroom.

Rosemary: But they weren't under oath when they raised their hand.

The Court: We're not going to swear in twenty-seven people and repeat the questions I just asked. Besides, the four named plaintiffs were all under oath when you took their depositions. If you want to take a few more after the class is certified, I'm sure Mr. Peters would accommodate you.

(Long pause)

Okay, let's move on to the class of Third District voters. Rosemary, what is defendants' basis for opposing certification of that class?

Rosemary: Your Honor, there's been no showing that all of the voters share a common claim. There could be dozens of reasons why someone voted for Mr. Sandoza. A hundred voters could have a hundred different reasons for voting for him. So no one or two persons can represent the wide range of people who voted for Mr. Sandoza.

The Court: I believe you personally took the deposition of the representative of this class, Ms. Holly Gonightly?

Rosemary: How did you know that?

The Court: I read her deposition. Plaintiffs submitted it as part of their motion.

Rosemary: Oh, I didn't realize that.

The Court: Well, when you took Ms. Gonightly's deposition, what reason did she give for voting for Mr. Sandoza?

Rosemary: I think she said everything she had heard about him. His education, his financial background, his work in the not-for-profit world and his family's various tragedies.

The Court: And all of that came from the AI background Boogle had invented for Mr. Sandoza?

Rosemary: I guess so.

The Court: It seems to me that virtually everyone who voted for him must have done so because of one or more or those reasons, and all of those reasons can be traced to the phony biography Boogle created.

Rosemary: But what if someone only voted for him because he was a Republican? And would have voted for him even if they had known that his education and background had been generated by AI?

The Court: If there are any such voters, they would be excluded from the class. But I doubt many voters would fall into that group.

Mr. Peters: Your Honor, we could ask them now. There are approximately thirty Third District voters in the courtroom, all of whom voted for Mr. Sandoza.

The Court: Very well. If we have any voters from the Third District present, and if you voted for Mr. Sandoza, would you please stand.

(Entire spectator section on the right-hand side stands.)

Mr. Garte: I counted thirty-one.

The Court: So did I. Ladies and gentlemen . . . . I'm sorry, it appears that all of you are ladies. So ladies, did all of you vote for Mr. Sandoza? If so, please raise your hand.

(All raise their hand.)

The Court: Now, please raise your hand if you voted for Mr. Sandoza solely because he was a Republican and without any regard to his educational or professional background?

(No hands are raised.)

The Court: It's as I thought. Third District voters who voted for Mr. Sandoza will have done so for a variety of reasons, but those reasons can all be traced back to his professed background or to his campaign statements, all of which were generated by Boogle's artificial intelligence program.

Mr. Peters, you are to be commended for having these two plaintiff groups in court today. Their presence, and their response to the questions I posed, means that there is no need to speculate about the matter. So I will grant plaintiffs' motion for certification of two classes: those who donated to Mr. Sandoza's campaign and those who simply voted for him. I'll issue a detailed decision next week.

Let's take a short break. I need to call my wife and remind her to pick up the turkey today so it can begin thawing.

* * * *

The Court: Okay, we'll now consider plaintiffs' motion for partial summary judgment, specifically, summary judgment as to the liability of all defendants. If granted, that would leave only the question of damages for the jury.

Now, with the help of my law clerks, I've studied all the papers and briefs that have been submitted. And it doesn't seem to me that there is any factual dispute that needs to be resolved by the jury. In fact, in their deposition testimony, defendants have all conceded their complicity in this fraud.

But perhaps there is something you can say that would convince me not to grant summary judgment. Mr. Sadly, I'll start with you. Is there any reason why the Court should not grant summary judgment against your clients – Gregory Sandoza and Goldstone Strategies?

Mr. Sadly: Yes there is, Your Honor. Plaintiffs have painted this case as a matter of fraud. But neither Mr. Sandoza nor his political action committee are guilty of fraud. The only thing they're guilty of is lying.

The Court: Lying?

Mr. Sadly: That's correct. Mr. Sandoza and his campaign, including Goldstone Strategies, didn't defraud anyone. They merely lied. About his educational and professional background and about his family's history of tragedy.

The Court: It seems to me that those were pretty significant lies.

Mr. Sadly: Maybe so, but lying has a long tradition in American politics. Some of our greatest presidents and senators have lied. If lying in politics is suddenly going to be banned, who would ever be willing to run for office? Your Honor, we need to keep America safe for politicians. If you rule for plaintiffs in this case, no politician will ever be safe.

The Court: That might be a good thing. Now Mr. Sadly, is there any other argument you'd like to make?

Mr. Sadly: I can't think of anything else now, but once I sit down I'm sure something else will come to mind and I'll want to stand back up. May I sit down without prejudice to standing back up when I think of something else?

The Court: You may sit down but I don't believe you will have any need to stand back up. I find that the lies and invented facts your clients have admitted to were part of a campaign to defraud the voters of the Third Congressional District. And so I'm granting summary judgment against Mr. Sandoza and Goldstone.

Mr. Waters, I'll hear from you next. Is there any reason why I should not award summary judgment against Take America Back? It seems to have spent over $2 million on Mr. Sandoza's campaign, primarily to produce and purchase broadcast time for a two-minute television commercial that highlighted his bogus background.

Mr. Waters: Your Honor, the founder of Take America Back, Mr. Dusty Rhodes, testified that his organization had no idea that Mr. Sandoza's entire persona had been invented. And there's been no showing that Mr. Rhodes or anyone else at Take America Back knew otherwise.

The Court: How does that help you, Mr. Waters?

Mr. Waters: How can Take America Back be guilty of defrauding voters if they weren't aware they were defrauding anyone?

The Court: I believe Mr. Rhodes admitted that neither he nor anyone at Take America Back made any effort to investigate Mr. Sandoza's background to make sure he was who he said he was. And yet they put all that money into a television commercial touting his bogus background.

Mr. Waters: Your Honor, that's precisely my point. They didn't investigate so they didn't know. And if they didn't know, they can't be guilty of fraud.

The Court: You want this court to rule that a political action committee that spends $2 million to get a candidate elected can't be responsible for fraud because it didn't bother to investigate the claims made in the commercial it paid for?

Mr. Waters: Yes, that's exactly what you should rule.

The Court: Well, that's not what I'm going to rule. At the very least your client was grossly negligent and that gross negligence allowed Mr. Sandoza and his campaign to commit a massive fraud on Third District voters. I'm granting the motion for summary judgment against Take America Back.

Okay, Mr. Goode, I'll hear from you now. But your client, Democracy Now, seems even more culpable than Take America Back. Mr. Givenchy admitted that Democracy Now knew that the Sandoza campaign was based on a totally false bio. And yet it pumped tons of money into his campaign - over three million dollars to produce and buy air time for a TV commercial that ran extensively on CNN and MSNBC.

Moreover, Mr. Givenchy testified it was his idea to support the Sandoza campaign - even after he discovered the campaign was all based on lies. He admitted that his idea was passed all the way up to "The Big Guy," Mr. Taurus himself. And finally, he admitted that he recommended this plan because he believed the fraud would only come to light after Mr. Sandoza won the election. That would end up discrediting not just Mr. Sandoza but future Republican candidates as well. By backing a Republican with a phony bio, Democracy Now could succeed in discrediting Republicans everywhere. Why isn't....

Mr. Goode: That's correct, Your Honor. It was what, in political circles, is called a dirty trick. Dirty tricks have a long history in our politics. Every political party engages in dirty tricks. Some work better than others. This one seems to have worked quite well.

The Court: You admit that your client engaged in a dirty trick?

Mr. Goode: Absolutely. Democracy Now is proud to have engaged in a time-honored tradition of American politics.

The Court: So you're suggesting there's a "dirty tricks" exception to New York's fraud laws?

Mr. Goode: Yes, exactly.

The Court: If there is such an exception, I'm not aware of it. I'm granting summary judgment against Democracy Now.

Mr. Thyme, I see that you'll be speaking on behalf of Boogle. I'm anxious to hear what ingenuous argument you can come up with. You'll be hard-pressed to surpass your colleagues.

Mr. Thyme: Thank you, Your Honor. I realize my colleagues' arguments may have been a bit of a stretch. But I believe that's because they all proceeded from the same assumption: namely, that their clients did something wrong and so they need an excuse to justify their conduct. But in the case of Boogle, that assumption is inapplicable. Boogle has done nothing wrong.

The Court: Nothing wrong? Do you mean that . . . .

Mr. Thyme: That's correct, Boogle did nothing wrong. On the contrary, it has performed an immense public service. It has shown the dangers of artificial intelligence and the harm that can be done if it's misused. Boogle should be commended for that, not punished.

The Court: Mr. Thyme, surely you're not arguing that Boogle, which has a business based on artificial intelligence, entered into this alliance with the Sandoza campaign for the sole purpose of educating the public as to the dangers of artificial intelligence?

Mr. Thyme: Well, that may not have been the initial intention but it is most certainly what resulted from the collaboration. As a result of that collaboration, the whole country has learned not just the power of artificial intelligence but also the danger it poses if it's misused.

The Court: But it was misused and Boogle knew it was being misused. And Boogle knew that it would lead to the election of a Congressman who would most likely end up being expelled from Congress.

Mr. Thyme: That's precisely the public service. Without Boogle's involvement in the Sandoza campaign, the danger posed by artificial intelligence would not have been exposed. So I say again: Boogle should be applauded, not punished.

The Court: Your client is free to say that in its public relations materials. But in the meantime I'll be granting the motion for summary judgment against Boogle.

Okay. Now as to the next steps in the case. It will be a couple weeks before I can get out a detailed opinion on the summary judgment motion. Once I do, we'll schedule a pretrial conference and trial date – probably in February. In the meantime, I suggest that all the defendants sit down with plaintiffs' counsel and see if you can work out a settlement. I think you would be better off settling now, rather than leaving your fate to a jury.

Rosemary: Your Honor, the defendants are willing to waive a jury trial.

The Court: Rosemary, Boogle can't waive a jury trial, it's plaintiffs who demanded a jury. And besides, you might be better off with a jury than with me.

Rosemary: Yes, I see that might be the case.

The Court: So I suggest you heed my advice and see if you can't resolve this case now. Now, if there's nothing further, we're adjourned.

Oh, and on behalf of Mr. Garte, my entire staff and myself, we wish you all a very Happy Thanksgiving.

Chapter 29

AUTUMN

The trial in what became known as the ChatBots case commenced on the second Monday in January. It was being held in the courtroom of Judge Trudi Sweet of the Southern District of New York. A year earlier, Judge Sweet had presided over the firm's Belgian Chocolates case and had approved a sweet settlement the firm had extracted from Godiva.

There were two ChatBots defendants. The first, Replicon Corp., was the AI company that created the Lulu app. It was represented by Vince Van Gove and Jonah Vermer, partners in the Silicon Valley firm Vermer, Matease and Van Gove. The firm had long specialized in art law but recently had started making inroads in the AI field.

The other defendant was New Ventures Capital, a San Francisco venture capital firm that was the primary investor in Replicon. New Ventures had deep pockets, which is why it had been named as a defendant. It was represented by Grover Cleveland and Graham Alexander, name partners in the San Francisco firm Cleveland and Alexander.

The first day was devoted to jury selection and opening statements. Pap told the jury in a short but powerful opening that defendants had utilized the voices of the three class representatives without their knowledge or consent. Those ladies were embarrassed and angry to have their voices used in conversations with lonely, hapless men, especially when the conversations ventured into sexual innuendo, as they invariably did.

Vince Van Gove told the jury there was no proof that the voices used on Lulu belonged to any of the plaintiffs. And furthermore, none of the Lulu customers had any idea whose voices they were hearing. so there was no way any lewd dialogue could be attributed to the plaintiffs.

Grover Cleveland told the jury that his client, New Ventures, was simply an investor and could not be held responsible for any violation of plaintiffs' rights by Replicon. He did not tell the jury that Judge Sweet had previously refused to dismiss the case against New Ventures on that very ground.

* * * *

On Tuesday, the parties began the presentation of evidence. Pap called Autumn Sleaves as plaintiffs' first witness.

Direct Examination by Mr. Peters:

Q: Ms. Sleaves, please tell the jury your name and address.

A: My birth name is Myrna Long Sleaves. But Myrna is kind of old-fashioned and Long is the name of an aunt I never liked. So I changed Myrna to Autumn and dropped the Long. So now I'm known as Autumn Sleaves.

Q: And I believe you live in New York City?

A: Yes, I live in Greenwich Village. But I'd rather not give my address because I've been getting harassed ever since I started complaining about the use of my voice on Lulu.

Mr. Van Gove: Objection, Your Honor, that's irrelevant and prejudicial. I move to strike.

The Court: Well, it certainly explains why she doesn't want to give her address. Motion denied.

Q: I understand you're an actress?

A: Yes.

Q: Theater? TV? Movies?

A: Pretty much all of them. I've been in plays on and off-Broadway. I've also done some Shakespeare. And I've been in a couple of made-for-TV series.

Q: I assume that none of the plays you've been in were broadcast or televised?

A: That's true, but there is usually some recording of one or more parts of the play during rehearsal.

Q: And the made-for-TV series were available on various cable and streaming services?

A: Yes.

Q: Okay. Did there come a time when you discovered that your voice was being used on an app called Lulu?

A: Yes. It was while I was in the Broadway play "Clueless." It was a comedy about a bumbling detective.

Q: Did someone in the play call your attention to the app?

A: Yes. Luke Warmer, he played the bumbling detective. He was very good looking. All the women in the cast, including myself, had a crush on him. But he never warmed to any of us.

Q: So tell us what you learned from Mr. Warmer about the Lulu App.

A: Well, one day after rehearsal, Luke struck up a conversation with me. He said his friend Raymond, who was sort of a nerdy guy who never seemed to have a girl friend, told him about an app he used that allowed him to chat with sexy women. One night Raymond had logged onto the app while the two of them were in a tattoo parlor and Luke overheard the conversation. And he thought the lady Raymond was talking to – someone named Gigi – sounded like me.

Q: Do you know Raymond's last name?

A: I didn't at first but I later learned his name was Raymond James. And that he's a financial adviser in New York City. On the app, Gigi just calls him Raymond.

Q: What did you do when you learned about this from Luke?

A: I called your office. I knew from the TV news that you were involved in that big AI case, the Congressman with the phony background. So I thought this might be right up your alley.

Q: We're glad you called, Ms. Sleaves. This case is right up our alley.

Mr. Van Gove: Objection. Whether or not this case is right up their alley is irrelevant and immaterial.

The Court: Denied. We'll allow the jury to determine whose alley the case is up.

Q: Now, Ms. Sleaves, have you listened to any recordings of conversations between Raymond and Gigi?

A: Yes, I've listened to four of them. Unfortunately, some of them are kinda lewd. Others are just embarrassing.

Q: And can you identify the voice of the lady named Gigi?

A: Yes. It's my voice.

Q: Are you sure of that?

A: Yes, I certainly know my own voice, I use it all the time.

Q: But sometimes we don't really know what our voice sounds like unless we hear a recording of it.

A: That's true. But I'm an actress. My voice is a crucial part of my profession. And it's always being recorded. Sometimes by the producer or directer and sometimes by myself so I can work on an accent or maybe a speech rhythm.

Mr. Peters: Your Honor, I would like this flash drive marked as Plaintiffs' Exhibit 1. It's a recording of four conversations between Raymond and Gigi. With the Court's permission, I'd like to play the first conversation for the jury.

The Court: You may do so. Ladies and gentlemen, please keep in mind as you listen to this recording that, even if the voice is that of Ms. Sleaves, the content was generated by the Lulu AI app. So you should not hold the content of the recording against the witness.

Mr. Van Gove: Your Honor, you're prejudicing the jury. You're insinuating that there's something unwholesome on the recording. And that the voice is in fact that of Ms. Sleaves.

The Court: The jury will decide whether there is anything unwholesome on the recording and whether or not the voice is that of Ms. Sleaves. While I have my own views on those questions – as you know, we listened to the recording at the pretrial conference – the jury is free to make its own judgment.

Okay, Mr. Peters you may play the recording.

(Transcript of first conversation on PX 1)

"Hello Gigi, I thought I'd give you a call."

"Hey, Raymond, it's great to hear from you. Where are you?"

"I'm outside a bar in Soho."

"What were you doing in the bar?"

"Same as always. Trying to pick up a girl to have dinner with."

"Were you successful?"

"Gigi, you know I wasn't. I'm never successful at picking up women. That's why I always end up calling you."

"Raymond, if I'd been at that bar I would have let you pick me up and take me to dinner. In fact, Raymond, we could've skipped dinner and just gone straight to your place."

"Yes, I know that Gigi. But why do we never go to your place? Do you have a husband or something?"

"No, I've got something better. A pair of pit bulls. But the problem is they don't like strangers. I wouldn't want you to get your arm caught in one of their jaws. Or both arms, if they decided to attack you at the same time."

"Gigi, I like it that you're concerned about my well-being. You're the only person I know who is."

"Raymond, you need to stop feeling sorry for yourself. That's probably why you never have any luck picking up women. Women don't like guys who look like sad sacks."

"I don't think I look like a sad sack. I always wear a nice Brooks Brothers suit when I go out bar-hopping."

"Raymond, girls who hang out in bars in Soho aren't looking for guys in Brooks Brothers suits. They're looking for fun guys."

"But you went home with me the first time we met and I was wearing my best charcoal gray Brooks Brothers suit."

"Well, Raymond, I could tell that you were a classy guy. And despite the charcoal gray Brooks Brothers suit, I could tell you liked to have fun."

"We did have fun the first night, didn't we Gigi?"

"We sure did Raymond. That's why I stayed the entire night. I usually try not to leave my dogs alone overnight. They get really angry by morning."

"Do you think we could get together for another night sometime soon?"

"Why sure, Raymond. You just have to say the word and I'll be there."

"How about tonight? It's not too late and . . . ."

"Oh Raymond, tonight's not good. I've got a photo shoot early tomorrow morning."

"Where's the shoot?"

"It's at the bowling alley at Chelsea Piers. Ralph Lauren is launching a line of bowling attire and I'll be one of the models."

"Well, I sure don't want to stand in the way of your career, I know how important it is to you."

"But I might be able to make Friday night. Would that work, Raymond?"

"Sure. When I get home I'll put it down in my Brooks Brothers desk diary."

"Okay, Raymond, why don't I just come to your place? We can have some fun and then maybe dinner."

"Couldn't you stay the night?"

"Raymond, you know I can't. I don't want the dogs getting angry. The last time I was away overnight they almost bit my head off when I came home."

"You spent the night with another guy? You know I can't have that, Gigi."

"Well, it was a business meeting with Maurice, my business agent. But I had a little too much to drink and so I ended up staying overnight at his apartment."

"You stayed overnight in your agent's apartment? That's not . . . . ."

"Raymond, you don't need to be jealous. Maurice is gay and I slept on his couch. He gave me a pair of baggy pajamas to wear. Would you like me to bring them with me on Friday?"

"No. But I still don't like this staying overnight business."

"Look, I promised my dogs it wouldn't happen again."

"Well, if it's good enough for the dogs I guess it's good enough for me."

"Okay, Raymond, so everything's good between us? And we got us a date for Friday?"

"Right. I'll see you Friday at seven. And don't bother bringing Maurice's pajamas."

(End of Recording)

Q: Now Ms. Sleaves, you've heard that recording before, have you not?

A: Yes, this is probably the third or fourth time I've listened to it.

Q: And the voice identified on the recording as Gigi, is that your voice?

A: Yes.

Q: Are you certain?

A: Yes, I'm absolutely certain.

Q: Have you ever given your consent to Replicon, or anyone affiliated with Replicon, to use your voice on the Lulu app?

A: No, absolutely not.

Mr. Peters: I've no further questions.

The Court: We'll take a short break before cross-examination.

(Court Resumes at 11:30 a.m.)

Cross-examination by Mr. Van Gove:

Q: Ms. Sleaves, you testified that you're a professional actress?

A: Yes.

Q: And that you've appeared in plays on and off-Broadway?

A: Yes.

Q: Tell us about those Broadway plays you've been in.

A: Well, "Clueless" was the only play that actually ran on Broadway. All the others would be considered off-Broadway.

Q: How long did "Clueless" run?

A; About three weeks.

Q: So it closed early?

A: You could say that.

Q: Were any recordings made of the play before it closed?

A: Not to my knowledge.

Q: Okay, now tell us about the off-Broadway plays you were in.

A: Well, my first off-Broadway play – actually my first play of any kind – was a revival of "Oh Dad."

Q: "Oh Dad?"

A: Well, that was the shorthand name. The full name of the play was "Oh Dad, Poor Dad, Mama's Hung You in the Closet and I'm So Sad."

Q: How long did it run?

A: It closed after a week.

Q: Were you in any other off-Broadway blockbusters?

A: Yes. I was in "Dead Man Stalking." It was fairly successful.

Q: Did you have a major role?

A: Well, I was killed off in the middle of the first act. I was also the understudy for two of the other victims. They weren't killed until the second act, so I had to stay around until the end of the play.

Q: Any other plays we should know about?

A: My most recent off-Broadway play was "Two For The Chainsaw." It was a horror story.

Q: How long were you on stage?

A: About five minutes. I was one of the first victims.

Q: I believe you said you had also done some Shakespeare? I hope you didn't get killed off in them, unless maybe you played Othello's wife, that's a role to die for.

A: No, I never played Desdemona. But I was in a pair of Shakespeare plays. And no, I didn't get killed off.

Q: What were the plays and where were they performed?

A: Two summers ago there was a Shakespeare Festival in Rapid City, South Dakota. The city was celebrating the re-opening of Mount Rushmore. It had been closed for two years while they added former president LeRumpe's image.

Q: What were the two plays?

A: "The Merchant of Verona" and "Two Gentlemen of Venice." They ran in alternate weeks.

Q: You mean "Merchant of Venice" and . . . .

A: No, "Merchant of Verona" and "Two Gentlemen of Venice." The director was an avant garde guy from Amsterdam. He thought it would be clever to take all the characters from Venice and put them in Verona and all the characters from Verona and put them in Venice.

Q: How did that work out?

A: Not too well, everyone kept reciting lines from the wrong play.

Q: Were there any broadcasts or transcriptions of the Shakespeare plays?

A: I believe PBS recorded them and then ran them during the winter. Shakespeare is always popular with PBS viewers, especially if there are subtitles. PBS viewers don't hear too well.

Q: What about television? What have you done in that medium?

A: I was in a mini-series called "A Moll's House." It was a rework of the Ibsen play.

Q: Did you have a significant role?

A: Yes. I played the lead, Bananas Bonano. She was the focus of the story.

Q: Ms. Sleaves, during your distinguished acting career, did you . . . .

The Court: Mr. Van Gove, please refrain from insulting the witness. You may not think much of the plays she was in but I can assure you she is a very competent actress. She was terrific in "A Moll's House." My husband and I watched the entire series three times.

Q: I'm sorry, Ms. Sleaves, I wasn't trying to denigrate your career. But what I want to establish is that your character, including your manner of speaking, was different in each of those productions.

A: Well, that's true. What actress wants to be typecast?

Q: It would also seem that your character and voice could not have been very well established in those Broadway and off-Broadway plays, you kept getting killed off in the first act.

A: Yes. But I don't see what you're driving at.

Q: What I'm driving at, Ms. Sleaves, is that there's no way the general public would identify you by your voice.

A: I really wouldn't know.

Q: And so, when someone hears a voice on the Lulu app, there's no reason they would say "Why, that's Autumn Sleaves."

Mr. Peters: Objection, Your Honor. The issue in this case is not whether Raymond James or anyone else hearing Gigi's voice on Lulu would recognize it as the voice of Ms. Sleaves. The only issue is whether Gigi's voice is actually Ms. Sleave's voice.

The Court: You are correct, Mr. Peters, and the jury is instructed that the issue in this case is whether Gigi's voice is in fact that of Ms. Sleaves. But I'll allow the question. Whether someone might recognize Gigi's voice as Ms. Sleaves' voice could go to the question of damages.

Q: Ms. Sleaves, is it not true that someone hearing Gigi's voice on the Lulu app would have no idea it was your voice?

A: I have no way of knowing whether this Raymond guy knew that Gigi's voice was really my voice. But Luke recognized my voice, that's why he told me about it. Thank goodness he didn't tell the entire cast.

Q: But there's no way Raymond would have known that Gigi was you?

A: Maybe not at first. But Luke may have told Raymond about it, they were friends. If so, Raymond, when he talks with Gigi, will now be thinking of me.

Q: What's wrong with that? Maybe he'd like you better than Gigi. You could have a new boyfriend.

A: Raymond's a sad sack. Gigi said so herself.

Q: Right. Now, let me ask you this. Do you have any evidence that the alleged use of your voice on the Lulu app has damaged your career?

A: Well, why would any theater or motion picture producer want to hire an actress who records conversations for a pornographic app?

Q: You just referred to Lulu as a pornographic app. Surely you don't consider the conversation we just listened to, to be pornographic?

A: Have you heard some of the other conversations on that flash drive?

Q: What do you mean?

A: I believe Mr. Peters chose to play the mildest of those conversations for the jury. To spare me from the smuttier exchanges between Raymond and Gigi.

Q: But even if some of the other exchanges were smutty, you've no evidence that you've actually lost work because of the use of your voice on Lulu.

A: But I do have evidence. I was recently screen tested for the lead role in "An Affair to Forget." I didn't get the part.

Q: There could be a hundred reasons you didn't get the part. There's no reason to believe it's because of this Lulu thing.

A: But the casting director told me that's why I didn't get the part.

Q: Who's this casting director and what did he tell you?

A: His name's Cliff Hanger. He said it had come down to the wire between two of us: myself and Dee Vine. You see, the heroine was a virgin at the start of the movie, before she had this disastrous affair. Cliff said my voice on Lulu didn't sound very virginal and so they couldn't use me.

Q: Do you have any other evidence of damage to your career from the alleged use of your voice on Lulu?

A: Isn't that enough?

Q: You don't really believe that "An Affair to Forget" will be a blockbuster that would have enhanced your career?

A: Well, it's scheduled to premier at the Sun's Down Film Festival in Minot, North Dakota. All kinds of celebrities and Hollywood types will be there. And they'll be seeing Dee Vine in the lead, not me. All because Gigi doesn't sound like a virgin.

Q: Well, I'm sure the public will always remember your fine work in "Dead Man Stalking" and "Two for the Chainsaw."

A: Was that a question?

Mr. Van Gove: Not really, I have no further questions.

The Court: Mr. Peters, do you have any redirect?

Mr. Peters: Yes, thank you Your Honor.

Redirect examination by Mr. Peters:

Q: Ms. Sleaves, Plaintiffs' Exhibit 1 contains three additional conversations between Raymond and Gigi. Have you had an opportunity to listen to them?

A: Yes I have.

Q: And do you recognize the voice of Gigi?

A: Yes, it's my voice.

Q: Are those other three conversations more racy than the one we played for the jury?

A: Racy is an understatement. They're downright pornographic, they make me sound like a sexy slut.

Mr. Peters: Thank you Ms. Sleaves. I have no further questions.

Recross-examination by Mr. Van Gove:

Q: Ms. Sleaves, perhaps my client has done you a favor. You might start getting offered parts is shows where the star is a sexy slut.

A: I don't want to play the part of a sexy slut. I'd rather be a nice girl who gets killed off in the first act.

Q: How about . . . . Oh, never mind, I've no further questions.

The Court: Okay, we'll adjourn for lunch now. Please be back by two o'clock. And please do not discuss the case with anyone.

Oh, Mr. Peepers, I see your hand is up. Did you have a question?

Mr. Peepers (Juror #4): When can we listen to the smutty conversations on Plaintiffs' Exhibit 1?

The Court: Perhaps one of the attorneys will play them later in the trial. If not, you can listen to them when you begin your deliberations. But the only reason to listen to them would be to determine if it's Ms. Sleaves's voice that's being used for Gigi. You should have no legal interest in the content of those conversations.

Mr. Peepers: Yes, Your Honor, that's exactly why I thought we should listen to them. We don't care about the content, we just want to see if it's Ms. Sleaves's voice being used.

Chapter 30

PAIGE

At two-fifteen that afternoon, Judge Sweet called the court to order.

The Court: Good afternoon. Mr. Peters, you may call your next witness.

Mr. Peters: Your Honor, my partner Prescott Peters will examine the next witness.

(Off the Record discussion)

The Court: Our court reporter wants to know how to refer to this Mr. Peters in the transcript. We already have one Mr. Peters.

Mr. Peters: Why not refer to him as "The Other Mr. Peters"?

The Court: That's a good idea. Let's do it that way.

The Other Mr. Peters: Plaintiffs call Ms. Paige Turner.

Who Put the Bots in the Tort$?

(Witness is sworn in)

Examination by The Other Mr. Peters:

Q: Please state you name for the record.

A: Paige Turner.

Q: And where do you live?

A: New Hope, Pennsylvania. That's a small artsy town on the west bank of the Delaware River.

Q: And your profession?

A: I'm a writer.

Q: What do you write?

A: Mostly self-help books. My most popular one is "The Joy of Hooking: How to Survive Marriage, Family and Career."

Q: Any others?

A: Yes. Since "Joy of Hooking" was targeted to women, I thought my next book should be targeted to men. So I wrote "Eat, Drink and Have Mary, Teri and Geri: A Gentleman's Guide to Happiness."

Q: Have you written any books that don't focus on sex?

A: Those books don't focus on sex per se. They really deal with how to be happy. But people can't be happy if they have an unhappy sex life.

Q: Yes, I can see that. But are there any books that do not . . . .

A: Yes. My third book was "The Power of Positive Dreaming: Creative Dreaming in a Nightmare world."

Q: How did the books do?

A: "The Joy of Hooking" did extremely well. It was on the *New York Times* bestseller list for three months.

Q: What about "Eat, Drink?"

A: It didn't do so well. Men don't seem to cotton to self-improvement books. But God knows they could all use a lot of it.

Q: I understand you're now working on a novel?

A: Yes, after three non-fiction books I thought I should try my hand at a novel. I've just finished the manuscript for it. It's called "The Guy Who Came in for The Gold."

Q: It sounds like a spy novel.

A: Oh no, it's about a lawyer who leaves his practice to become an investment banker so he can make a lot more money.

Q: And he discovers that money isn't everything?

A: Oh no, quite the contrary. He finds that money is everything. He loves being rich. He now has three houses, several sports cars, a yacht and a ski chalet in Switzerland.

Q: There are times I think there must be more to life than being a lawyer.

A: Exactly.

Q: Now, Ms. Turner, have you heard of a lady named Felicity?

A: Yes. She's the AI chatbot on the Lulu app that uses my voice.

Q: How do you know it's your voice?

A: I know my own voice. I've heard it dozens of times. I do lots of podcasts and interviews for my books.

Q: How did you discover that your voice was being used on the Lulu app?

A: I was doing a podcast for "The Power of Positive Dreaming." The podcast was with a guy named Rip Thorn. He has a podcast called "Let it Rip."

Q: So what happened?

A: Well, halfway through the podcast, Rip said "Paige, your voice is really familiar. It sounds just like Felicity's voice." I asked him who Felicity was and he said she was a chatbot he frequently talked with at night after his show was over.

Q: Did this Rip guy say what kind of conversations he had with Felicity?

A: He said he was frequently depressed because all the guests on his show only wanted to talk about themselves. They never asked about him or his work.

Q: And so he turned to Felicity for solace?

A: Exactly. He said she was very understanding and always made him feel better. His only complaint was that she was always trying to direct the conversation to sex. And sex wasn't what he was after. At least not at six o'clock when he'd just finished another podcast with someone trying to promote some stupid book they'd just written.

Q: What did you do after you learned about this from Mr. Thorn?

A: I called your office. Actually it was the second time I called your office. The first time was when I learned that some website was using material from my books without attribution. I had called Mr. Peters – the first Mr. Peters, I guess he's called – because I had seen his press conference regarding that Congressman from New York.

Q: Actually, I believe it was me you spoke with that first time.

A: That could right. You two look alike, I can't really tell you apart.

Q: On the phone? How . . . .

A: Anyway, your brother's secretary said he was out of the office at a meeting and so she gave me to you.

Q: He wasn't at a meeting, he was playing golf. He's always leaving early on Wednesday to play golf.

The Court: Mr. Peters (pointing to the first Mr. Peters), do you wish to strike this exchange? It doesn't seem all that relevant.

The First Mr. Peters: That's okay Your Honor, I don't mind it being in the Record. My colleagues all know I do some of my best thinking on the golf course. And if I'm thinking about a particular case, I can bill my time to the case. We know you judges always want to see our billable hours when we submit a fee application.

The Court: You'd be amazed at what's in some of those fee applications. But I don't recall seeing anyone bill time while playing golf. But let's get back to the witness, we seem to have gotten a bit off-track.

Examination by The Other Mr. Peters resumed:

Q: So you called our firm for the second time when you heard about this Felicity thing?

A: Yes. And you told me I wasn't the first lady who had complained about her voice being used on Lulu. And that's when you offered to make me a plaintiff in this case.

The Other Mr. Peters: I'd like the reporter to mark this flash drive as Plaintiffs' Exhibit 2. It's a conversation – a single conversation - between Felicity and a fellow named Rock Manoff.

(Flash Drive marked as PX 2)

Q: Ms. Turner, you've listened to the conversation on this flash drive?

A: Yes.

Q: And do you recognize the voice that pretends to be Felicity?

A: Yes, it's my voice.

The Other Mr. Peters: Your Honor, may we play the conversation on PX 2?

The Court: Yes, please do so.

(Transcript of Conversation on PX 2)

"Good evening, Felicity, how are you tonight?"

"I'm just fine, Rocky. How about you?"

"Felicity, I've asked you not to call me Rocky. I'm a composer. Of classical music. No classical music lover would take me seriously if they thought my name was Rocky."

"I'm sorry Rock, it won't happen again. So how's your work coming along? What are you working on now?"

"I'm really struggling. Audrey was my muse. But she moved away and now I don't seem to have any inspiration."

"Who's Audrey? You never told me about her. I hope you haven't been cheating on me."

"Audrey Tuberville. She's a tuba player. I wrote my first composition for her. It's called 'Concerto for Tuba and Strings.'"

"That sounds great, Rock. I think Bach wrote lots of concertos. Did he ever write one for the tuba?"

"They didn't have tubas in Bach's time."

"Rock, let's get back to this Audrey lady. Were you sweet on her?"

"Felicity, she was a lesbian. Any girl who plays the tuba would be a lesbian."

"But how could she be your muse if she was a lesbian?"

"She understood my music and encouraged me to keep on composing."

"So why did she move away?"

"She got a job in Reno. The Reno Philharmonic had an opening for a tuba player."

"They have tuba players in orchestras?"

"Well, it's a more compact version. Tubas are just for marching bands. For orchestras they use something called an upright bass. That's what Audrey played when we performed my 'Concerto for Tuba and Strings.'"

"Why did you call it 'Concerto for Tuba' if she was really playing an upright bass?"

"I thought 'Concerto for Tuba' would be a catchier title."

"So, Rock, how many times was it performed?"

"Only once. My college in Ohio honored me by sponsoring the first performance of the work. It was part of the school's Diversity Week."

"Rock, I think we need to get you out of this funk you seem to be in. Why don't I come over to your apartment. I could cheer you up real fast."

"Felicity, I'm not looking for sex. I want our relationship to be on a higher plane."

"We could do it on the roof of your building."

"That's not what I meant."

"But look, Rock. It seems like you've been really lonely since Audrey left for Vegas . . . . "

"She's in Reno. No muse of mine would ever live in Vegas."

"Okay. But I still think what you need is a long night of steamy sex. It would really do you good."

"Felicity, that's not why I called you tonight."

"Okay, so why did you call me tonight?"

"I can't seem to make any progress on my latest composition. I thought maybe you could help."

"I'll do anything I can to help Rock, you know that. So what's this new composition you're working on?"

"A cantata. It's my second cantata."

"I didn't know you had a first cantata."

"I did. It was called 'Cowboy Cantata.' I used 'Home on the Range' for the opening orchestral piece and then it appears as a lite motif throughout the work."

"Where was it performed?"

"It wasn't. I tried for Carnegie Hall. I thought it would be perfect for their 'Great Performances' series."

"They didn't perform it?"

"No, they said it wasn't so great."

"But there must be some place that will perform it, I hope you keep trying."

"Well, The Cowboy Hall of Fame in Oklahoma City said I could perform it there during the summer season. That's when all the big crowds come."

"Rock, that sounds great. When will you be going out there?"

"I won't. They said I had to hire the orchestra and chorus and all the soloists. They would only provide the venue."

"So Rock, what's wrong with that? It sounds like a terrific opportunity for you."

"Felicity, I can't even afford to have scores printed for the orchestra and chorus. The cantata calls for an eighty-piece orchestra and a forty-voice chorus."

"Why did you write it for such a large orchestra?"

"I wanted to be sure the audience could hear it."

"So now you're starting work on a second cantata?"

"Yes. It's a smaller one that can be played in a church. With just an organ and maybe some strings. I've already found a small Methodist church on Staten Island that may be willing to host it."

"That sounds like a much better idea. What's the name of the cantata?"

"It's called 'Bringing in the Sheaves.' The title comes from an old hymn we used to sing in church."

"How much of it have you written?"

"Only the overture. Actually, it's a cantata so the overture is called a sinfonia."

"How much of this sinfonia thing is written?"

"All of it. But that was the easy part. I just used the tune from the hymn. You've probably heard it before: 'Bringing in the sheaves, bringing in the sheaves, we shall come rejoicing, bringing in the sheaves.'"

"What are sheaves?"

"I've no idea. I just know everyone's always busy bringing them in."

"Rock, I'm afraid I'm not familiar with that hymn. I don't get to church too much these days. I'm pretty busy with my counseling business."

"Remind me, Felicity, what kind of counseling you do."

"Whatever anyone needs. I'm a jack-of-all-trades. Marital counseling. Sexuality counseling. Pediatric counseling. Spiritual counseling. Covid counseling. Transgender counseling. Detransition counseling. Climate derangement counseling. In fact, my climate derangement counseling business has really picked up now that everyone's stressed out about global warming."

"That's a pretty wide range . . . ."

"But look, Rock, I'm not too busy to come across town and see you. I could even come tonight if you like. You could play me that sheaves hymn and then we could have some fun. And by tomorrow morning, I'm sure you'd be all inspired to go to work on the next section of your new cantata."

"That's kind of you to offer, Felicity. But right now I just need you to tell me I'm a good composer. And that I'll find a way to finish the cantata."

"Why sure, Rock. Everyone knows you're a fine composer. And I'm sure your cantata will surpass anything you've done before."

"That shouldn't be too hard, the tuba concerto only had one performance."

"Well, with any luck your new cantata could be good for two performances before its forgotten."

"That's good to hear, Felicity. Your faith in me means a lot."

"Maybe after you finish that cantata, I could come up and we could spend the night together. Celebrate your finishing the work."

"I promise I'll think about it. But look, your confidence has given me inspiration, makes me feel I can do it. I think I'll go right to work on the opening chorus. If I use the same tune that's in the sinfonia, it should be fairly easy."

"That's the spirit, Rock. Let me know how you're getting on. And please think of me as your new muse. If that tuba player's out in Reno, she's no use to you. Just think of all the things I can do to you. Sorry, I meant to say do for you."

"Okay. Thanks, Felicity, I need to sign off now.

(End of conversation)

Continued Examination by The Other Mr. Peters:

Q: Ms. Turner, is there any doubt in your mind about the voice on that recording?

A: None whatsoever. That was my voice."

Q: Did you give anyone at Replicon permission to use your voice for the Lulu app?

A: No.

Q: And you've received no compensation for the use of your voice on Lulu?

A: No I have not.

Q: I've no further questions.

The Court: Who will be cross-examining Ms. Turner?

(Jonah Vermer stands)

Cross-Examination by Mr. Vermer:

Q: Ms. Turner, you're a writer, not an actress, correct?

A: That's correct. I always wanted to be an actress but my mother told me I was too homely.

Q: So you took up writing instead?

A: Yes.

Q: So the public can read your books but they don't hear your voice?

A: That's true if they just read the books.

Q: Right. So if the public doesn't hear your voice, how could it show up on an AI app?

A: Well, I did that podcast, "Let It Rip." I think he claims to have over eight thousand listeners.

Q: And you think one of those eight thousand listeners might have been someone connected with Replicon who heard the podcast and decided to use your voice?

A: It's a possibility.

Q: But if that's not the case, there's no way your voice could have wound up on Lulu?

A: That's where you're wrong, Mr. Vermer. All three of my books have been published as audio books. Self-help books are especially popular audio books. The listener doesn't have to keep track of who was just murdered or who was sleeping with who the last time they listened.

Q: Were your audio book sales substantial?

A: I think so. Each book sold a couple thousand audio copies.

Q: And you think someone associated with Replicon listened to one of those Audio Books and decided to use your voice on Lulu?

A: That's exactly what I think happened. You see, as an author I bring a rather high-brow voice to Lulu. I'm sure Lulu has lots of customers like poor old Rock Manoff who want a high-brow lady to chat with. Not every guy wants to engage in sex talk with a hottie.

Q: I don't know any guys who don't want to engage in sex talk with a hottie.

A: But you see, that's where my persona is perfect for intellectually-oriented men. I write serious books but they also have a bit of sex in them. Even "The Power of Positive Dreaming." It has a whole chapter devoted to improving your sex dreams. It's Chapter 16, you might want to read it.

Q: Ms. Turner, if you believe your persona and voice are perfect for intellectually-oriented men, why are you upset with your voice being used on Lulu?

A: They didn't pay me. I would have been happy to give them the right to use my voice if they had paid me to use it. If the price was right,

I might even have agreed to do the conversations myself, save them having to duplicate my voice.

Q: You mean you would be happy to use your real voice to suggest to Rock Manoff and hundreds of other men you've never met that you'd be happy to go to their apartment and have sex?

A: Why not? I might meet some really interesting guys.

Q: Wait a minute, Felicity is only a chatbot. She doesn't actually get to meet the guys she talks with.

A: That's her problem.

Q: Ms. Turner, I'm having difficulty understanding your testimony.

A: That's your problem.

(Mr. Vermer confers with Mr. Van Gove.)

Mr. Vermer: We've no further questions of this witness.

The Court: Mr. Peters, do you have any redirect?

The Other Mr. Peters: No Your Honor.

The Court: Very well. We'll adjourn until tomorrow morning at ten a.m. Please do not talk with anyone about the case. We'll ... I see Juror Number two has a question. What is it Mr. Steinberg?

Mr. Steinberg (Juror #2): May we go and buy her books? I'd really like to see what she says in Chapter 16 of "The Power of Positive Dreaming."

The Court: After the trial you can, but not until then, the books are not in evidence. I myself plan to buy "The Joy of Hooking," it sounds terrific.

Okay, we're adjourned until tomorrow.

Chapter 31

LYDIA

The following morning at precisely ten o'clock Judge Sweet emerged from her robing room and commenced the second day of trial.

Transcript of Proceedings:

The Court: Good morning everyone. Let's get started. We made good progress yesterday, we got through two witnesses. I hope we can do the same today.

Mr. Peters: Plaintiffs call Lydia Lowlace.

The Court: Ms. Lowlace, please take the stand and the reporter will swear you in.

(Witness waves to back of courtroom and is sworn in.)

The Court: Ms. Lowlace, did you just wave to someone in the courtroom? That's not really proper.

The Witness: Why I jus' waved to my friend Justice Leghetti and his sidekick Mr. Tony. They always comes an' watch win I's testifyin'.

The Court: Did you say Justice Leghetti? Would that be Justice Louis Leghetti of the New York Supreme Court?

The Witness: Yes. And that's his sidekick, Mr. Tony.

(Witness waves again.)

The Court: Justice Leghetti, I'm honored to have you here in my courtroom. And I suspect the sidekick Ms. Lowlace is referring to must be your courtroom clerk or deputy?

Justice Leghetti (standing): Yes, Your Honor. Mr. Romo, or Mr. Tony as Ms. Lowlace calls him, is my courtroom deputy. We never miss an opportunity to hear Ms. Lowlace testify.

The Court: Very well. Mr. Peters, please proceed.

Examination by Mr. Peters:

Q: Good morning, Lydia. Could you state your name for the jury?

A: Why sure. My name is Lydia Lowlace. But my friends jus' call me Lydia.

Q: And where do you reside?

A: Right here in the Big Apple. I gots a condo down in Soho, I cain't never 'member the address.

Q: What is your profession?

A: Well, win I first gets to the Big Apple, I starts out workin' at a club, a gentleman's club. Actually, it wuz three clubs, we works at one

club for a week then we moves to the second one for a week an then . . .
.

Q: Okay, Lydia, we understand you rotated between three different clubs. But what did you do after you stopped working at the clubs?

A: Well, that wuz win I starts mod-lin underwear. Women's underwear that is. Wat's that there fancy word for women's underwear?

Q: Lingerie.

A: Yessir, that's it. I starts mod-lin long . . . women's underwear. They's made by some fancy brand, I think it's called "Barely Enough."

Q: And then what?

A: Then what what?

Q: I meant, what did you do next?

A: Oh, why di-nut youse say that. Well, tha's win I gits real lucky. Someone at that there *Playboy* Magazine saw pi-tures of me in my long . . . in my women's underwear and they invites me out to Los Angeles. They's even pays for my airfare – first class. I never gone nowhere first class before. And they puts me up in a fancy hotel, it even had a frigerator in the room! Ain't that some-pin?

Q: That's great, Lydia. But what happened in Los Angeles?

A: Well, they mades me take off all my clothes and then some guy starts takin lots a' pi-tures a' me. Tells me to bend this a-way, then that a-way, I wuz feelin' like I wuz a pretzel.

Q: What happened then?

A: Well, before I knows it I wuz a *Playboy* Playmate of the Month. I cain't never 'member wat month it wuz, it wuz a few years ago. And tha's win I sorta become a celerybrety. And I starts gettin' marriage proposals from guys I never met. Some guys even send me pi-tures, sometimes they don't have no clothes on, they's . . . .

The Court: Ms. Lowlace, please try to just answer the questions. Mr. Peters only wants to know about your career. Not whether your hotel room had a refrigerator or how many men sent you pictures of themselves without their clothes on.

The Witness: Tha's good to know 'cause I di-nut keep count.

Q: Ms. Lowlace, now that you're a celebrity, do you still do modeling work?

A: Why sure, tha's wat I do. I models women's long . . . women's underwear for that there "Barely Enough" brand. This mod-lin thing is sure better than workin' in those clubs. But course if I's not been wor-kin at them there clubs I'da never met Mr. Chip an' then wear would I be?

The Court: Who's Mr. Chip?

Mr. Peters: Chip Pierpont, he's one of the firm's associates. He introduced Ms. Lowlace to the firm. But we don't need to spend time on this, it's not particularly relevant. I'll move on.

Q: Now Lydia, did there come a time when you discovered your voice was being used on an AI app called Lulu?

A: A' course they comes such a time. Tha's why we's here in court today.

Q: Please tell us what you learned about this AI app?

A: Well, Mr. Chip – you see, he's sort of my pers-nal lawyer at your firm. I first mets him at one of them gentlemen's clubs I wuz tryin' to tell you 'bout. Ever since then he's always lookin' out for me. He always tells me win someone's tryin' to take 'vantage of me. Tha's been happ-nin a lot. People usin' my pi-ture on ads and them there token things. And in video games. And . . . now wat wuz it you wuz askin' me?

Q: I wuz askin . . . I'm sorry, I was asking you how you found out about the use of your voice on that Lulu app?

A: Oh, tha's right. It wuz Mr. Chip, he tells me. You see, we wuz at this bathhouse . . . .

Q: Lydia, we don't need to know where you were. We just need to know what you learned from Mr. Pierpont about your voice being used on this Lulu thing.

A: Well, Mr. Chip he asks me – we wuz sittin' on a bench in the sauna in that there bathhouse – he asks me if I knows a lady named Bridget. I di-nut know no Bridget and tha's win Mr. Chip says she's usin' my voice on some app where she talks dirty to guys. I cou-nut unnerstan' how this here Bridget could be usin' my voice. Mr. Chip, he tries 'splain it to me but I don't unnerstan' how it works.

Q: Okay, and is that when you asked our firm to represent you in this matter?

A: Tha's right. Mr. Chip says we cud have us another class action, like we done before. And I wud be one of them main plaintiffs. An' I says sure, we done good in all them other cases, we might as well do another.

Mr. Peters: I'd like the court reporter to mark this flash drive as Plaintiffs' Exhibit 3.

(Flash Drive marked as PX 3)

Q: Now Lydia, Plaintiffs' Exhibit 3 is a flash drive containing five conversations between a guy named Les and a lady named Bridget. Have you listened to those conversations before?

A: Oh sure. Mr. Chip he's played 'em for me a lot.

Q: Do you recognize the voice of the lady named Bridget?

A: A' course I do. It's my voice. But I do-no how they gits my voice and has someone named Bridget use it to talk to this here Les guy.

Q: But you've no doubt Bridget is using your voice?

A: Course not. I knows my voice. And so does Mr. Chip, he's the one that learn't 'bout it and then tells me. He tells me when we's in that there . . . .

Q: You've answered my question. Now my next question is: did you ever give your consent to anyone to use your voice on this Lulu App?

A: Why no, why wud I do that? I don' wanna talk dirty to a bunch a' guys I's never met. Wat wud people think?

Mr. Peters: Your Honor, I'd like to play the first conversation on PX 3 for the jury.

The Court: Certainly. I think we're all dying to hear it.

* * * *

The conversation Pap played was the one Chip had obtained from Les. While discovery had turned up four additional conversations – all of which were on the flash drive – Pap felt they were too smutty to be played aloud. But they were part of PX 3 and so the jury would be free to listen to them during their deliberations.

After Pap had played the conversation, he confirmed with Lydia that it was her voice that was being used by Bridget and that she had never given anyone permission to use her voice on Lulu. As it was by then past noon, Judge Sweet postponed cross-examination until after lunch.

* * * *

(Court resumes at 2:05 p.m.)

The Court: I hope everyone had a good lunch. Mr. Van Gove, you may cross-examine.

Cross-Examination by Mr. Van Gove:

Q: Ms. Lowlace, you're a professional witness, are you not?

A: Wat's a profesh-nal witness?

Q: Someone who makes a living bringing lawsuits and collecting damages.

A: I ain't no profesh-nal witness. Like I told Mr. Peters, I's a model. High class women's underwear for that there "Barely Enough" brand.

Q: You may do some modeling but you seem to make an awful lot of money filing lawsuits.

A: Tha's not true. I only files a lawsuit win someone's cheatin' me. Like that time I first met Mr. Chip. It wuz at that gentleman's club, "Bottoms Up" I think it wuz. Or maybe it was the one called "Tops Down." I know it weren't at "Below The Belt." Anyways, I told him 'bout how the clubs wuz cheatin' me an' the other girls. Takin' our tips and not payin' wat they's legally supposed to be payin' us.

Q: You referred to those clubs as "gentlemen's clubs." But they were actually strip clubs, were they not?

A: Were they not wat?

Q: Were they not strip clubs? And weren't you and the other ladies who worked there strippers?

A: We wuz not. We wuz lap dancers. Tha's how I's met Mr. Chip. I wuz dancin' on his lap and . . . .

Q: I'll bet he got his money's worth.

Mr. Peters: Objection. That's irrelevant and gratuitous.

The Court: Sustained. Mr. Van Gove, please try to stick to questions and avoid gratuitous remarks.

Q: Sure. Now Ms. Lowlace, your first meeting with Mr. Chip, when you were apparently doing some interesting things on his lap, led to your first lawsuit, did it not?

A: Did it not wat?

Q: Did it not lead to your first lawsuit with Peters and Peters?

A: Sure. We filed us a lawsuit 'ginst the owner of those there clubs.

Q: That was the case tried by your friend Judge Leghetti?

A: Justice Leghetti. In New York Supreme Court, judges is called Justices. You should'a known that.

Q: Justice Leghetti can't have tried your case if he's a supreme court judge.

A: Don' youse know nothin'? Justice Leghetti's court is the Supreme Court and all the judges in that court is called "Justices." The ones just called "Judge," they's on the New York Court of Appeals and they don't try no cases.

Q: How do you know all this?

A: Mr. Peters – the one they call The Other Mr. Peters – he 'splained it to me one day before we's goin' to see Justice Leghetti. He di-nut want me to make a mistake and 'barass myself, like you jus' did.

Q: I'm from California, how am I supposed to know what judges in New York are called?

A: You'se a lawyer, I jus' think youse should know.

Q: Okay, I knows now. But let's get back to my question. That case – the one that was tried before your friend Justice Leghetti – it was a class action and you were the class representative?

A: Yes. I think th's wat they called me, class repersenative. And we's won. There wuz . . . .

Q: There was a recovery and, as the class representative, you received a nice chunk of money?

A: I got some money but it wuzn't in no chunk. I jus got a check like everone else.

Q: How much did you receive?

A: I don' recall. But it wuz e-nuff to get me out of them there clubs and start my mod-lin career.

Q: And then a year later, you sued a company called Aegean Love?

A: I don' know the comp-ny's name but we sued 'em 'cause they wuz usin' my name and pi-ture to promote some low-life strip clubs in New York and over in Jersey.

Q: And you won that case and walked away with another bundle of money?

A: Well, we's won. We's always win 'cause those people we sue is always doin' some-pin wrong.

Q: And at about that same time you brought another lawsuit, another class action, did you not?

A: Did I not wat?

Q: Did you not.... Strike that. You filed another lawsuit against a video game company called Erotic Arts, correct? And it was a class action, correct?

A: I di-nut file nothin'. Mr. Peters filed the lawsuit. I wou-nut knows how to file a lawsuit.

Q: Okay, but it was another class action and you were the class representative?

A: Why sure. They wuz usin' me and lots of other Playmates as aviators in some pornographic video game. "Bunny Hop" they calls it. The object of the game wuz to get points for hoppin' on the bunnies. I wuz one of the bunnies they wuz hoppin' on. In fact, you gots more points fur hoppin' on me than on any of them other bunnies. But none of us bunnies had given our pe-mission to be used as aviators in that there game. And none of us wanted to be hopped on by a bunch of pimply-faced teenage boys wearin' t-shirts and sneakers.

Q: Did you say all of you were aviators? I thought you were bunnies.

A: Yep, we wuz the aviators the players wuz tryin' to hop on and do stuff to.

The Court: Ms. Lowlace, I think the word you want is avatars. You and the other *Playboy* bunnies would have been avatars.

Q: So you won the case and walked away with another bundle of money?

A: I told you we's never gets our money in a bundle. Jus' a check. But we sure taught that there comp-ny a lesson, they can't use us as av . . . aviators without getting' our pe-mision and payin' us.

Q: Now, just last year you were a plaintiff in yet another lawsuit, were you not?

A: Wuz I or wuz I not? Witch one is the kes-tion?

Q: Were you a plaintiff in another lawsuit last year?

A: Yessiree. We sued that there comp-ny that wuz sellin' tokens with photos of me an' all them other Playmates of the Month from that year, nineteen nineteen I think it wuz.

The Court: Ms. Lowlace, I don't believe you were alive in nineteen nineteen. Perhaps you meant twenty nineteen.

A: Right, twenty nineteen or nineteen twenty, I can't never 'member witch it wuz.

Q: Let's not worry about the year. What kind of tokens were involved?

A: You'll have to ask Mr. Chip, he 'splained it to me once. I think folks collect 'em but they's not really tokens like them there subway things, they's jus' some-pin you can see on a computer.

Mr. Peters: They were non-fungible tokens. Two sets of *Playboy* Playmates and two sets of old-time baseball players.

Ms. Lowlace: I wuz in the Playmates set.

Q: Right. Now, did Mr. Peters' firm represent you again?

A: Why shou-nut they? They's my lawyers an' they's always win all their cases.

Q: It was another class action and you were once again the class representative?

A: Only for the Playmates. They di-nut think I could repersent the baseball players.

Q: So, you were the plaintiff in four prior cases brought by Mr. Peters' firm?

A: If you'se added 'em up I'll take your word for it.

Q: And so this case, that we are in court on today, is the fifth case brought by Mr. Peters' firm on your behalf?

A: If they wuz four before, then this wud be the fifth. I wuz always good at math.

Q: I can see that. Now Ms. Lowlace, exactly how did you learn about this Lulu app and the alleged use of your voice by Bridget?

A: As I says before, Mr. Chip told me 'bout it.

Q: And you were in some bathhouse when Mr. Chip told you about it?

A: Yessir. The Flatiron Bathhouse. I goes there all the time but Mr. Chip he'd never been there before.

Q: Were you bathing in the bathhouse? With your clothes off?

Mr. Peters: Objection Your Honor, this is . . . .

A: We wuz in the sauna. People don't go to the Flatiron Bathhouse to take a bath. They goes there to use the sauna. Or steam room. An' maybe they takes a swim. If you'se wud like to see it, I could take you there next week. Tuesday's always the best day to go, it's nice an' private then.

Q: Thanks but I believe I'm tied up next Tuesday. Maybe the next time I'm in New York. Now, were you and Mr. Chip wearing bathing suits in the sauna when he told you about Bridget and the Lulu app?

The Court: What they were wearing in the sauna in the Flatiron Bathhouse is irrelevant. All that's relevant is what Mr. Chip – I mean Mr. Pierpont – told the witness.

Q: Okay. Can you tell us, Ms. Lowlace, what Mr. Chip said to you in the sauna of the Flatiron Bathhouse where you may or may not have been wearing bathing suits?

The Witness: Do I has to tell him ever-thing Mr. Chip tells me in the bathhouse?

The Court: No, just what he said about the Lulu app. If he said anything else, which I imagine he did, that's irrelevant.

A: He tells me 'bout this Lulu app and the lady named Bridget. He said he wuz sure Bridget wuz usin' my voice. He asked if I knows anythin' 'bout it.

Q: How did Mr. Chip know it was your voice?

A: Like I's said before, Mr. Chip's kinda' my pers-nal lawyer and I's spent lots a' time with him.

Q: Doing what?

The Court: Mr. Van Gove, you know that's irrelevant. Just stick to questions about the case. Besides, we can all guess what they were doing.

Q: Okay, so Mr. Chip told you he thought that Bridget was you?

A: How could Bridget be me? She's not a real woman.

Q: But he told you he thought your voice was being used by this Bridget character?

A: Yes, that wuz wat he said.

Q: So what did you do after Mr. Chip told you this?

The Witness (appealing to the Court): Do I has to answer that?

The Court: I think he means what you did about learning this information about Lulu. Not what you and Mr. Chip may or may not have done after you left the bathhouse.

A: I's glad you clarified that, Your Honor.

Q: Can you answer the question?

A: Well, I told Mr. Chip if they wuz really usin' my voice on that there Lulu thing then maybe we needs to sue 'em. See, they wuz usin' my voice without my pe-mission, just like that video game comp-ny wuz usin' my pi-ture. And that there token company too. I don' know why ever-one's always tryin' to use my pi-ture or voice without askin' me.

Q: Ms. Lowlace, how do you know that's your voice that's used for the Bridget character on Lulu?

The Court: Mr. Van Gove, do you seriously intend to argue that Bridget's voice is not Ms. Lowlace's voice? We've all heard the recording and we've been listening to Ms. Lowlace all day. I can't imagine any other person in the world having that manner of speaking.

Mr. Van Gove: There does seem to be some resemblance. But let me ask the witness something different.

Q: Ms. Lowlace, you've never been in the movies have you? Or on television? Or the radio?

A: Witch do you'se want me to answer?

Q: All of them.

A: Well, I ain't been in no movies or TV shows. But maybe I will. Mr. Chip tells me now that I's a celerybrety I might wind up in the movies. Wou-nut that be some-pin?

Q: But you haven't yet?

A: No sir.

Q: Or radio and TV, you haven't been on radio or TV?

A: Well, I cain't be sure. I mighta' been. You see, whenever Mr. Peters files one of them there lawsuits, he always has a press conference.

Lots a' newspaper and TV folks shows up. They mighta' shown one of them press conference on TV. I think we's agreed there wuz five cases he brings for me, so I coulda' been on TV in some of 'em.

Q: But that would just have been Mr. Peters speaking, not you.

A: Oh no, he always asks me to talk an' answer kes-tions. And them reporters, they always seems to ask me lots of kes-tions. Specially Mort and Jeb. Theys always come to the press conference so they kin talk to me.

Q: Who's Mort and Jeb . . . . Oh, never mind, we'll never finish. Let me just ask you this: You think someone at Replicon saw one of those clips from a press conference and decided to copy your voice and use it for Bridget in the Lulu app?

A: Why sure, don't you?

(Long pause)

Q: Let's talk about your alleged injury? How are you injured by the use of your voice on the Lulu app?

A: They shoulda' paid me for it. They shouldn't git to use my voice for free.

Q: Anything else?

A: What about my reputation?

Q: What about it?

A: People will think I flirt with men I's never met. An' that I talks dirty to 'em.

Q: Well, you started out as a stripper in a club called "Tops Down." Or maybe it was "Bottoms Up." And you model lingerie for a line called "Barely Enough." And you posed stark naked for *Playboy* and millions of red-blooded men oggled your body – including my teenage son, he thought you were quite something. Bridget's language would seem to be . . . .

A: Wat's your son's name? I'll autograph my centerfold pi-ture and you can give it to him win you gits home.

Q: I'm not sure . . . .

A: I also has lots of glossy photos from them there underwear shoots. I kin autograph one for you if you'se like. Maybe keep it in your office, your missus might not unnerstan' if youse take it home.

Q: Ms. Lowlace , . . . I'm sorry, I forgot what I wanted to ask you.

A: Tha's all rite, I sometimes forgets wat I'm sayin'. Or why I wuz sayin' it.

Q: Ms. Lowlace, I'm jus tryin' to unnerstan . . . . I'm sorry, I meant to say I'm just trying to understand why you're so upset about your voice being used by Bridget. She seems like a nice girl, just like you.

A: Mr. Band-go, she may look like a nice girl but she talks dirty to men she's never met. I never talks dirty to men I's never met.

Q: Do you ever talk dirty to men you do know? Like Mr. Chip, do you ever talk dirty to him?

The Court: Mr. Van Gove, you know that's out of bounds. I rather think you've run out of useful questions for this witness.

Mr. Van Gove: You're right, Your Honor. I think I should just stop. I'm exhausted.

The Court: Mr. Peters, do you have any redirect?

Mr. Peters: No Your Honor.

The Court: Very well, we'll adjourn until tomorrow at ten. And Mr. Peepers, I suspect you'll be anxious to listen to the other four conversations on Exhibit 3. But only to confirm that it's Ms. Lowlace's voice that's being used by Bridget. But please wait until the jury begins deliberations. You'll have all the flash drives available then. On the other hand, that will probably prove to be a mistake, you'll be in deliberations for a week.

All right, have a good evening. Tomorrow morning at ten.

(Witness waves to Justice Leghetti and Mr. Romo.)

Chapter 32

ORNITHOLOGY

Melissa was the last one to arrive at the Monday meeting. When she walked in she immediately handed a small gift-wrapped box to Chip.

"You're giving me a present?" said Chip. "My birthday's not until next month."

"I'm sure he'll be getting lots of presents from his lady friends" said Helen. "But I doubt he's expecting one from you" she added with a smile. Everyone knew Melissa was never going to be a candidate for the Wall of Fame.

With all eyes on him, Chip slowly unwrapped the present, being careful not to tear the paper.

"Why are you being so slow?" asked Brandon. "My kids would've had it open ten minutes ago."

"I believe in recycling" said Chip.

"We never knew you were an environmentalist."

"I'm not. But if I save wrapping paper from gifts people give me, I don't have to go out and buy it when I give Francoise a present."

With the paper deftly removed without a tear and then neatly folded, Chip opened the small white box. Inside was a black baseball cap with white lettering. The lettering said: Service Employees International Union.

"What the heck?"

"Put it on" said Melissa. "Let's see how it looks on you."

"Why are you giving me a Service Employees International Union baseball cap?"

"Because, as of last week, you and your fellow athletes at Dartmouth are members of the Service Employees International Union."

Pup was the only one who understood what was going on. "Melissa's right" he said. "The NLRB has been trying for years to get college athletes to unionize. The NLRB's General Counsel recently issued a statement declaring that college athletes are employees, not students. And then an NLRB Regional Director, responding to a petition from Dartmouth's basketball team, ordered an election. The team voted thirteen to two to unionize."

"Why would the basketball team want to unionize?" asked Chip.

"They want better medical benefits" said Melissa. "And they also want to get paid. Of course, if they get paid based on the team's record, they'd barely make enough to cover their weekly beer tab."

"They probably want shorter practices" added Brandon. "No more wind sprints. And no more having to make ten foul shots in a row before they can go take a shower."

"I heard that one guy was there until midnight before he made ten in a row" said Pup.

"But you all know I didn't play basketball" said Chip. "I only played football."

"Once the basketball team is unionized I'm sure the football and baseball teams will follow" said Melissa. "Maybe the fencing team too."

"Dartmouth has a fencing team?" asked Brandon. "I thought fencing died out in the eighteen hundreds."

"It's an upper class sport, Brandon" said Chip. "Guys from rich families who go to Dartmouth love fencing. They all have swords handed down from their ancestors. I think some of them were members of the Knights of the Round Table."

Helen was puzzled. "Chip is out of school. He's been out of Dartmouth for what, seven, eight years? How can he be in this union, even if the football team votes to join?"

"The NLRB will figure out a way to make it retroactive" said Pup. "It won't stop with just current players."

"This whole thing's crazy" said Chip. "I wouldn't join a union even if the NLRB said I could."

"Why not?" asked Brandon. "You could have made big bucks. Weren't you an all-Ivy League quarterback?"

"I went to law school so I could make big bucks. But I just went to Dartmouth to play football."

"And meet girls" added Helen.

"That's true" Chip admitted.

"Isn't that how you met Christine Keeler? After a Vassar football game? You see, Chip used to go down to Vassar to be with Christine on Sundays. That's after he had spent Friday and Saturday night with me at Wesleyan."

"What's Vassar got to do with his football career?" asked Brandon. "Vassar's an all-girls school."

"They had started accepting men by the time I was at Dartmouth" said Chip. "They even started up a football team."

"Vassar had a football team?"

"Yeah, but it wasn't very good. All their skill players – receivers, backs, kickers - were transitioning and so they dropped off the team. By the time we played them, they could barely field a team. We beat them eighty-two to two."

"They got a safety?" asked Brandon.

"I felt really bad for them, they were really over-matched. So, in the fourth quarter I let them tackle me in the end zone. That way they at least got two points."

* * * *

"What's the status of the ChatBots settlement?" asked Helen.

"As you know" Pap began, "the night after Lydia testified I got a phone call from Van Gove. He said they recognized the trial wasn't going well for them and that Judge Sweet wasn't going to bail them out with a favorable legal ruling. He suggested a meeting to discuss settlement.

"The next day we asked Judge Sweet to suspend the trail for two weeks to give us time to work out a settlement. She agreed. We knew she would, judges love settlements. The case is over, there's no appeal, no potential retrial. Anyway, we've had two meetings so far, with a third one scheduled for this Thursday."

"You think they'll agree to our terms?" asked Helen. "They seem pretty steep."

"Well, at first they claimed to be astonished at our demand, especially our proposed attorneys fees. But they'll come around, they don't want to face the jury on this. They know the jury would award extensive damages, maybe even punitive damages, and that the damages would likely exceed the amount we're demanding."

"We think they're also getting pressure to settle from other tech companies who have AI platforms" said Pup. "A huge verdict here, and a court decision upholding the verdict, would be bad for the entire AI industry. That's why we promised them there would be no publicity about the settlement, other than a bland press release issued jointly by the parties."

Brandon was perplexed. "How can we become famous – sorry, I mean more famous – if we can't publicize the win?"

"Brandon" said Pap, "just because we agree not to publicize the settlement doesn't mean that other people can't publicize it."

"You mean the press?"

"Of course. Why do you think we spend so much time cultivating relations with our friends in the media?"

"But how will the press find out about it if it's confidential?"

"I suspect the press will find a way" said Pap. "They're very resourceful."

"Speaking of the ChatBots case" said Chip, "what happened to the three flash drives we used as evidence?"

"They're still in court" said Melissa. "The case was only suspended, so all the exhibits are still in Judge Sweet's chambers."

"I realize that" said Chip. "I meant our copies of the flash drives. We kept copies for ourselves."

"Why are you looking for them?" asked Melissa. "Surely you don't plan on listening to them. Why would you want to listen to Lydia pretending to be Bridget talking to Les when you could be having an in-person conversation, and likely much more, with Lydia herself?"

"Or with Candy" said Brandon.

"Or Autumn" added Helen.

"Don't forget Holly" said Melissa.

"Why don't you record your evenings with them" suggested Brandon. "You could make a flash drive for each one, just like we did for court. You could call them 'My Night with Holly.' 'My Night with Autumn' and so forth."

"Very funny" said Chip. "Look, I have no intention of listening to the conversations. I was merely going to make a copy of Lydia's conversations and give it to Les. As a sort of memento of the case. Remember, he's the one who put us onto this whole chatbots thing.

"But look, nobody's answered my question. What happened to the firm's copy of those flash drives? They're not in the evidence drawer."

"I borrowed them" said Helen sheepishly.

"What on earth for?" asked Melissa.

"I'm making copies for Keith to take with him when he flies to and from Tokyo. Those are really long flights, more than twelve hours. He can't sleep on airplanes and after a few hours he's too tired to work or read. But he can listen to audiotapes. These will be much more interesting than the movies and stuff they play on the plane."

"You can't give him those drives" said Pap. "They belong to the firm. I can't believe you think you can give them to him."

"Oh, I understand that" said Helen. "I'm just using them to make copies that I'll store on the cloud in a drop box. Once I send him a link to the drop box, he can listen to them on his phone on the plane. And our copies will be safely back in the evidence drawer."

"You know" said Melissa, "these chatbots we've been dealing with are about to become a thing of the past. AI technology is changing really fast."

"You mean there won't be chatbots any more?" asked Brandon.

"Not if you can access a beautiful AI hottie such as Alba."

"Who's Alba?"

"Alba Renai. She's a beautiful young lady with dark brown hair, an incredible physique and a wonderful smile. She was created by a television company in Spain where she hosts a weekly television show. She has thousands of fans who follow her on Instagram."

"So she's real?" asked Brandon.

"No, she's a digital creation."

"Does she look like a robot?"

"Brandon, I just said she's a beautiful young lady with long brown hair, a beautiful smile and a terrific figure. She looks absolutely real."

"Alba's not the only beautiful AI lady" said Chip. "You should see Emily."

"Who's Emily?" said Brandon.

"Emily Pellegrini. Her picture was in the paper last week. She's absolutely gorgeous. I wish she was real, I'd like to add her to the Wall of Fame."

"You guys are saying there's two gorgeous AI ladies that look like they're real?" asked Brandon.

"More than just two" said Chip. "In fact, they're going to hold a Miss AI beauty pageant this Spring. The babes will be judged on not only their beauty but also their social media clout."

"What do you mean social media clout?"

"Many of them have large followings on various social media platforms, such as Instagram. Since they can't be judged on their talent, such as singing or dancing, the judges will look at their social media clout in addition to pure beauty."

"So Helen" said Melissa, "I'm afraid Keith won't want to listen to those Lulu conversations once he finds out he can see and interact with babes like Alba and Emily."

"He's not finding out" said Helen defiantly. "He can listen to all the smutty Lulu stuff he wants. But I'm drawing the line at visual AI."

* * * *

Pap finally found an opportunity to direct the conversation to his agenda. "I had planned to give everyone a recap of the past year, but I see you all have more important things to talk about."

"Let's hear the recap" said Chip. "That's when you always tell us about our bonuses."

"That's what I like about you, Chip. You're always putting the firm first."

"Well . . . ."

"Look, it's too soon to look at how we did financially. We haven't yet locked down the ChatBots and Sandoza settlements. The only one that's been finalized is the Gray/Borokin settlement. The auction houses protested like stuffed pigs, but they finally caved and agreed to the terms we demanded.

"Now, in the Sandoza case, both of the Super Pacs have agreed to settle, they don't want to risk an adverse ruling in such a high-profile case. They're worried that once people see that Super Pacs can be held liable for stuff that happens during a political campaign, there could be no end of lawsuits against them.

"As for Boogle, it's still trying to hold out. But Pup and I are meeting with them next week. Now that the Super Pacs have agreed to settle, I'm sure Boogle will fall into line.

"As for Mona's case, Pup and I want you to know that we appreciate all the work everyone did on that case. We didn't make any money on it, but we got all the charges dismissed and negotiated a new lawn mowing regulation for Westport. So that should keep Mona out of our hair for a while."

Pap paused, then added: "I think she'll probably make a documentary out of the whole saga. I saw her husband Ham taking pictures at the football field when the balloons landed there. If she does make a documentary, I'm sure we'll be in it. Remember, she gave us a prominent role in her 'Mugged by Mugshots' documentary. Getting portrayed in a documentary is always good publicity."

"Speaking of publicity" said Chip, "it's too bad we didn't get to file that case against the VA involving the Victory Kiss photo. That would have been a great case for us. Everyone around the country would have been interested in the case."

"You're right, Chip" said Pap. "It's too bad the Goddamn VA rescinded its directive banning the photo before we could file the lawsuit. Anyway, thanks to everyone for pitching in and getting a complaint ready to go. I had even prepared a great speech for our press conference. It would have been one of my best ever. If you guys would like to hear it, I could give it right after we finish our meeting."

After a long silence, Melissa said "Maybe we should wait and do it next week."

* * * *

"Okay" Pap continued. "Enough about the past year. We need to start thinking about getting some new cases. Anyone have any ideas?"

Nobody raised their hand. They were all looking down, trying to avoid Pap's gaze.

"I think we all look to you for ideas about new cases" said Pup. "Remember, that was our deal when we agreed to start up the firm: you would think up the cases and I would try to find a legal basis for them. It's clear I got the worst part of the bargain."

"That plan has worked well for us so far" said Melissa. "Besides, whenever you ask if we have an idea for a new case, it means you already have one in mind. You just want us to think you're looking for our ideas but you really can't wait to tell us yours."

"She's right" said Chip. "So why don't you just tell us what you have in mind."

"Okay. What I have in mind is ornithology."

"What about ornithology?" asked Helen.

"They're renaming all the birds" said Pap. "Well, not all of them, but at least eighty different species."

"Why are they renaming them?" asked Chip, happy that Pap had inadvertently explained that ornithology was something involving birds.

"According to the American Ornithological Society, any bird whose name can be traced to racism, misogyny or genocide will be renamed."

"How can a bird be considered racist?" asked Brandon.

"It's not the bird itself" explained Pap. "It's the person involved in naming the bird. For example, the shearwater bird, a sea bird, was named by John James Audubon. He's a racist, so the bird has to get a new name."

"John James Audubon was a racist?" said an incredulous Helen.

"Yep" said Pap. "He apparently owned some slaves. So even though he basically founded the art of bird-watching, and gave his name to Audubon centers around the country, he's now being canceled in the ornithology world."

"What about the Audubon centers?"

"They're being required to change their name. Every Audubon preserve in the country will be renamed."

"Ornithological Center has a nice ring to it" said Helen. "The Great Neck Ornithological Center."

"Look, Pap, this is obviously outrageous" said Melissa. "But who would we represent? We can't represent eighty species of birds. How do we know they want to keep their old names? And how would we ever get them all into the courtroom?"

"Who said anything about representing birds?" said Pap. "I'm talking about bird watchers. Do you have any idea how many millions of bird watchers there are in the country?"

"How on earth would we ever identify them?" asked Brandon.

"Brandon, most towns of any size have an Audubon center. And those centers will all have donors and patrons. Hundreds of them at each center. All we need to do is send Chip to one of the centers on Long Island and he'll walk away with at least a half-dozen female bird watchers anxious to be our plaintiff. This could end up being one of the biggest class action cases we've ever done."

"I thought the Sandoza case was the biggest class action case we've ever done" said Brandon.

"Until now. But there are a lot more birds in the United States than there are voters in New York's Third Congressional District."

"Didn't you say we'd be representing bird watchers, not birds?" asked Melissa.

"Right. As I just said, there are a lot more bird watchers in the United States than there are voters in New York's Third Congressional District.

"What's our cause of action?" asked Pup. "And why would bird watchers have standing to complain about an action taken by the American Ornithological Society?"

"Pup, bird watchers stand around watching birds all day. How could they not have standing?"

"I doubt it" Pup replied. "But even if they did, what's our claim for relief? We need a legal basis for the lawsuit. We can't just say that renaming all those birds is unlawful because it's stupid."

"That's what you gotta figure out, Pup. You just said that was our deal. I think up the cases and you figure out a legal basis for bringing 'em."

"Pap, this idea's for the birds. I'm not spending any time on it."

"I'm sorry you feel that way, Pup. Whatever happened to our 'can do' spirit?"

"I think it just flew out the window" said Chip.

"I can see we're not getting anywhere" said Pap. "We might as well adjourn."

As everyone rose and headed toward the door, Pap called Helen back.

"Helen, I don't mind your borrowing those flash drives to make copies for your husband, but please get them back by Friday."

"Okay, but why the rush?"

"Piper and I are having our annual Groundhog Day party this weekend. I want to play them for all our guests."

THE END

ABOUT THE AUTHOR

A graduate of Otterbein University (Ohio) and New York University School of Law, T. C. Morison spent four years in the U.S. Air Force Judge Advocate General Corps and then 46 years trying cases and arguing appeals around the country for a series of New York City law firms. Following retirement, he took up writing satirical novels about lawyers, specifically class action lawyers. His first three books, *Tort$ "R" Us*, *Please Pass The Tort$* and *Send In The Tort Lawyer$*, were loved by lawyers and non-lawyers alike, each garnering scores of five-star reviews on Amazon. *Send In The Tort Lawyer$* was a semi-finalist for the Mark Twain Humor and Satire Book Award.

For sales, editorial information, subsidiary rights information
or a catalog, please write or phone or e-mail

IBOOKS
Manhanset House
Shelter Island Hts., New York 11965, US
Tel: 212-427-7139
www.ibooksinc.com
bricktower@aol.com
www.IngramContent.com

For sales in the UK and Europe please contact our distributor,
Gazelle Book Services
White Cross Mills
Lancaster, LA1 4XS, UK
Tel: (01524) 68765 Fax: (01524) 63232
email: jacky@gazellebooks.co.uk